D1349727

UNDERSTANDING THE ENTREPRENEUR

This book is dedicated to Despina Tsonoglou, a source of inspiration and support to all those who knew her.

Understanding the Entrepreneur

An Institutionalist Perspective

CHRISTOS KALANTARIDIS
University College Northampton, UK

ASHGATE

© Christos Kalantaridis 2004

Published by
Ashgate Publishing Limited
Gower House
Croft Road
Aldershot
Hants GU11 3HR
England

Ashgate Publishing Company
Suite 420
101 Cherry Street
Burlington, VT 05401-4405
USA

Ashgate website: http://www.ashgate.com

British Library Cataloguing in Publication Data
Kalantaridis, C. (Christos)
    Understanding the entrepreneur : an institutionalist
    perspective. - (Alternative voices in contemporary
    economics)
    1.Entrepreneurship
    I.Title
    338'.04

Library of Congress Cataloging-in-Publication Data
Kalantaridis, C. (Christos)
    Understanding the entrepreneur : an institutionalist perspective / Christos Kalantaridis.
        p. cm. -- (Alternative voices in contemporary economics)
    Includes bibliographical references and index.
    ISBN 0-7546-3344-6
    1. Entrepreneurship. 2. Business people. 3. Institutional economics. I. Title. II. Series.

    HB615.K35 2004
    338'.04--dc22
                                                                              2004001035

ISBN 0 7546 3344 6

Printed and bound in Great Britain by
Athenaeum Press Ltd., Gateshead, Tyne & Wear

Contents

List of Figures

List of Tables

Preface

It is now six years since I was first acquainted with the work of the old institutionalists in general, and that of Thorstein Veblen in particular. That was a chance encounter, with the work of 'a strange man ... [an individual who] walked through life as if he descended from another world' (Heilbroner, 1956, p. 166). To someone who spent a number of years conducting empirical research on the entrepreneur and the entrepreneurial function, what seemed perplexing was how unfamiliar the ideas of Thorstein Veblen were to the field of entrepreneurial studies. In the large, and rapidly growing, body of accumulated literature in entrepreneurship the ideas developed by the founder of the old institutionalism and his disciples remained virtually unknown. This is despite the fact, that this school of thought in economics attempted to develop an alternative to the mainstream conceptualisation of human action: one that is purposive but also contextual. As a response, old institutionalists pursued an agenda that concentrated upon understanding phenomena in different socio-economic milieus. This book constitutes an attempt to develop a contemporary approach in the study of the entrepreneur, which draws upon the suggestive ideas of Veblen, and a number of other scholars who were influenced by his work. The institutional approach illustrated in this book aims to stimulate debate upon a number of issues that form the intellectual core of entrepreneurial studies. In order to do so, the approach advanced here is placed within the context of earlier theoretical constructs in the field.

Acknowledgements

The production of any book is inevitably the work of a number of people and I would like to acknowledge the support I have received, over many years, in producing this work.

To begin with I would like to thank my parents, Odysseus and Soultana, and my sister Despina, whose sacrifice and support for many years helped make my aspirations a reality.

To the large number of former and present students, I am grateful for their probing and challenging questions. One research student, Matthew Dutton, has been particularly helpful in editing this book in its entirety.

My colleagues at University College Northampton can not go without mention. Marie Gerrard for assisting with the compilation of the work as a whole and all the colleagues in the Marketing and Entrepreneurship group for their support.

My thanks go, also, to the following reviewers for their comments and suggestions at various stages in the development of the ideas presented here: Professor John Pheby, University of Luton, Professor David Smallbone, Middlesex University, and Professor Warren Samuels, Michigan State University.

I would like to take the opportunity to thank my publishers, Ashgate, and especially Brendan George, for giving me this opportunity.

Last but not least to acknowledge the support of my family: my lovely wife, Tina, and my two young children, Rowena and Odysseus. When I have not been at the university lecturing or travelling for research I have been working on this book. For me it has been challenging and exciting. However, it is my family who has had to make a sacrifice. I would like to thank them for their love and unending support that helped me to persevere and complete this work. To Tina particularly, who has always been there to help me maintain a balanced perspective on life and living.

Christos Kalantaridis
1st June 2003

Chapter 1

Introduction

Entrepreneurship: A New Field of Study?

Since the publication of Cantillon's (1755) pioneering work, there has been considerable growth in that body of literature exploring the function and attributes of the entrepreneur. Scholarly and applied research emanating from a wide array of disciplinary backgrounds, such as economics, anthropology, sociology and psychology, provides useful insights in understanding this influential but elusive economic agent. However, entrepreneurship research has failed to grow of age as a coherent field of study within the social sciences (Bull and Willard, 1995; Julien, 1998). This could be attributed to the fragmentation of the field and the ensuing lack of integration of distinctive research routes (Wortman, 1987). Divergence of paths in theory-building lead to a 'a profound lack of consistency of terminology and method' (Brazeal and Herbert, 1999, p. 29). This prevents the creation of a community of scholars, who hold similar beliefs about the boundaries and concepts of the field, and engage in dialogue about a specific set of problems (Gartner, 2001).

One reason behind the failure to develop a broadly accepted conceptual and methodological framework for the study of entrepreneurship is the multidisciplinary character of earlier work. Kilby (1971) in his seminal contribution likened research in this field with the hunt for the

> ...Heffalump. The Heffalump is a rather large and very important animal. He has been hunted by many individuals using various ingenious trappings, devices but no one so far has succeeded in capturing him. All, who claim to have caught sight of him report that he is enormous, but they disagree on his particularities. Not having explored his current habitat with sufficient care, some hunters have used as bait their own favourite dishes and then tried to persuade people that what they caught was the Heffalump (Kilby, 1971, p. 1).

Following on from this Brazeal and Herbert (1999) suggest that scholars in the field seek to understand their object of enquiry, each from his or her specific and differentially conceived viewpoint. In fact, it is fair to suggest that there is precious little debate, in the sense of an active and ongoing controversy between a number of contemporary scholars, in the area of entrepreneurial studies.

Another reason behind the inability to clearly articulate a coherent and consistent set of concepts, methods and research questions, is the appropriateness - or otherwise - of over-arching and all-embracing generalisations in the study of a phenomenon such as entrepreneurship. Entrepreneurs operate in and are influenced by their context. At the most elementary, the importance of contextualisation is apparent in the assumption (explicit or implicit) that entrepreneurs act differently from everyone else (innovate), or have a unique perception of economic activity that enables them to deal with uncertainty and/or recognise opportunity[1]. For entrepreneurs to be able to conform with this assumption, they require knowledge of the needs and resources of the entirety of those who can not identify opportunities or deal with uncertainty, society as a whole. This makes the argument (inherent in the bulk of work emanating from economics), that society does not influence entrepreneurial behaviour unsustainable. The influence of the context extends to the accumulated body of knowledge shared by those belonging to a socio-economic milieu, and the emerging cognitive frameworks and boundaries of behaviour. Thus, some of the diversity in theoretical constructs and empirical evidence could arise from consequential differences in the environment within which entrepreneurs emerge and operate. This seems increasingly plausible considering the mosaic of historical contexts that underpin research in entrepreneurship. These range from pre-industrial structures in continental Europe (Hoselitz, 1963), and traditional cultures in contemporary less developed countries (Leff, 1979), to post-industrial modern Western formations (Casson, 1993; Kyrro, 1998). The function of the socio-economic milieu in determining the incidence, and influencing the attributes of entrepreneurship is dealt with in that body of literature adopting a sociological perspective, which in many ways is closer to practical reality than the ambitious writings to be found in economics (Swedberg, 2000).

Yet despite the considerable difficulties involved in the study of entrepreneurship, conceptual and empirical research in the field has intensified during the past twenty years or so. This renaissance of research in the field has been underpinned by developments in the 'real world'. Changes in the prevailing technological paradigm, which question the role of multinationals as the sole means of attaining economic advancement (Piore and Sabel, 1984), and the diminished influence of government in the co-ordination of economic activity (Falk, 1996) underline the significance of the entrepreneur. More or less at the same time, the decline and eventual collapse of the formerly Socialist economies of Central and Eastern Europe resulted in the demise of the only 'real' alternative form of organising economic activity to the market system (Smith, 1998). These developments led to enthusiastic proclamations that 'a free enterprise revolution is sweeping around the world. ... Never in the history of mankind has there been more need to understand entrepreneurship than today' (Bygrave, 1995, p. 129). Following long periods in the shadows of scholarly enquiry, it is now widely held among researchers that the entrepreneur constitutes a key influence in conditioning the pace and direction of economic change.

The prominence given to the role of the entrepreneur in the function of the market process resulted in a substantial growth of scholarly enquiry in the field. Centres of excellence in entrepreneurial studies emerged first in the US, and subsequently in Europe and Southeast Asia. There has been a mushrooming of new journals and national and international research conferences. More importantly, however, a number of doctoral programmes have been developed 'fostering' new generations of researchers. In that respect, i.e. the prospect of continuity of work, the accumulation of a critical mass of intellectual energy is qualitatively different from earlier revivals of interest in the entrepreneur. Admittedly disparate and lacking consistency of terminology and method, entrepreneurial studies are here to stay, not so much because of the strength of theorisation to date but more importantly because of the realisation of the importance of the subject of enquiry.

Understanding the Entrepreneur

Despite the considerable fragmentation of scholarly inquiry, past research in the field of entrepreneurial studies has provided us with suggestive insights into the 'life and the works' of the entrepreneur. Theoretical constructs emanating from distinct disciplinary settings shed light upon different aspects of entrepreneurship. Economists, especially those outside the mainstream, were able to explore the function performed by entrepreneurial economic agents. We now appreciate that the characteristics of the society, within which entrepreneurial actions are realised, matter. Attempts to delve in the entrepreneurial psyche provided us with insights in the motivational influences that drive individuals to become involved in the process of business enterprise. More recently there have also been considerable advances in grasping the role of information and knowledge in the cognitive processes of the entrepreneur. However, our ability to develop a coherent and consistent theory of the entrepreneur has been hampered on account of two key problems.

The first problem with the theorisation of entrepreneurship revolves around the balance between free will versus social determinism. Though not exclusive to entrepreneurial studies the parameters of this problem have been well articulated by Mark Granovetter. He states that modern sociology conceptualises

> people as overwhelmingly sensitive to the opinions of others and hence obedient to the dictates of consensually developed systems of norms and values, internalized through socialization, so that obedience is not perceived as a burden ... Classical and neo-classical economics operates, in contrast, with an atomized, undersocialized (sic) conception of human action (Granovetter, 1985, p. 482).

Reflecting this divide, attempts at theorisation emanating from economics and psychology, concentrated heavily upon the individual leaving little - if any scope - for the exploration of social influences. In contrast, sociologists, anthropologists, as well as many economic historians commit the opposite error to that of mainstream economists, i.e. oversocialisation. Entrepreneurial behaviour in this disciplinary setting is defined by social values: thus action can be understood from what people have been taught (or raised) to think. Resolving this issue is of particular importance (we contend) as the balance between agency and context matters more in the field of entrepreneurial studies than in other areas of the social sciences. This is because the entrepreneur more than any other economic actor is involved in purposive decision-making and the implementation of actions that differ from the norm. Schumpeter conceptualises this in terms of the innovativeness of entrepreneurship, while von Mises and Kirzner use the notion of alertness to opportunities. For Shackle this involves the entrepreneur's ability to imagine future states of affairs, whilst for Casson this entails the ability to take judgemental decisions. Whereas there is profound disagreement among scholars regarding the manifestations of purposive action, there is near universal agreement that agency matters in entrepreneurial decision-making, in that, it is agency that makes it entrepreneurial. At the same time, however, there is an apparent need to understand entrepreneurial behaviour within the context where it is realised (as discussed in some detail in the previous Section).

The second problem revolves around the process of entrepreneurial decision-making in settings characterised by ambiguity and fundamental uncertainty. More specifically, how do entrepreneurs, use their cognitive frameworks and finite calculative abilities, in order to deal with imperfect as well as unknowable information? This problem, which reflects the situation confronting entrepreneurs in the process of economic interaction, is one of considerable complexity. It has four distinct dimensions, which, individually, have been explored extensively in the literature but have not been dealt with, together, in a single approach. These four dimensions also cut across and are influenced by the interface between agency and context. The first dimension includes the cognitive framework used by the entrepreneur in the process of his or her decision-making process. This framework is undoubtedly shaped by the pervasive influence of the local setting, however, it is not defined by it. Competing arguments have been advanced by those researchers exploring the sociology and those focusing upon psychology of the entrepreneur regarding the formation of cognitive frameworks. However, it is Greenfield and Strickon who have been instrumental in providing a suggestive synthesis revolving around the notion of the entrepreneurial learning. The second dimension involves the degree to which an entrepreneur can process problems of infinite complexity. This introduces the notion of bounded rationality, which has been developed significantly within the discipline of economics. The third dimension revolves around the availability of information regarding the problem confronting the entrepreneur. This is information that exists but may or may not be held by all economic agents. The parameters of this dimension have been investigated extensively by Casson. The final dimension concerns information that could assist the entrepreneur in his or her decision-making process but simply does not exist. This unknowable information derives from the fact that the entrepreneur interacts through time with other economic agents, and the outcomes to his or her actions depend to a considerable extent upon the actions and reactions of other agents. Advocates of the Austrian tradition have been instrumental in defining this dimension of the entrepreneurial decision-making process.

Institutionalism and Entrepreneurship

Early institutionalism emerged in late nineteenth and early twentieth century in the United States. Scholars working within this tradition set out to create an integrated theoretical system of the stature and scope of that of Karl Marx, Alfred Marshall, Leon Walras or Vilfredo Pareto. Central to the institutionalist thinking are the role of habits in economic activity, the conceptualisation of human agency, and the deployment of an evolutionary (non-teleological) perspective in economic science. The importance of these issues for entrepreneurship research is evident. How does the (social and economic) context influence individual actions? How can we move beyond the restrictive assumptions of neo-classicism and understand the impact of the motivational and the cognitive upon the decision-making process of economic agents? How can we understand change, from the point of view of individual economic actors who exist in an ever-changing present? These issues could form the core of the research agenda in the area of entrepreneurial studies.

However, early institutionalism failed to influence or even inform entrepreneurship research. This is despite the fact that the leading exponent of institutional ideas, Thorstein Veblen, and his work were well known to both Joseph Schumpeter and Frank Knight, who led the revival of entrepreneurship research. In fact, it was Frank Knight who advanced Veblen's candidacy for the Presidency of the American Economic Association. This raises the question why the ideas of old institutionalists remained detached from entrepreneurship research. One reason for this is the inability of early institutionalists to provide a systematic and viable alternative approach to economic theory (Hodgson, 1998). Those who followed the intellectual footsteps of Veblen were unable to agree upon a theoretical core that would underpin institutionalist research. Another reason for the detachment of institutionalism from entrepreneurship research was the dramatic decline of the former in the US after 1930. Indeed, it was not until the 1980s that the ideas of the old institutionalists grew into prominence again, partly as consequence of the emergence of a new generation of scholars in the tradition, and partly by association with the New Institutional Economics. The third, and final, reason is the changing disciplinary underpinning of entrepreneurial studies. Indeed, as economics became increasingly dominated by the mathematical style of the neo-classical school, those exploring the entrepreneurial phenomenon sought inspiration from other disciplines: such as economic history, sociology and psychology.

Institutional and evolutionary analyses first appeared in the field of entrepreneurial studies in the 1980s, and were widely used in the 1990s. The review of the literature of the psychology and the sociology of the entrepreneur (Chapter 3) suggests that these notions enhance our understanding of entrepreneurship. However, the bulk of this work in the new field of study draws upon the very influential New Institutional Economics, rather than the old institutionalist approach adopted here. Thus, it is appropriate to discuss briefly the disparities between the two traditions (for detailed comparisons see Mayhew, 1989; Hodgson, 1998), and how these may impact upon theorisation in the field of entrepreneurial studies. Indeed, there is a profound difference of perspective between the old and the new institutionalisms: whereas the former emerged as a critique and an alternative to the mainstream tradition in economics the latter constitutes an attempt to introduce institutions in mainstream analysis. In doing so, New Institutionalists rely upon some long established assumptions concerning agency. In this context 'the individual, along with his or her assumed behavioural characteristics, is taken as the elemental building-block' (Hodgson, 1994, p. 397). It is this atomistic, but at the same time agnostic, idea of the abstract individual that is fundamental to New Institutional Economics[2]. These individuals, in the process of economising the cost of transacting create institutions. Institutions are efficiency solutions that subsequently provide external constraints, conventions or openings, to the individual, which are taken for granted. In contrast old institutionalists do not take the individual as given. The behaviour of individuals is influenced by institutions. Thus 'institutions play an essential role in providing a cognitive framework for interpreting sense data and in providing intellectual habits or routines for transforming information into useful knowledge' (Hodgson, 1993, p. 16). However, institutions do not prescribe behaviour enabling individuals to take volatile decisions and instigate change or experience failure. Finally, old institutionalists adopt evolutionary analysis: it embraces diversity, and qualitative and quantitative change. Overall, the main thesis advanced here is that old institutionalism provides a more suggestive platform for the study of entrepreneurship than the New Institutional Economics.

The Argument

The entrepreneur is defined here as putting together factors of production, as well as contracts with other entrepreneurs and economic actors in a network of production and distribution[3]. The entrepreneur, unlike the salaried manager, is in a position to realise, and, make judgemental decisions about the process in its entirety. The entrepreneurial function is commonly, though not exclusively, performed by individuals. Indeed, other units of analysis (some of them emanating from pre-capitalist or non-capitalist milieus) may act in an entrepreneurial manner. Although the approach developed here acknowledges entrepreneurship beyond the entrepreneur, it concentrates upon the individual entrepreneur. This is partly because individuals have historically provided us with the most elementary building blocks in social science. Focusing upon the individual (rather than other analytical units) enables us to place the approach developed here within the broad theoretical framework of entrepreneurship research. Another reason behind the emphasis placed upon the individual economic agent is analytical simplicity. Attempting to enhance our understanding of the entrepreneur using a single analytical unit is an onerous task. Exploring entrepreneurship in different units of analysis is a near impossible task. Before going any further, we would like to stress that there have been many instances in the literature where entrepreneurial behaviour was manifested by units other than individuals (Stewart, 1989; King Whyte 1996; Lounsbury, 1998). However, the extension of theoretical constructs, developed originally to study individual economic agents, to the analysis of alternative analytical units, needs careful consideration. Simply perceiving units such as the family as a mere collection of individuals, replicates the error of neo-classical economists who delved into the economics of the household. This is an issue we will return to in the Conclusions of this book.

The Research Agenda

The main aim of the book is to develop a consistent and coherent approach for the study of the entrepreneur. The theoretical context developed here is influenced by the ideas of old institutionalists. Within this setting, our paramount objective is to provide an alternative conceptualisation of the entrepreneur that does not simply relax but breaks away from the restrictive assumptions that constrained the development of the field in economics. In doing so, particular emphasis is placed upon the interface between agency and context. We then go on to deploy this conceptualisation of the entrepreneur in the process of decision-making during economic transacting.

The ideas developed here differ in two significant ways from previous work in the field. Firstly, the underlined aim is not to pursue the development of a general theory - such as those commonly found in physics - applicable to a mosaic of socio-economic contexts. In manner reminiscent of Darwinian biology, the book identifies some general principles by which origin and development can be explained, which could be combined with data regarding specific historical settings. Secondly, the approach advanced here is not so much a creation *de novo*, but a process in which some individual contributions, such as those of Thorstein Veblen, Karl Polanyi and Mark Granovetter, are central.

Agency and Context

The cornerstone of this approach is the interaction between two core concepts (see Figure 1.1): the innate attributes (defined here as instincts) and the socio-economic environment (habits). Instincts can be clustered into two broad categories: self-regarding and other-regarding. The propensity to acquire and competitiveness fall in the former category, whilst workmanship and co-operation fall in the latter category. Outside these two grouping stands idle curiosity: the essence of the entrepreneurial process. Idle curiosity embodies the human propensity towards experimentation and creative intelligence. This could lead to new and improved ways of thinking and doing. Despite the universality of instincts, they are not rooted in the biological constitution of humans. Instincts are more than simple reflective reactions, involving consciousness and intelligence. Instincts may cancel one another through the sheer force of the contrary pull on the same body. Habits, in turn, can be one of two things: habits of thought (hereafter institutions) and technology. Institutions are defined as social constructs regarding the validity, expediency or merit of a given line of conduct or deliberation. The second type of habits is based on matter-of-fact knowledge, meaning mechanical cause and effect. Technology is the embodiment of matter-of-fact knowledge accumulated by previous generations. Moreover, the habits (institutions and technology) prevailing in a society may encourage one class of instincts at the expense of others. This leads us to the formulation of our first proposition that *the actions of the entrepreneur are shaped by the interaction between purpose and context* (see Figure 1.1).

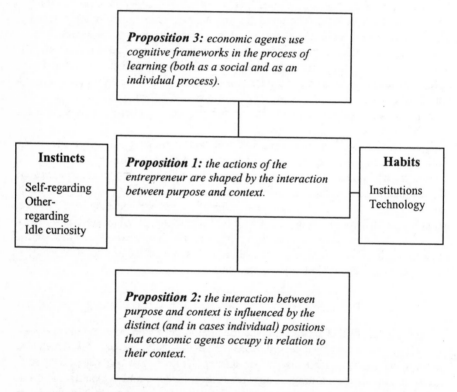

Figure 1.1 Core Concepts and Propositions

The interaction between agency and context differs significantly not only between but also within socio-economic milieus. The findings of previous research in the field of entrepreneurial studies provide support to diverging arguments regarding the integration (Weber, McClelland) or alienation (Hagen, Hoselitz, Kets de Vries) of entrepreneurial individuals from their setting. In order to resolve this issue (the tension between free will and determinism) that plagued earlier attempts at theory building, the concept of embeddedness is deployed. The individual's attempt at purposive action is examined within the context of concrete, ongoing systems of social relations (Granovetter, 1985). This raises two key issues that are instrumental in the development of an alternative approach to the study of entrepreneurial behaviour. The first revolves around the identification of the level or degree of embeddedness between members of the same milieu. The second focuses on the question: embeddedness to what? The latter is particularly relevant in the case of multicultural societies, where different and interacting institutional settings exist within the same location. These two dimensions define the 'position' of the economic agent in relation to his or her context. This leads us to the formulation of our second proposition: *the interaction between purpose and context is influenced by the distinct (and in cases individual) positions that economic agents occupy in relation to their context.*

Individuals operating in specific socio-economic settings form cognitive frameworks, that enable them to understand and interpret information (sense-data). Economic agents operating in the same context develop broadly similar cognitive frameworks that facilitate communication and social interaction. These cognitive frameworks are deployed in transforming information into meaningful knowledge (learning as a social process) as well as making sense of the experiences generated in response to individual actions performed by the economic agent (learning as an individual process). This enables us to formulate our final propositions that: *economic agents use cognitive frameworks in the process of learning (both as a social and an individual process).*

Entrepreneurial Decision-making

The contextual entrepreneur, by virtue of his or her finite calculative abilities, can not simultaneously engage in decision-making regarding a large number of complex, ambiguous and uncertain situations. Thus, situations that have been present in many instances in the past, and thus are familiar to the entrepreneur (i.e. involving a very narrow gap between the individual's capabilities and the difficulty of the situation) may be excluded from judgemental decision-making. The same is the case for situations that involve a very wide gap between the individual's capabilities and the difficulty of the situation. In both types of situation the entrepreneur may chose to tap into his or her experiences (repertoire of actions) and merely replicate actions that have been used in the past. Having identified a situation where judgemental decision-making is required, mapping its parameters is a key entrepreneurial task. In doing so, the entrepreneur is using his or her cognitive framework to interpret the information available (see Figure 1.2). However, the availability of information as well as cognition may differ between economic agents on account of the distinct and often individual positions that they occupy in relation to his or her context (Proposition 2). As a result, the entrepreneur's understanding may be at best partial or at worst misplaced.

Nonetheless, it is this understanding that guides the task of devising a number of alternative potential actions.

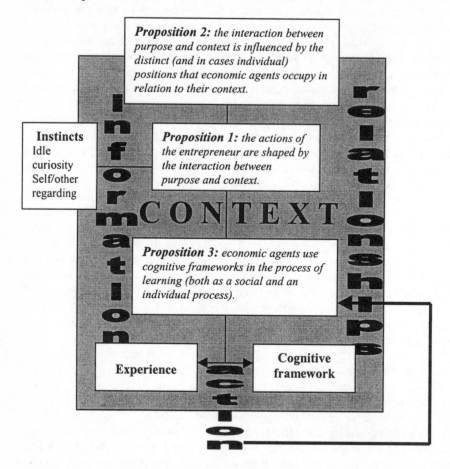

Figure 1.2 Entrepreneurial Decision-making

Idle curiosity, which constitutes the source of inquisitiveness and creative thinking, is instrumental in the development a complement of such actions. However, the ability of the individual to exploit idle curiosity (and thus the wealth of alternatives available) in his or her decision-making process is conditioned by the interaction between purpose and context (Proposition 1), which itself is defined by the position that the agent occupies (Proposition 2). As a consequence, when confronted with the same problem, different entrepreneurial agents may identify diverse complements of potential actions. Having defined a number of alternative potential actions, the entrepreneur has to identify and implement the one which is most appropriate for the situation in question. In doing so, he or she has to take into consideration the reaction of other economic agents to his or her decisions.

The reaction of other economic agents is constrained by the boundaries of acceptable behaviour that is specific to the contextual setting. The position (Proposition 2) of the entrepreneur, and the ensuing web of already existing relationships, assist him or her to second-guess the reaction of economic agents who are key in the realisation of the objectives of the decision. Lastly, the entrepreneur's own experiences are used as a proxy of potential actions of all the other economic agents who may respond to the entrepreneurial decision.

The adoption and implementation of one course of action in response to an ambiguous and uncertain situation initiates a process of generating new information and experiences. The emerging information and experiences lie at the heart of continuous entrepreneurial learning: prompting to review and revise his or her actions.

Entrepreneurship and Public Policy

During the early post-war era, academics and policy-makers appeared convinced that increased size concentration and the resulting large enterprises would be the main engines of economic growth. Consensus around this thesis was underpinned by theoretical constructs from neo-classical economics and beyond. Advocates of the mainstream tradition stressed the importance of economies of scale in generating gains in productive efficiency (Williamson, 1968). Outside the mainstream, Schumpeter (1942) and Galbraith (1956) argued that innovative capability increases with the size of the firm. Within this context, economic policy focused upon the maximisation of the benefits obtained through increased concentration of productive activities, while avoiding the costs imposed by the centralisation of economic power in the hands of a small number of large corporations (Audretsch, 2002). This view was questioned during the 1970s and challenged during the 1980s. At that time, there was a growing body of empirical evidence supporting the thesis that smaller, entrepreneurial ventures were not inefficient organisations surviving at the margins of economy, but significant sources of wealth and employment generation (Bolton, 1971; Birch, 1981; Drucker, 1986). Moreover, it was also shown that such ventures were important contributors to the overall process of innovation (Rothwell and Zegveld, 1982; Bound et al, 1984; Pavitt et al, 1987)[4].

In this changing setting the question of how we can facilitate the ventures of practising and latent entrepreneurs and, thus, create entrepreneurial economies has emerged as a key issue confronting policy-makers the world over. The rationale behind this public policy interest derives from the assumption that entrepreneurship is a key factor in the process of economic growth. Indeed, the relationship between economic growth and entrepreneurship has been the subject of a large number of studies. The findings of this research are far less conclusive than the commitment of policy-makers in promoting enterprising behaviour would let us believe.

Early research around the role of entrepreneurs in the process of economic growth focused upon the historical processes recorded in, what are now, advanced industrialised economies. More specifically, Habakkuk (1953) concludes that, during the seventeenth century, English landowners were primarily consumers rather than investors and contributed little to the development of the sector. In a seminal study exploring the processes of industrial development in Britain, France, Prussia-Germany, the United States Japan and Russia, Wilken concludes that 'entrepreneurship was of little causal significance in the industrial transition in these societies' (Wilken, 1979, p. 253). Based upon the findings of an altogether different empirical context, that of Less Developed Countries, Leff lends support to this thesis, arguing that 'earlier theoretical concerns that lack of entrepreneurship would prove a serious barrier for economic development have turned out to be much exaggerated' (Leff, 1979, p. 60).

In contrast, a growing number of recent studies[5] support the contrary argument, i.e. that there is a relationship between entrepreneurship and economic growth. More specifically, Thurik (1994) in a cross-sectional study of OECD countries for the 1984-1994 period, argues that increased entrepreneurship, measured in terms of business ownership rates, is associated with higher rates of employment. Audretsch and Thurik (2002) take this argument further, suggesting that increases in entrepreneurial activity tends to result in higher growth rates and a reduction in unemployment in subsequent time periods. The Global Entrepreneurship Monitor (Reynolds et al, 2002) also establishes an empirical link between entrepreneurship and employment change[6]. The existence of evidence supporting two opposing arguments could be explained in part by the diverse conceptual frameworks and methodological approaches adopted by individual researchers. Another plausible explanation is that the relationship between entrepreneurship and economic growth may be context specific, and, thus, differ from one socio-economic milieu to the other.

Despite the lack of conclusive evidence regarding the ability of entrepreneurs to act as catalysts of economic growth, governments pursue with great vigour the development of more entrepreneurial economies. The means of attaining this objective vary considerably. A number of public policy initiatives aim at influencing the demand for entrepreneurial ventures. Establishing well-functioning markets, providing a stable macro-economic environment, and simplifying and reducing the burden of taxation are key measures with this context (Glancey and McQuaid, 2000). The theoretical underpinning of this approach draws broadly from neo-classical economics (discussed in some detail in Chapter 2): getting the economic fundamentals right will ensure the emergence of entrepreneurs. Alternative theoretical constructs (such as those discussed in Chapter 3) suggest that economic factors are necessary but not sufficient conditions for the emergence of entrepreneurship. Instead, issues such as the legitimacy of entrepreneurship as a career path, attitudes towards risk and co-operation are instrumental in determining the supply of entrepreneurial economic agents (OECD, 1997). In response, governments have gradually moved away from the exclusive use of traditional policy instruments towards policies aiming to enable entrepreneurial activities (Audretsch, 2002). In this setting it is argued that

[f]ostering a culture of entrepreneurship requires a two fold strategy. On the one hand it involves measures to encourage individuals to become an entrepreneur and to equip them with the necessary skills to make their business successful, including reforms in training and education systems, cultural changes and measures to remove obstacles to business start-up. On the other hand, encouraging entrepreneurship also implies creating a business environment which is conducive to start-ups, growth and successful transfer of businesses (EC, 1998, p. 3).

This led to the introduction of the concept of entrepreneurship policy, which is used to denote the

measures taken to stimulate entrepreneurship, that are aimed at the pre-start-up, start-up and post-start-up phases of the entrepreneurial process, and designed and delivered to address the areas of motivation, opportunity and skills, with the primary objective of encouraging more people in the population to consider entrepreneurship as an option, to move into the nascent stage of taking steps to get started and to proceed into the infancy and early stages of a business (Lundstrom and Stevenson, 2001, p. 132).

Thus, the domain of entrepreneurship policy is potentially large. It can include activities at different levels of government (from local to supranational), and multiple dimensions. In response to the potentially wide remit of such policy, there has been an attempt by scholars in the field to distinguish between entrepreneurship policy on the one hand, and public policy that shapes the context for entrepreneurial ventures on the other. The key criterion used for this purpose is the time-scope of policy; with entrepreneurship policy focusing upon 'intermediate conditions', rather than background or short-term conditions (Hart, 2001; Reynolds et al, 2002). The rationale behind this choice is two-fold. The first concerns with the need to identify some well-established boundaries among policy domains. The second reason behind the emphasis placed upon 'intermediate conditions' is that the time-scale concerned allows policy-makers (and why not scholars) 'the possibility of perceiving (and perhaps taking credit for) the consequences of their efforts' (Hart, 2001, p. 8). Thus, education policy or macroeconomic policy fall outside the boundaries of entrepreneurship policy.

Entrepreneurship policy is also perceived to be different from traditional policies aiming at supporting small and medium-sized enterprises (hereafter SMEs). The later is fairly well-established, invariably the domain of ministry or governmental agency in advanced industrialised countries, whilst no such agencies exist to promote entrepreneurs (Audretsch, 2002). Moreover, SME policy revolves around supporting existing organisational structures (businesses), whilst entrepreneurship policy focuses upon individuals, economic agents who want to pursue opportunities. Thus, entrepreneurship policy embraces four areas, which fall outside the confines of SME policy: entrepreneurship education, reduction of entry and exit barriers, the promotion of an entrepreneurial culture, and specific measures to help individuals though the nascent and start-up stages (Stevenson and Lundstrum, 2002). A broad range of public policy measures fall within these four areas, including attempts to increase entrepreneurship awareness through the introduction of enterprise into the school and college curriculum, provide finance and mentoring to special groups (such as younger and older workers, females, and disabled individuals) where rates of enterprise creation are very low, developing entrepreneurial skills through the provision of training and mentoring to practising entrepreneurs, seeking to minimise the administrative burden on small and/or new firms, increasing the supply of equity capital through tax breaks for wealthy individuals who want to become business angels (for a review see Storey, 2003).

Entrepreneurship policy is a relatively new domain in public policy, but seems likely to become of increasing importance. It is becoming increasingly sophisticated, recognising the need for segmentation, and is informed by the outcomes of scholarly research. The strength of the relationship between academics and policy-makers augers well for the future: i.e. generating the knowledge needed in order to address policy questions. Although the book focuses squarely upon theoretical issues it is our intention to return to the issue of public policy, exploring the implications of our approach.

The Structure of the Book

The Book is organised into three distinct entities. The first, comprising of Chapters 2 and 3, explores the literature. The main aim of these two Chapters is to define the dimensions of the two key research questions, and to identify the characteristics of approaches that have provided significant insights in the study of the entrepreneur as well as the features of other less productive theoretical constructs. The review of the literature is organised along the lines of disciplinary setting: the main divide being between economics on the one side, and other disciplines from the social sciences on the other. The rationale behind the decision to dedicate a separate Chapter on economics and the field of entrepreneurial studies rests squarely with the disciplinary origin of the approach advanced here, rather than any value judgement regarding the suggestiveness - or otherwise - of elements of the entrepreneurship literature. The second composite part of the book, including of Chapters 4 and 5, develops an institutionalist approach in the study of the entrepreneur. The third distinct element of the book, consisting of Chapter 6, examines the analytical power of the proposed approach using some empirical evidence.

More specifically, Chapter 2 reviews earlier theoretical constructs in the field of entrepreneurial studies emanating from economics. Whilst no single economic theory of the entrepreneur acquired a position of dominance, continuity and the evolution of ideas is apparent. Thus, the work of economists enables us to gain considerable insights upon the influence of time upon entrepreneurial decision-making. Moreover, economists explore both cognitive and motivational influences – depending upon their conceptual point of departure. Reviewing the literature exploring the sociology and psychology of the entrepreneur – outside economics – constitutes the main purpose of Chapter 3. Conceptual schemata emanating from disciplines such as sociology, psychology, anthropology and economic history is disparate and lacks even the tentative links apparent in economics. However, they enhance our understanding of the interface between agency and context. Moreover, rather perversely, it is work from disciplines other than economics that introduces notions such as institutional and evolutionary analyses into the field of entrepreneurial studies[7].

Chapter 4 introduces the main component elements of the institutionalist approach advanced here. Because of the lack of consistency of terminology among advocates of old institutionalism, conceptual clarity is considered essential. Therefore, the concepts of instincts and habits are defined and analysed. Then we go on to deploy the core theoretical propositions of our approach in understanding entrepreneurial behaviour. In the following Chapter we utilise the alternative conceptualisation of the entrepreneur in order to explore the entrepreneurial decision-making under conditions of less than perfect (in the mainstream sense of the term) information and bounded rationality. Particular emphasis is placed upon situations that may result in predictable or unpredictable behaviour.

The following Chapter (6) examines the explanatory power of the approach developed here, in relation to other theoretical constructs in the field of entrepreneurial studies. In doing so we focus upon the analysis of the voluminous body of scholarly research regarding the origins of entrepreneurial economic agents in post-socialist Russia.

The final Chapter attempts to conclude by drawing the different themes into a coherent approach that enhances our understanding of the entrepreneur. The book ends where it begins, by using the approach developed in order to explore the implications upon method and the direction of future research in the field of entrepreneurial studies, as well as examining the impact of the proposed approach upon entrepreneurship policy.

Notes

1 This could be either as a result of entrepreneurial foresight (Knight, 1921) or access to information not readily available to the population at large (Casson, 1982).
2 Although the bounded nature of the rationality of economic agents is acknowledged by advocates of the New Institutional Economics.
3 Placed within the context of existing theoretical constructs, the definition used for the purposes of this study follows on a lengthy tradition of functional definitions emanating from economics (see Chapter 2 for a more detailed discussion of such definitions).
4 This shift can be explained in large part by a technology induced shift in the prevailing technological paradigm. Thus, whereas the large-scale assembly-line production technologies of the early post-war era encouraged mass production, this was not the case with information and communication technologies. The latter enabled the production of a wide and changing array of customised products, shifting the balance towards flexible

specialisation (Piore and Sable, 1984; Hirst and Zeitlin, 1991).

5 Apart from those studies reviewed here, Birch (1981), Storey and Johnson (1987), Weigant and Audretsch (1999) and Audretsch et al (2002) support the thesis that there is a relationship between entrepreneurship and growth, measured invariably in terms of employment. Davis et al (1996) and Wagner (1995) present recent critiques of this thesis.

6 The adoption of a quantitative methodology by recent studies creates particular difficulties in establishing causation. Thus, in most instances there is evidence about the presence of a relationship between entrepreneurship and economic growth but precious little indication regarding the direction of the relationship.

7 This is despite the fact that institutional and evolutionary analyses are becoming increasingly important in economics. In fact, it is the work of economists which influenced especially sociological research in the field.

Chapter 2

The Entrepreneur in Economics

Introduction

It is widely held in the literature that the entrepreneur constitutes a key influence in conditioning the pace and direction of change as few - if any - other economic agents are able to do. But this much having been acknowledged, it has been proved more than usually problematic to incorporate the entrepreneurial function into the mainstream models of value theory or the theory of the firm (Baumol, 1995). A number of arguments have been put forward regarding the exclusion of the entrepreneur from the mainstream tradition (discussed in some detail later in this Chapter). These arguments do not only provide an explanation why the theoretical firm is entrepreneurless, but also underline the difficulty of the task of introducing the entrepreneur in the mainstream. The magnitude of this task is also manifested by the limitations of the handful of attempts to introduce the entrepreneur in the neo-classical analysis during the past thirty years or so. As a consequence, a number of suggestive theoretical constructs regarding the entrepreneur and his or her function in the market process are to be found within alternative traditions in economics.

Earlier attempts at understanding entrepreneurial decision-making, rather than a comprehensive review of the accumulated knowledge, constitute the main focus of our investigation in this Chapter[1]. In doing so we decided to organise the accumulated body of literature in chronological order. We believe that this is the most appropriate structure as it enables us to identify the (admittedly selective) continuity in the field. In order to assist the reader follow these – often ambiguous – linkages we created Table 2.1, which illustrates the evolution of ideas on the entrepreneur in economics, through time and across intellectual traditions. Many scholars in economics may find the divide between early and classical, mainstream, Austrian and radical too broad, concealing considerable disparities in the intellectual origins of scholars. In response we would like to stress that this divide is a purposeful one: attempting to explore the tentative linkages in the economic theories of the entrepreneur. Moreover, this divide is only partial in that it focuses only upon those ideas developed within the field of entrepreneurial studies. This is particularly important as to most economists the entrepreneur was part of a broader research agenda. Lastly, we contend that given the four groupings the categorisation of scholars is correct. Only Schumpeter presented us with a dilemma regarding his inclusion (or not) in the Austrian tradition. We believe that his work on entrepreneurship is significantly different from that of the Mises-Hayek-Kirzner continuum to warrant separate examination.

Table 2.1 Economic Theories of the Entrepreneur

	Early and Classical	Mainstream	Austrian	Radical
18th and 19th century	Cantillon, 1755 Say, 1803	-	-	-
1900-1933	Hawley, 1907	Knight, 1921	-	Schumpeter, 1928
1934-1966	-	-	Mises, 1949 Hayek, 1937; 1948	-
1967-to date	-	Baumol, 1968; 1995 Casson, 1982; 1998	Schakle, 1970 Kirzner, 1981; 1997	Choi, 1993 Harper, 1996

Early Conceptualisations of the Entrepreneur

It is now widely acknowledged that Cantillon, in the first half of the eighteenth century, provides the earliest attempt at exploring the entrepreneurial function in economics. He developed a hierarchical theory of social classes (Schumpeter, 1994 [1954]). The landed aristocracy, which occupies the top of the economic and social order, is financially independent by virtue of its property rights over natural resources. The rest of the inhabitants are financially dependent and

> they may be divided into two classes, namely the Entrepreneurs and Wage Earners; and that the entrepreneurs work for uncertain wages, so to speak, and all the others for certain wages ... The General who has a salary, the Courtier who has a pension, and the Domestic who has wages are in the latter class. All the others are Entrepreneurs, whether they establish themselves with a capital to carry on their enterprise, or are Entrepreneurs of their own work without any capital, and they may be considered as living subjects to uncertainty; even Beggars and Robbers are Entrepreneurs of this class (Cantillon, 1932 [1755] p. 54).

Cantillon, thus, sets very low entrance requirements to the entrepreneurial class - providing probably the broadest definition in the accumulated literature. Beggars and robbers as well as farmers[2] are some of the elements comprising the entrepreneurial class within this theoretical framework.

The ability to take decisions within conditions of uncertainty emerges as the defining feature of entrepreneurial activity. This uncertainty derives from the fact that future market demand is unpredictable; specifically where expenditures are known and certain but incomes are unknown and uncertain (Binks and Vale, 1991). The entrepreneur's success lies with an ability to perceive and predict the actions and reactions of his or her counterparts better than they can predict his or her own. The unique characteristic of Cantillon's entrepreneur is foresight and confidence to operate under conditions of uncertainty (Casson, 1982). The resulting entrepreneurial profit derives from risk-bearing rather than 'orthodox effort'.

Cantillon went on to explore what determines the supply of entrepreneurial talent in an economy. In doing so he drew upon his idea that the economy is an organised system of interconnected markets that operate in such a fashion as to achieve equilibrium. Therefore, according to Cantillon entrepreneurs are allocated through the same mechanism that allocates labourers or goods

> All these Entrepreneurs become consumers and customers of each other... They adjust their numbers in the State to their Customers or to their market. If there are too many Hatters in a City or in a street for the number of persons who buy their hats there, those having the fewest customers will have to go bankrupt; if there are too few, it will be a profitable enterprise, which will encourage some new Hatters to open shop there, and it is thus that Entrepreneurs of all kinds, at their own risk, adjust their numbers in a State (Cantillon, 1932 [1755] p. 56).

Cantillon's contribution lies with the fact that he emphasised the existence of a third category of individuals beyond the landowners and labourers. He gave a name to those persons who are not involved in the production process and whose contribution in terms of wealth creation is unobservable and intangible: entrepreneurs. He went on to provide a systematic exposition of what distinguishes the entrepreneurial function and behaviour.

Jean Baptiste Say aspired to provide a systematic exposition of Smith's main ideas, which was effectively an alternative to Ricardo's interpretation, that identified and explored the function performed by entrepreneurs (Roll, 1992). Though acknowledging the importance of all three factors of production (land, capital and labour) he identifies labour as the key to production. He develops a tripartite division of labour between theory (the study of laws and course of nature), application (of the theory for a useful purpose) and execution (Barreto, 1989). Each function of human industry is identified with a specific agent: the philosopher who studies the theory, the entrepreneur who creates useful products, and the workman who supplies manual labour.

Thus, Say regards the entrepreneur as a rare phenomenon who is able to co-ordinate and combine the factors of production. The overriding characteristic of the condition in which the entrepreneur operates is the variety of inputs and markets that must be successfully combined (Binks and Vale, 1991). The emphasis is not restricted in the final product markets as is the case with Cantillon. The entrepreneur is also confronted with other factor markets such as those for raw materials, labour, finance, land and plant and equipment.

However, following on from Cantillon's early works, Say was the first to explicitly distinguish between the function of the entrepreneur and that of the capitalist (Schumpeter, 1994 [1954]). The entrepreneur is the active agent in the production process who may work from capital borrowed by capitalists (Koolman, 1971). In return for the co-ordinating role of the entrepreneur s/he receives a wage which can be theoretically separated from the interest received by the capitalist.

This divide between the capitalist and the entrepreneur influenced Say's exploration of the factors which determine the supply of entrepreneurial talent. In doing so, he moves away from Cantillon's mechanistic interpretation. Say argues that the entrepreneur does not have to be rich

> for he may work upon borrowed capital; but he must at least be solvent, and have the reputation of intelligence, prudence, probity and regularity .... [he must have] a combination of moral qualities that are not often found together. Judgement, perseverance, and a knowledge of the world (Say, 1830 [1803], p. 285).

Another limit to the supply of entrepreneurship is sheer bad lack.

Say also realises the role of uncertainty. In fact, it is uncertainty that makes the entrepreneurial function difficult. Thus, he conceptualises the entrepreneur as a specialist at accommodating the unexpected and overcoming problems. The entrepreneur 'is called upon to estimate, with tolerable accuracy, the importance of the specific product, the probable amount of demand, and the means of its production' (Say, 1830 original 1803, p. 285). However, uncertainty is not the result of imperfect information. Indeed, in Say's theory information is essentially a free good. Uncertainty emanates partly from the fact that the entrepreneur has to estimate fairly accurately the importance of a product and the probable amount of demand.

Say's contribution in the broad area of entrepreneurial studies derives from the association of entrepreneurship with the combination of factors of production into a producing organism. Thus, the entrepreneur's main function is that of a central processing unit, which receives information from a variety of sources, and makes production decisions. Say realises to some extent, that a greatly improved theory of economic process may be derived by making the entrepreneur the pivot on which everything turns. But, 'he certainly failed to make full use of it and presumably did not see all its analytic possibilities' (Schumpeter, 1994 [1954], p. 555). Moreover, in a manner typical of his era Say assumes free access to information. Finally, he goes to considerable lengths in stressing the significance of the entrepreneur: the work of the scientist and the workman is necessary, but it is the entrepreneur who drives the productive forces by the useful application of theory and the direction of execution (Barreto, 1989).

The theoretical constructs of Cantillon and Say possess apparent limitations: they fail to examine the dynamics of the entrepreneurial process, and shed no light on what influences the supply of entrepreneurship. However, their work is still relevant. This is because they identify entrepreneurship as a distinct analytical category, and, define the parameters of further research – emanating from economics - in the field of entrepreneurial studies. After, these early works interest on the function of the entrepreneur diminishes. For classical political economists, and especially those influenced by Ricardo, the entrepreneur is synonymous with the capitalist, whilst the entrepreneurial function becomes the realm of the 'invisible hand of the market'.

Hawley's Enterpriser

Following a long period in the shadows entrepreneurship re-emerged as the focus of economic enquiry during the early twentieth century. Frederick Barnard Hawley attempted to integrate the entrepreneur (identified in his work as the enterpriser) in classical theory. His ideas, though suggestive, have failed to make any impact in the field of entrepreneurial studies to date[3]. His inability to influence scholarly inquiry could be explained in part by his attachment to the classical tradition at a time when the static equilibrium framework was growing into prominence, and the fact that his work was subsequently overshadowed by the ideas of Knight. Moreover, Hawley's choice of terminology, calling his theoretical construct 'the risk theory of profit' and the use of enterpriser instead of entrepreneur, lead post-Knightian economists to tend to ignore him.

Hawley argued that enterprise was a crucial missing element in economics. Enterprise is not a factor of production (like land, labour and capital) but 'the assumption of responsibility in industrial undertaking' (Hawley, 1907, p 108). Production factors are the tools, whilst enterprise is the head of the productive process (Barreto, 1989). Thus, the enterpriser has a key function in the production process: using the means of production, s/he decides what to do. However, the enterpriser operates in a world of uncertainty. Therefore, it is the enterpriser who assumes the responsibility of the use of factors of production. Hawley conceptualises the enterpriser as the motivator and uncertainty bearer who will decide what shall be produced, how much of it, and by what method, in order to attain his/her own ends (Hawley, 1907).

Hawley's contribution is limited, though admittedly purposefully so. Whilst he acknowledges the role of the enterpriser in motivating production and dealing with uncertainty he remains agnostic about either the cognitive or motivational influences of such individuals. To do otherwise it would require a move beyond the assumptions of the classical tradition. However, his work is of interest, as it constitutes an intermediate stage between Cantillon and Knight.

Schumpeter on Entrepreneurship

Joseph Alois Schumpeter was undoubtedly more responsible than any other economist of his time for the revival of interest on the function and characteristics of the entrepreneur. He was educated, and influenced, by von Bawerk and von Wiser: two leading scholars of the Austrian School. As a consequence, and with some justification, Schumpeter is often grouped together with Ludwig von Mises as the two most distinguished exponents of the second generation of Austrians. However, his treatise on entrepreneurship differs significantly from that Mises-Hayek-Kirzner tradition. Thus, for the purposes of this study Schumpeter's contribution stands alone, too idiosyncratic to fit with the orthodoxy of any one school of thought (Stolper, 1968).

Schumpeter detaches the entrepreneur from risk-bearing: the latter is the function of the capitalist or of the banking sector who lend the money to the entrepreneur. Instead, the entrepreneur is defined as the innovator, the individual who introduces new combinations of production factors. He argues that

> the essense of entrepreneurship lies in the perception and exploitation of new opportunities in the realm of business ... it always has to do with bringing about a different use of national resources in that they are withdrawn from their traditional employ and subjected to new combinations (Schumpeter, 1928, p. 380).

Schumpeter goes on to identify five types of innovation: the introduction of a new good; the introduction of a new method of production; the opening of a new market; the conquest of a new source of raw materials; the creation of a new type of industrial organisation. Therefore anyone who performs any of these functions - either an independent businessman or a director of a larger organisation - is an entrepreneur.

One interesting and not frequently discussed aspect of Schumpeter's work revolves around the identification of appropriate units of analysis. For someone who contributed to the advancement of methodological individualism, Schumpeter, rather unexpectedly, acknowledges that the entrepreneurial function does not have to be embodied in a single physical person. Instead, the economic agent who acts entrepreneurially is specific to the characteristics of the socio-economic milieu. Using an example from the US he argues that

> the practice of farmers in this country has been revolutionized again and again by the introduction of methods worked out in the Department of Agriculture, and by the Department of Agriculture's success in teaching these methods. In this case then it is the Department of Agriculture that acted as the entrepreneur (Schumpeter, 1949, p. 70).

Schumpeter (1949) goes to considerable length in distinguishing between the entrepreneurial function and the entrepreneur. Drawing from Say's tripartite division of labour (see above) Schumpeter identifies a clear division between invention and entrepreneurship: the latter being the remit of economic agents who get things done (Say's application) whilst the former of those engaged with the production of new (scientific) ideas (Say's abstract labour). The ideas generated by inventors are not by themselves of any importance for economic activity (Schumpeter uses the example of ancient Greeks who had produced all that is necessary to create a steam engine but actually did not build one), whilst not all innovations need to embody something that is scientifically new (Schumpeter, 1947). In some cases invention and the entrepreneurship are combined within the same economic agent, however, they remain distinct analytical categories. Similarly, Schumpeter provides a distinction between management and entrepreneurship. The former is perceived to be

> an exceedingly simple matter and essentially a matter of administration if the combinations that have been carried into effect in the past had simply to be repeated subject to those adaptations which common business experience suggests in the face of conditions that change under the influence of external factors ... but if we confine Say's definition to cases in which combinations that are not inherited from the past have to be set anew, then the situation is different and we do have a distinctive function before us (Schumpeter, 1949, pp. 67-68).

Although there is no clear dividing line between the managerial and the entrepreneurial function, Schumpeter suggests that this is a useful divide that conveys an essential difference. He goes on to argue that entrepreneurs do not only and always perform the entrepreneurial function. The entrepreneur is also performing a number of non-entrepreneurial functions. The entrepreneur is also his or her own technical expert, his own buying and selling agent, the head of his or her office, his or her own personnel manager and even his or her own solicitor. Thus, Schumpeter concludes that although it may make sense to consider business activity as a whole (including both managerial and entrepreneurial functions), the distinctive element of entrepreneurship should not be lost from sight[4].

Having distinguished the entrepreneurial function from those of invention and management Schumpeter stresses the importance of the former. He argues that the entrepreneur changes the conditions of supply, combines resources in new ways and thereby sets a new production function (Martinelli, 1994). He explores the revolutionary character of the entrepreneur with the same admiration that Marx showed for the proletariat. In fact, Schumpeter is responsible for the conception of the entrepreneur as the heroic figure of capitalist development. Thus, talented entrepreneurs are a very scarce breed.

The scarcity of entrepreneurial talent however, does not lie in their cognitive processes, an argument originally made by Cantillon and further advanced by Frank Knight (see Section below) one of Schumpeter's contemporaries. A preference for saving and investment is one of the distinguishing characteristics of the entrepreneur. More importantly, however, entrepreneurship calls for a specific type of personality and conduct which differs from the rational economic man. The entrepreneur takes advantage of rationally based components of his environment, but he is not the average product of capitalist culture. S/he is the bold leader, willing to break through a wide array of ordinary constraints; this sets him apart from the manager (Martinelli, 1994). S/he is defined by a unique set of motivational factors. These include the dream and the will to establish a private kingdom; the will to conquer, to fight, to prove oneself superior to all others, to succeed for the shake of it not the fruits of success; and the joy of creating.

So how does the entrepreneur fit in the process of creative destruction? The argument goes that the climate most favourable to innovation is when the economy is approaching equilibrium, for then the future seems relatively easy to foresee. The first innovations are made by the most talented entrepreneurs who in return enjoy greater profits. Their success encourages less talented entrepreneurs to enter the market. Because they are adapting ideas - which have already been tried and tested by pioneers - the capitalists perceive the risks of backing less talented entrepreneurs are relatively low. A wave of innovation follows but as the market becomes more cluttered, the rate of profit falls and innovative activity diminishes.

It is difficult to overestimate Schumpeter's contribution in the field of entrepreneurial studies. He revived scholarly interest in entrepreneurship and its function in the process of economic development, among economists, whilst also supporting the Harvard Centre for Research in Entrepreneurial History (see Chapter 3). Moreover, the Schumpeterian entrepreneur is a contextual agent, embedded in a historically conditioned milieu. However, Schumpeter's work on the process of entrepreneurial decision-making is short on detail. He states that 'the interaction of institutional forms and entrepreneurial activity … is, as has already been intimated, a major topic for further enquiry' (Schumpeter, 1947, p. 153).

Knight: Entrepreneurship, Uncertainty and Risk

Frank Knight's work appeared more or less at the same time as that of Schumpeter, and contributed significantly in the revival of scholarly interest in entrepreneurship. Drawing upon the work of Cantillon and Hawley who conceptualise entrepreneurship as decision-making under conditions of uncertainty, Knight advances a sophisticated analysis of the entrepreneur (Casson, 1995). In doing so he places the entrepreneur in the centre of the free enterprise system, securing and directing co-operative effort in a social group.

His point of departure is a distinction between risk and uncertainty. He used the former notion to describe situations in which probabilities are available to guide decision-making, whilst the latter concept was reserved for situations in which information is too imprecise to be summarised by probabilities (Runde, 1998). In situations of risk, events can be insured against in some way, and the insurance cost added to the cost of production. In contrast, uncertainty is identified with a situation where the probabilities of alternative outcomes can not be determined either by a priori reasoning or statistical inference. Uncertainty is a ubiquitous aspect of business decisions because production takes time (Knight, 1921). Decisions on inputs must be made now in order to create output for the future. Households, as factor owners demand spot payment for their services. At the same time they are unwilling to commit themselves on future demand for the product, because they anticipate that unforeseeable changes will occur. Knight then argues that

> [W]hen uncertainty is present and the task of deciding what to do and how to do it takes ascendancy over that of execution, the internal organisation of the productive groups is no longer a matter of indifference or a mechanical detail. Centralisation of this deciding and controlling function is imperative, a process of "cephalization" such as has taken place in the evolution of organic life, is inevitable, and for the same reasons as in the case of biological evolution (Knight, 1921, pp. 268-269).

The presence of uncertainty leads economic agents to the voluntary specialisation of decision-making on the basis of (i) their knowledge and judgement, (ii) their degree of foresight, (iii) their superior managerial ability (i.e. foresight and an ability to control others), and (iv) their confidence in backing their judgement with actions. Entrepreneurs are those individuals who can foresee the future, who can develop correct hypothesis regarding uncertain future events. Moreover, the entrepreneurs take responsibility and control, as they

> ... "assume the risk" or "insure" the doubtful and timid by guaranteeing to the latter a specified income in return for an assignment of actual results (Knight, 1921, pp. 269-270).

The result is the enterprise system, characterised by the emergence of a social group of business people, who specialise in the function of responsible direction of economic life: the entrepreneurs. In return for their actions the entrepreneurs are the recipients of pure profit. Profit is the residual income available after all contractual payments have been deducted from the revenues of the enterprise. It is the reward to the entrepreneur for bearing the costs of uncertainty.

What distinguishes entrepreneurs from other (non-entrepreneurial) individuals is their

> capacity by perception and inference to form correct judgements as to the future course of events in the environment ... Of special importance is the variation in the power of reading human nature, of forecasting the conduct of other men... (Knight, 1921, pp. 241-242).

In understanding entrepreneurial action, as the judgemental element of human action in general, Knight extends the boundaries of the mainstream, as he explores behavioural aspects of the discipline. On the issue of the ends he claims that although economic agents behave as if they are trying to maximise something, this differs from the fixed quantitative utility functions of the mainstream. Every end is more or less redefined in the process of achieving it, and this is one of the reasons for desiring the activity[5] (Knight, 1935). He believes that people behave as if they are trying to maximise something. However, he goes on to argue that the real ends are not the concrete quantitative utility functions.

In the pursuit of changing ends, each economic agent engages in the 'competitive game': playing the game generates its own satisfaction in addition to those of winning (Casson, 1995). However, play is to a large extent a social activity, influenced by 'other-regarding' motives and desires, directed not to material things, but to forms of social relationships (Knight, 1921). Thus, it is important to understand what is happening on the inside of entrepreneurs. Knight's response is to emphasise the impact of the subconscious: i.e. thinking about something and then forgetting it, only for the solution to come to us at some point in the future 'out of the blue' (for a detailed discussion see Franz, 2002).

Knight's contribution to the area of entrepreneurial studies rests not only in the oft-commended distinction between risk and uncertainty. He develops a hybrid model that can be used in understanding entrepreneurial decision-making. However, this aspect of his work remains incomplete: Knight believes that the processes of the subconscious are so mysterious, that we have to accept the rationality solution as 'second best'.

The Neo-classical Exclusion

The work of Frank Knight, and particularly his distinction between risk and uncertainty, has been very influential upon advocates of the mainstream tradition in economics. However, entrepreneurship, a notion central to the ideas developed by Knight, faded into obscurity during the rise into prominence of the neo-classical tradition in the mid-twentieth century. As Samuelson and Hicks led the revival of the work of Walras and Pareto, general equilibrium models acquired a position of prominence in microeconomics (Cosgel, 1996). This precluded the emergence of a neoclassical theory of the entrepreneur, a point conceded even by advocates of the mainstream tradition[6] (Baumol, 1968; Blaug, 1986; Herbert and Link, 1988; Barreto, 1989). This exclusion has been graphically portrayed by William Baumol (1968) in his influential article in the *American Economic Review*. He argues that

> [t]he entrepreneur is at the same time one of the most intriguing and one of the most elusive characters in the cast that constitutes the subject of economic analysis. He has long been recognized as the apex of the hierarchy that determines the behavior of the firm and thereby bears a heavy responsibility for the vitality of the free enterprise society ... In more recent years ... he has ... virtually disappeared from the theoretical literature (Baumol, 1968, p. 64).

A number of competing arguments have been advanced in order to explain the exclusion of the entrepreneur from the mainstream tradition. The first argument attempts to explain the difficulty of addressing entrepreneurship in neoclassical economics on account of the very nature of the subject - especially as defined by the Schumpeterian tradition. It circumscribes what the theory is able to do. Indeed, the decision-making process of the innovative entrepreneur revolves around the introduction of something unprecedented and unexpected. This precludes any useful description of such a function into the language of mathematics, which in turn rules out systematic optimisation. Hebert and Link also argue that 'the entrepreneur was squeezed from economics when the discipline attempted to emulate the physical sciences by incorporating the mathematical method' (Hebert and Link, 1988, p. 158). Another explanation of the neo-classical exclusion takes issue with the emphasis on equilibrium. Mainstream theory describes the conditions for competitive equilibrium, but can not explain the way in which market forces bring about adjustments in process and quantities and the introduction of new products and processes (Harper, 1996). As a result, Mark Blaug argues that 'so long as economic analysis is pre-occupied with the nature of static equilibrium under conditions of perfect competition, there is simply no room ... for a theory of entrepreneurship' (Blaug, 1986, p. 223). On a similar note Demsetz (1983) attributes the neglect of the entrepreneur by the mainstream tradition to several problems associated with the study of economic change. The inability to introduce the entrepreneur in mainstream analysis is also on account of the basic assumption that the individual has free access to all the necessary information required for effective decision-making, combined with the notion of rational, maximising behaviour by economic agents (Barreto, 1989). These assumptions divorce the entrepreneur from all elements of responsibility and judgement (Martinelli, 1994). Many mainstream economists have tried to advance the conceptualisation of entrepreneurship as a dependent variable in economic analysis, through the relaxation of the assumptions about access to information and rationality. This led to the introduction of new parameters in the model of human agency - such as ethics and judgement. The realisation of the implications of complex and uncertain environments upon the decision-making process of economic agents, has prompted advocates of the neo-classical tradition to revisit the assumption regarding the access and availability of information. However, attempts at addressing both issues were tempered by an innate desire to maintain the essence of the 'economic man' in one format or another. In a recent, and suggestive, contribution to the debate Young Back Choi centres upon the notion of maximisation. Questioning both method and assumptions he argues that

> [t]he mathematical tool of maximization has many undeniably useful applications ... in a deterministic or semideterministic environment, where the possession of perfect, or quasi-perfect, information can be taken for granted, objective functions are well defined, and alternatives and their expected values are known in full (Choi, 1993, p. 16).

However, these circumstances are not met when agents face genuine uncertainty, and as Frank Knight observes, the main difficulty confronting decision-makers is defining the problem to be solved. Introducing maximisation in order to resolve an incorrectly defined problem can result in error. In response, scholars of the neo-classical tradition attempted to model the problem of decision-making under uncertainty. Within this context, agents are assumed to maximise expected utility. However, the new model does not deal with uncertainty as defined by Knight but rather with risk (Hey, 1979), whilst still assuming away the issue of how the individual decision-maker arrives at the expectation based on what s/he maximises.

Whilst these arguments highlight several reasons for the neo-classical exclusion, and identify a number of problems in introducing the entrepreneur in the mainstream tradition in economics they fall well short of a satisfactory explanation. The mathematical method undoubtedly creates difficulties in introducing the entrepreneurial function, the emphasis placed upon equilibrium solutions tends to obscure the process of change, and the assumptions regarding information and human agency tend to 'de-skill' the decision-making process of economic agents. However, all these component elements of the mainstream are symptomatic of its origins and aspirations. In particular they have all been intentional features of theory, and have been present since neo-classical economics was born (Ackerman, 1999). The issue of origin must be traced back to the marginal revolution of the 1870s[7]. Philip Mirowski (1989) shows, drawing from published work and bibliographical information of pioneers of the neo-classical tradition and making comparisons to the physics of the time, that there is a penetration of mechanical analogies and mathematical thinking into economics. Thus, according to Mirowski, the marginal revolution is a shift in emphasis towards quantitative specification, laws of motion, causation, and equilibrium associated with the mechanistic metaphor[8]. Similarly, Ingrao and Israel (1999) content that original constructs in mainstream economics is a continuation of a major current of 19th century European social thought to identify law-like regularities in social life and organisation. Cosgel (1996) takes this argument further, suggesting that the shift towards a mechanistic metaphor has also produced heuristic metaphors such as the mind as a calculator and the man as a pleasure machine, that prevent altogether the introduction of the entrepreneur from the mainstream tradition[9]. Indeed, there is a growing body of scholarly opinion conceding the influence of physics in mainstream economics (Hodgson, 1998). The implications of this thesis are far reaching, suggesting that the adoption of an approach that is inherently mechanistic may preclude 'the solution to the problem of the entrepreneur through minor cosmetic adjustments within ...[the] ... adopted framework' (Cosgel, 1996, p. 74).

The origin of the mainstream is inextricably linked with the aspiration of this tradition to raise the status of economics to that of the natural sciences. Equipped with methods that enable advocates of the mainstream to lay claim to certainties commonly identified with physics, economics is often reported to have risen above the other social sciences[10]. The adoption of instruments of the mainstream by sociologists, anthropologists, and political scientists is also perceived to be evidence of the probity of the approach (Choi, 1993). We argue that the neo-classical exclusion could be explained by its physics-like origin and aspirations. In this setting there is little – if any scope – to address an economic agent who thrives in uncertainty.

The explanation advanced here raises the question of the significance of the exclusion of the entrepreneur for the mainstream. Does the exclusion of the entrepreneur really matter? The parameters of this question have been set by Wilken (1979) in the context of economic development, when he distinguished between definitional and causal significance. He argues that

> [e]ntrepreneurship will have *definitional* significance in all situations, because, by definition, it is a term referring to the initiating activity of human actors ... money does not invest itself, labor does not hire itself, factories do not build themselves ... in terms of its *causal significance* ... our concern is with the extent to which entrepreneurship *adds to, or detracts from*, the influence of other factors affecting economic growth (Wilken, 1979, pp. 4-5).

The implications of the explanation of the neo-classical exclusion advanced here, if entrepreneurship is only of definitional significance, is an inherent inability to understand the entrepreneur, and fail to delve into a central 'black box' of economic science (a point discussed in Chapter 1). This impacts upon our ability to decipher the decision-making process of individual economic agents, with significant implication for both theory and policy. This is nowhere more apparent than in the handful of troublesome attempts to introduce the entrepreneur in the mainstream (discussed in considerable length in a subsequent Section of this Chapter). Within this context (of simply definitional significance of the entrepreneur), however, the inability to incorporate the entrepreneur into mainstream microeconomic theory appears to be unfortunate and disappointing but not detrimental upon the robustness of existing theory. The implications of the explanation developed here, if entrepreneurship is of causal significance, are grievous. It means that existing theoretical constructs of the mainstream are at best incomplete, failing to account for a factor that influences economic activity. To date, there have been precious few studies exploring the issue of the definitional or causal significance of entrepreneurship (see Chapter 1). Rather disappointingly, the issue of the implications of the neo-classical exclusion remains.

The Austrian School and the Process of Entrepreneurial Discovery

The Austrian School provides one of the most coherent and suggestive theoretical constructs in entrepreneurial studies. This is not particularly unexpected given the emphasis placed upon states of disequilibria and the individual by exponents of this tradition. Thus, radical subjectivism, methodological individualism, and the purposiveness of human action have been deployed with some success in enhancing our understanding of the function of entrepreneurs in the market process.

Continuity (illustrated in this Section through the Mises-Hayek-Kirzner schema), and the evolution of ideas by generations of Austrians led to a position of growing intellectual prominence in the field.   However, an inherent emphasis on hermeneutics rather than predictive ability restricted the ability of Austrian constructs to reach and influence entrepreneurship researchers outside the field of economics.

Mises

Mises' influence in the field of entrepreneurial studies has been modest, predominantly through the work of his student, Israel Kirzner.   However, the Misesian analysis of the entrepreneur as the 'acting individual' is both sophisticated and insightful and merits careful consideration.   Within this context, the entrepreneur is the economic agent who applies reason to changes occurring in the market.   This conceptualisation of entrepreneurship is inclusive, encompassing all action in the market economy that is human (Gunning, 1997; Kirzner, 1997).   Thus, '[in] any real and living economy every actor is always an entrepreneur' (Mises, 1949, p. 253).

The identification of all human action (hereafter entrepreneurial action[11]) with entrepreneurship is because of the impact of time.   Individuals must act from an ever moving and changing present between an irrevocable and cumulative past and an unknown future (Oakley, 1996).   Thus every 'action is always directed toward the future; it is essentially and necessarily always planning and acting for a better future' (Mises, 1966, p. 100).   The end state towards which the entrepreneurial action is directed must be conceived *ex ante*, and there is no way of knowing beforehand the extent to which the action will attain the sought end.   The crucial problem for each entrepreneur is to form an opinion about how other economic actors (entrepreneurs) will act.   In doing so, the entrepreneur has to draw upon his/her experience of other actors' past value judgements and actions, although it is impossible to use experience to deduce with certainty the future conduct of other economic actors (Oakley, 1996).   Thus, uncertainty prevails even in short-run activities.

A defining attribute of entrepreneurial action is that it is purposeful, i.e.

> [a]ction is will put into operation, and transformed into agency, [it] is aiming at ends and goals, [it] is the ego's meaningful response to stimuli and to the conditions of its environment (Mises, 1966, p. 11).

On the issue of the driver of entrepreneurial actions, Mises emphasises the importance of satisfaction or not of the individual's needs. It is the entrepreneur's 'dissatisfaction with expected future conditions as they would probably develop if nothing were done to alter them' (Mises, 1966, p. 100) that prompts the individual to consider action. Uneasiness with the future - if nothing is done - is combined with an ability to *imagine* future conditions that are better suited to the needs (ends) of the entrepreneur. Mises did not address the issue of how ends are set, but instead focused upon entrepreneurial actions as a manifestation of the mind.

According to Mises the mind possesses

> a special quality that enables man to transform the raw material of sensation into perception and the perceptual data into an image of reality. It is precisely this specific quality or power of his intellect – the logical structure of his mind that provides man with the faculty of seeing more in the world than nonhuman beings see (Mises 1990, p. 48).

However, the entrepreneur sees reality not as it is but only through the structure of his or her mind and senses. Without these the individual would be unable to discern and take action. Whilst certain aspects of a situation may be grasped through applied natural science, others will be of human origin and require interpretation on the basis of past experiences. This may lead to errors, inefficiency and failure (Mises, 1958). However, these do not mean that entrepreneurs are irrational, but rather that they are rational though fallible (Mises, 1966).

The Misesian entrepreneur is a complex creature: undoubtedly an individual both in the sense of the ends pursued, but also in terms of the structures of the mind and his or her experiences. Driven by an inherent dissatisfaction with his/her ability to satisfy his or her ends, the entrepreneur has the ability to imagine new combinations of means in the face of uncertainty. The main instrument in dealing with uncertainty is his or her ability to predict the behaviour of other entrepreneurs on the basis of past performance. Thus, the actions of the entrepreneur are purposeful and rational. Actions could be wrong but are rationally derived. In fact, the erroneous actions of one entrepreneur emerge as market opportunities for another. This is a profoundly different conceptualisation, less heroic but more inclusive, from that provided by Schumpeter enabling us to examine entrepreneurship beyond innovation. At the same time however it imposes a set of alternative restrictions, precluding any investigation of change instigated by the entrepreneur. Indeed, the Misesian entrepreneur is reactive to the challenges offered by specific situations. Moreover, the impact that the external environment - and specifically the institutional setting - has upon entrepreneurial actions, whilst acknowledged, remains unexplored: as 'the way to a cognition of collective wholes is through the analysis of individual actions' (Mises, 1966, p. 42).

Hayek

Hayek focuses upon the concepts of information and knowledge, rather than the issue of entrepreneurial decision-making. He sets out to identify the ways in which individuals involved in a complex and expanding division of labour, successfully co-ordinate their actions, when each individual possesses only local and idiosyncratic knowledge (Foss, 1994). Thus, a key element in Hayek's discussion of learning processes, was what he saw as 'a problem of the division of knowledge'

(Hayek, 1937, p. 50), i.e. the fact that different economic agents know different things.

The availability of information constitutes only the first of the constraints on individual decision-making. The capacity to process information (what Hayek refers to as 'mental processing') offers another set of constraints. This places considerable demands on the time, physical endurance, wakefulness, mental capability, and the senses of entrepreneurs (Tansey, 2002). Since individuals can not know everything, they must depend upon institutions (formations) for the transmission and sharing of information.

> The price system is just one of those formations which man has learned to use (though he is still very far from having learned to make the best use of it) after he had stumbled upon it without understanding it. Through it not only a division of labour but also a co-ordinated utilization of resources based on an equally divided knowledge has become possible (Hayek, 1948, p. 88).

Hayek visualises the world in which there is a continuous process of discovery: not major discoveries, but, mostly minor ones about individual wants at particular times and places. His description of the process of entrepreneurial discovery is as follows: individuals and societies are surrounded by pre-existing theories in the light of which events are interpreted. Perceptions of the accumulated experience of the species (knowledge) are shaped under the pervasive influence of the individual's own experience. These combined with the fact that access to information is partial and localised means that entrepreneurs are key economic agents in the acquisition of information and knowledge and the pursuit of equilibrium prices. Entrepreneurs generate hypotheses that are subsequently tested, and are confirmed or refuted[12].

Israel Kirzner

Kirzner's theory is explicitly founded upon the ideas developed by Mises (human action) and Hayek (information and knowledge) (Gloria-Palermo, 1998). His conceptualisation of the entrepreneur has been refined over a period of nearly a quarter of a century, and evolved to a considerable degree, in response to criticisms raised by fellow economists of the Austrian School (Lachmann, 1991; Gunning, 1997). As a result, Kirzner's later work (and especially his 1997 article in the *Journal of Economic Literature*) offers one of the most convincing attempts at theorisation[13].

Natural 'alertness' to possible profit opportunities constitutes the defining attribute of practising entrepreneurs.

> ... opportunities are created by earlier entrepreneurial errors, which have resulted in shortages, surplus, misallocated resources. The daring, alert

entrepreneur discovers these earlier errors, buys where prices are "too low" and sells where prices are "too high" (Kirzner, 1997, p. 70).

Previous entrepreneurial errors combined with continuous change in tastes, the resources at hand, as well as technological developments mean that opportunities for entrepreneurial profit are present in each market. Within this context, the process by which opportunities are noticed and grasped in an inherently uncertain environment constitutes the essence of a market economy. In response Kirzner advances the notion of entrepreneurial discovery.

His point of departure is Hayek's conceptualisation of the market as a process of continuous mutual discovery (discussed in greater detail above). Discovery differs from neo-classical constructs about research for information

> ... (which one know one had lacked) is that the former (unlike the latter) involves that surprise which accompanies the realization that one had overlooked something in fact readily available (Kirzner, 1997, p. 72).

Thus, the entrepreneur is at all times engaged in a systematic and purposeful scanning of the market for opportunities, without knowing exactly what s/he is looking for. Entrepreneurial alertness refers to an attitude of receptiveness to available - but hitherto overlooked - opportunities. Each discovery is accompanied by a sense of surprise of what the entrepreneur had previously overlooked. This previously 'unthought-of knowledge', is the result of entrepreneurial boldness and imagination in a market defined by Knightian uncertainty[14].

The identification of the entrepreneur with the alert and imaginative economic agent who discovers previously unthought-of knowledge, offers an alternative conceptualisation of the market process from that of the neo-classical tradition. In the latter, economic agents are buying or selling identical products or services at uniform prices, performing a static task bereft of any element of intelligence and creativity that seems far removed from the reality of competition. In the former, the entrepreneur actively seeks to outdo his or her other rivals, by grasping opportunities overlooked by rivals that enable him/her to offer the best possible deal for customers. This dynamically competitive market process Kirzner defines as 'rivalrous competition' (Kirzner, 1997).

Kirzner's work has undoubtedly enhanced our understanding of the entrepreneur: s/he is more coherent and 'less subjective', but at the same time less complex and multi-dimensional from his or her Misesian progenitor. Moreover, and rather disappointingly Kirzner remains agnostic about why and how does the entrepreneur acquires flashes of superior foresight.

G. L. S. Shackle: Entrepreneurship and Decision-making

An alternative conceptualisation of the entrepreneur to that developed by Kirzner, from within the Austrian School, is provided by Shackle, who was a student of

Hayek's. Shackle's theoretical construct is radical, closer to the ideas of Schumpeter than those of Kirzner.

Shackle's work is inherently dynamic, casting the past as irrevocable and the future as unknowable. Within this context, 'like all humans, the business-man is the prisoner of time' (Shackle, 1970, p. 21), unable both to derive certainties for the future and to reverse or repeat events that happened in the past. This leads Shackle to argue that it is not knowledge that constitutes the key in understanding human action, but rather 'unknowledge', namely the inevitable uncertainties caused by the effect of time on the decisions of economic agents (Batstone and Pheby, 1996).

As a consequence, one of the main pillars of neo-classical analysis, economic rationality i.e. the ability to explain human actions in terms of past events and fixed preferences, is replaced with creativity and spontaneity (Backhouse, 1985). Shackle then argues that economic agents

> can choose only among imaginations and fictions. Imagined actions and policies can have only imagined consequences, and it follows that we can choose only an action whose consequences we can not directly know, since we can not be eyewitnesses of them (Shackle, 1970, p. 106).

Shackle's use of the term imagination does not imply that opportunities are mere illusions, but rather that any choice involves the exercise of imagining possible alternative future state of affairs (Ricketts, 1987). It is the very faculty of imagination that makes individual economic agents enterprising, and, since everyone faces choices, all economic agents are entrepreneurial. Instead, he uses the term 'enterpriser' to refer to those individuals engaged in decision-making in a business context. Shackle's enterpriser is not *'the helpless victim of uncertainty'* (Shackle, 1970, p. 21). Instead, competitive advantage can also be created by the enterpriser, through the promotion of uncertainty. This is because s/he hopes to discover and apply new knowledge that will enable him or her to outdo his or her rivals (Shackle, 1973).

In addressing the question of how economic agents are able to take decisions about an unknowable future Shackle identifies two approaches (for a detailed exposition see Batstone and Pheby, 1996). The first entails the identification of the worst (focus loss) and best (focus gain) consequences of an action. Against these two extremities the possibilities of alternative sequels to an action can be measured. The second, involves the assessment of how surprised the enterpriser would be by the occurrence of each outcome (potential surprise). The actual procedure of decision-making may involve the use of a partial method of analysis, using the *ceteris paribus* assumption. This means that whilst the

> ... problem is really indivisible and the most advantageous course depends upon the whole circumstances ... there may in practice be no escape from considering different aspects of ... [the]... problem in succession (Shackle, 1970, p. 22).

The advancement of Misesian ideas (such as the impact of time, and the notion of imagination) is apparent in the work of Shackle. However insightful, his overall theoretical construct leaves some key questions unanswered: after all his approach to the entrepreneur was only by implication, an integral part of his theory of individual choice.

The Revival of Interest in the Entrepreneur in the Mainstream

The acknowledgement of the mainstream (Baumol, 1968) exclusion has prompted a number of calls for a revival of scholarly interest on the entrepreneur and his or her decision-making process. In response, a small number of theoretical constructs have emerged attempting to resurrect the entrepreneur in the mainstream. The approach adopted in order to explore entrepreneurship in the mainstream varied considerably: ranging from thoughtful and appropriately qualified schemata (Baumol and Casson) to brave extensions of the neo-classical analysis in a new field of study (production function approaches[15]). In this Section we focus squarely upon the former.

William Baumol

Baumol's work[16] in the area of entrepreneurial studies is unlike that of most other scholars emanating from economics. Whilst the latter attempt to devise conceptual schemata – invariably through the relaxation of neo-classical assumptions either about rationality or access to information or both - that enhance our understanding of entrepreneurial decision-making, he sets out to understand entrepreneurship with existing analytical instruments, whilst acknowledging the limitations of the exercise (Baumol, 1968).

Baumol (1995) distinguishes between two entrepreneurial prototypes: the firm-organising, who creates, organises, and operates a business enterprise, and the innovating, as conceptualised by Schumpeter. The activities of the former prototype can be examined using standard analytical instruments regarding the allocation of resources and price determination in perfectly competitive or contestable markets. It is the Schumpeterian entrepreneur that does not fit easily in existing neo-classical theoretical constructs. He goes on to identify two areas in which one can learn more about innovating entrepreneurs: the attributes of the individual, and the issue of how of entrepreneurship is allocated. As far as the former area is concerned that

> the discovery of the attributes of an entrepreneurial personality, is certainly promising ... [B]ut the task seems to fall outside the purview of economic theory (Baumol, 1995, p. 22).

This prompts Baumol (1990) to focus on the second task. He develops the thesis that entrepreneurship is present in all economic structures, however, the manifestations of it vary. Indeed, at certain instances entrepreneurial activity may be unproductive or even parasitical, and thus damaging to the economy as a whole. The allocation of entrepreneurship in productive, unproductive and destructive activities is heavily influenced by the (changeable) rules of the competitive game and the ensuing reward structures.

Baumol's work highlights the fact that neo-classical theorisation of entrepreneurship is possible - an approach followed by other contemporary scholars. Moreover, his discussion of the productive or otherwise nature of entrepreneurship has been suggestive. However, for all his brave efforts Baumol's work provides evidence to the limitations of mainstream conceptualisations.

Mark Casson: An Eclectic Synthesis

Mark Casson sets out to develop an economic theory of the entrepreneur that fits alongside neo-classical constructs. In doing so he acknowledges the significance of emotional rewards and the cost of accessing information, whilst remaining detached from the idiosyncratic nature of some earlier scholars (Schumpeter and Kirzner) regarding the motivation of the entrepreneur that are incompatible with 'rational action' (Casson, 1998). He utilises insights gained from previous researchers in the area of entrepreneurial studies as well as the micro-economic analysis of the new institutionalists.

Casson (1982) distinguishes two approaches regarding definition: the functional (i.e. what does an entrepreneur do) and the indicative (which provides a description by which the entrepreneur may be recognised). Whilst a functional definition may be quite abstract (and all the economic definitions examined in this Chapter fall in this category), an indicative definition is very down to earth. It describes an entrepreneur in terms of his legal status, his contractual relation with other parties, his position in society and so on. He argues that part of the difficulty in defining entrepreneurship arises from a failure to integrate these two approaches. Thus, he defines the entrepreneur as the person 'who takes judgmental decisions about the co-ordination of scarce resources'[17] (Casson, 1995, p. 80).

The need to exercise judgement in the decision-making process is evident when an individual deals with new and complex situations, where objectives are ambiguous. It emanates from the uncertainty associated with change (volatility), especially as the decision made by other economic agents may influence outcomes. In later works Casson (1998) distinguishes between two types of change: transitory and persistent. The former is driven by small factors, and occurs frequently, whilst the latter is driven by varied factors and occurs infrequently. Planing in advance is the appropriate response transitory change, and this is the realm of management. The proliferation of factors, and the intermittent nature of persistent change mean that planning is inappropriate. Instead decision-makers have to deal with such change as and when it occurs, thus requiring the attention of entrepreneurial individuals.

His relaxation of the neo-classical assumptions begins with the recognition that individuals differ not only in their tastes but also in their access to information

(Casson, 1982). Individuals with similar tastes, acting under similar circumstances, but with different information at their disposal, may well make different decisions. This is partly due to the fact that information is costly, therefore individuals may opt to make decision on the basis of very limited information, and partly because the interpretation of information may differ as individuals use their own cognitive frameworks (Casson, 1998). It is important to stress that the treatment of information by Casson differs significantly from that provided by Kirzner and Mises. Whereas the latter refers to information that individuals do not know that exists (thus the element of surprise), the former refers to known-to-be available information which it is costly to produce (Stiglitz, 1994).

The entrepreneur believes that the totality of the information available to him or her, in respect of some decision, is unique (Casson, 1982). On account of this, he will decide one way when everyone else would decide another. 'The entrepreneurs ... believe that they are right, and the other are wrong. Other things being equal, it is the most optimistic and self-confident entrepreneur who will prevail' (Casson, 1998, p. 17). The essence of entrepreneurship is being different because one has a different perception of a situation because of differing access to information. The decision to act rests squarely with the optimism and confidence that drive entrepreneurial behaviour.

Thus, the demand for entrepreneurship (i.e. the number and nature of entrepreneurial roles – opportunities – that need to be filled) is highly subjective (Casson, 1993). The supply of entrepreneurs is governed by occupational choice. Drawing upon the neo-classical models developed by Lukas (1978) and Kihlstrom and Laffont (1979), Casson suggests that the decision to become an entrepreneur is influenced, at least in part, by the potential entrepreneurial rewards in relation to the prevailing wage levels. This could be graphically represented though a neoclassical supply-side curve. However, Casson extends this thesis by arguing that the position of the supply side curve depends on the number of able entrepreneurs, which in turn is determined by the distribution of wealth, the organisation of education, the social structure, the degree of social mobility, and the institutionalist framework (Casson, 1982).

Casson's contribution in the field of entrepreneurial studies has been significant: utilising insights provided by earlier scholars, he develops an approach that can complement neo-classical microeconomics. A defining feature of his work is the introduction of a social dimension that would criticisms about the under-socialised (Granovetter, 1985) theorisation of mainstream economics. More importantly, Casson has been successful in his venture. However, his work has not been extended or developed further by other scholars in the field of entrepreneurial studies. One could argue that this is because Casson has taken neo-classical economics as far as it would go, whilst maintaining consistency, in understanding entrepreneurial decision-making.

Choi on Uncertainty and Entrepreneurial Decision-making

Like Mark Casson, Young Back Choi is driven by the realisation of the inability of the mainstream tradition to decipher decision-making under conditions of uncertainty. However, unlike Casson who opts for the development of theory of the entrepreneur that can exist alongside the mainstream, Choi aspires to advance a rigorous alternative to the orthodox analysis of human agency. In doing so, he seeks inspiration from the philosophy of science, and particularly Kuhn's 'paradigm'[18] and Margolis notion of 'pattern'[19], rather than economics. The emphasis placed by Choi upon human agency, and the centrality of the notions of paradigm and convention, meant that his work influenced more debates between the old and new institutionalisms rather than the emerging field of entrepreneurial studies. Thus, the 'deviant' individual who breaks away from the prevailing conventions in the face of adversity (envy) remains little known among entrepreneurship researchers.

Given that Choi's point of divergence from the mainstream tradition is the influence of uncertainty upon the decision-making process of economic agents, it is appropriate to begin the review of his theoretical construct with the identification of the sources of this uncertainty. He identifies four such sources (Choi, 1993). The first concerns with the relative complexity of a calculation regarding a decision, in relation to the calculating capabilities of the individual. Thus, in some instances uncertainty may emerge by the fact that the agent is not capable of exploring all possible outcomes at any given situation. The second source of uncertainty is the unpredictability of the future. He explains that this is dependent partly upon the fact that there are factors that are beyond the control of economic agents, and partly because there is no guarantee that regularities observed in the past will continue in the future. This conceptualisation of the future as a source of uncertainty is somewhat narrower from that reported by advocates of the Austrian tradition[20]. This is apparent as Choi identifies the interdependence of human actions as a third, distinct source of uncertainty. The mental process of the individual economic agent, and the fact that s/he is not omniscient, creates the fourth source of uncertainty.

Choi then goes on to argue that decision-making may be divided into perception and logical choice. Whilst mainstream theory has developed elaborate models to explore the latter, it has failed to address the issue of perception, i.e. the process through which the economic agent identifies a situation as an instance of a broader phenomenon, even when the agent does not possess the totality of relevant information. Perception is the act of understanding a situation with enough confidence to support action. The outcome of this process is a model, defined as paradigm. Choi then develops a set of propositions that are meant to organise the behavioural consequences of this approach.

> The "first fact" ... is that every human action presupposes an associated paradigm; its identification is the crux of decision-making under

uncertainty. A direct corollary, and "second fact," is that individuals will continue searching for a paradigm until they find one (Choi, 1993, p. 7).

The relentless pursuit of a paradigm as a way of resolving uncertainty has the result that the decision-making process is also one of learning and experimentation. Thus, paradigm-seeking constitutes a dynamic and never perfected process of reasoning. However, this process of understanding situations does not take place in abstract, but within the boundaries and with the help of existing paradigms.

As Choi's analysis goes successively from less complicated (individuals in total isolation) to more complicated (individuals in heterogeneous groups with a high degree of interaction) models, possibilities for vicarious experimentation, imitation and interpersonal comparison emerge as implications of the relentless pursuit of paradigms. As a consequence, at the social level, conventions that govern behaviour, which impose routines, habits, and inflexibilities, emerge as the unintended outcome of dealing with uncertainty (Choi, 1993). Conventions, like individual paradigms, tend to be stable over time, which creates conformity, inertia, sub-optimal solutions, and unexplored opportunities.

It is these unexploited opportunities, that emerge as a result of the stability of conventions that create the potential for entrepreneurial activities. For Choi

> [e]ntrepreneurs are those enterprising individuals who dare to be different and risk envy and ostracism to reap possible personal gain from the exploitation of opportunities ignored by or even unknown to others. Sometimes they succeed and sometimes they fail. Entrepreneurs are emulated as they become successful through their unconventional actions, and, in the process, the innovations soon become conventions themselves (Choi, 1993, p. 153).

Thus, envy and the threat of being ostracised emerges as the main obstacle to entrepreneurial activity. This envy is the result of the conflict between the social tendency to preserve old conventions and entrepreneurs who want to try something new, something that may disrupt and at the same time rejuvenate society. The envy barrier to entrepreneurial activities is overcome by the influence of property rights.

Choi's ideas regarding paradigm seeking as a means of understanding different situations constitutes a significant, positive contribution in developing an alternative, to the mainstream, model of human agency. Not unexpectedly, his ideas were scrutinised and concerns were raised about the consistency of the two key notions (paradigm and convention) as well as their inter-relationship (Pressman, 1997). Our main concern rests, with the process of introducing change in Choi's conceptual framework. Entrepreneurs are hailed as 'convention breakers who want to try something new ... the driving force of market activities and society' (Choi, 1993, p. 9). However, they respond to pre-existing opportunities, which tend to be unnoticed, on account of the stable nature of conventions. Moreover, in identifying the process through which conventions lead to unexploited opportunities, Choi points to 'an exogenous shock of rather substantial proportion ... [or] improvements in the state of knowledge' (Choi, 1993, p. 100), depressingly familiar sources of change from the mainstream.

D. H. Harper and the Growth of Knowledge Programme

The work of D. H. Harper, a student of Mark Casson, constitutes a significant venture into radical subjectivism, that extends well beyond that of the Austrian tradition and is influenced by Popper's idea of the growth of knowledge[21]. His point of departure is the acknowledgement that learning processes are crucial to most of the phenomena which economists seek to explain. Thus, he sets out to develop a dynamic theory of entrepreneurial learning.

Entrepreneurship is defined by Harper as

> ...a profit-seeking activity aimed a identifying and solving ill-specified problems in structurally uncertain and complex situations. It involves the discovery of and creation of new end-means frameworks, rather than the allocation of given means in the pursuit of given ends (Harper, 1996, p. 3).

The entrepreneur is an agent who seeks to break outside the range of established routines and the existing framework of ideas. What distinguishes Harper from earlier theorists is that whereas they tend to emphasise the non-rational, intuitive faculties of the entrepreneur, he stresses the rational and critical aspects of entrepreneurship which are a prerequisite to acquiring knew knowledge.

The growth of knowledge model is organised around a handful of core propositions (for a detailed exposition see Harper, 1996). The unit of analysis is the individual, as it is only individual economic agents who have aims, conjectures and preferences and can make decisions. However, individuals when confronted with a problem do not automatically know its parameters. Instead, individuals must attempt to gain an understanding which is subjectively constructed – despite the fact that objective reality exists. More importantly, however, there is no method of testing whether one has found the truth. Thus, economic agents are fallible simply by virtue of their inability to test the assumptions upon which their actions are based. In response, individuals form tentative solutions to problems in a world of structural uncertainty, complexity and real time, and learn from the feedback provided by successive decisions. However, feedback is rarely optimal or perfect. Thus, although the entrepreneurs do not posses proven true knowledge, they can still make rational decisions. Rational decision-making in this context means evaluating rival schemes in the light of logic and experience.

As Harper himself recognises, the Growth of Knowledge Programme does not offer a complete and coherent alternative to neo-classical economics. However, unlike the work of Casson, it has the potential to be extended and resolve problems for which the neo-classical tradition is ill-suited[22].

Conclusions

Economic theories of the entrepreneur have advanced significantly since the pioneering works of Cantillon and Say. Despite, the mainstream exclusion economists have been successful in identifying a number of key considerations, often neglected by scholars from other disciplines (discussed in the following Chapter), that enhance our understanding of entrepreneurship and especially the cognitive processes involved. Firstly, economists introduce time and the passage of time upon the entrepreneurial decision-making. Entrepreneurs exist in an ever-changing present: drawing information from an irrevocable past, aiming to influence a future they do not know. The implications of acknowledging the impact of time are far reaching. Uncertainty becomes structural whilst decisions are mere manifestations of the imaginative creations of the mind. This brings us to the second important consideration emanating from economic theories of the entrepreneur: the cognitive processes. Rational processes of optimisation are the instruments used, either by choice (Baumol, Casson) or necessity (Knight). In contrast, those adopting a subjectivist stance (Austrians and Harper) attempt to derive more complex explanations. Whilst the subjectivist alternative lacks coherence and is by no means complete it offers a potentially fruitful line of enquiry in entrepreneurial studies. The third key considerations emanating from economics concerns with those factors that influence cognitive frameworks. Some scholars emphasise the influence of the subjective, the individual, whilst others stress the importance of the (shared) knowledge, accumulated over the centuries of human existence, that enables us to communicate with each other. This is particularly important for the interpretation of information, the fourth key consideration. Most scholars agree with the relaxation of the neo-classical assumption about free access to all the information the entrepreneur needs in his or her decision-making process. In response, some scholars include the costs of accessing information and contracting - when less than perfect information is available - drawing upon the ideas of those new institutionalists clustered around the 'Transaction Costs Economics'. In contrast, other economists introduce the concept of unknowledge, i.e. knowledge we do not even know that it exists. A final consideration involves the motivational influences that drive individuals to entrepreneurial decisions. The importance of motivation is explicitly conceded by many scholars (Hawley, Schumpeter, Knight, Mises, Kirzner). However, economists have failed to make significant inroads in this direction: this is nowhere more apparent than in the works of Knight who developed a hybrid model, and then abandoned it as it moved into the realm of psychology and consequently outside the remit of economics.

Our exploration of the theorisation of the entrepreneur in economics also underlines the limitations of a mechanistic approach, inspired by physics, such as that of the mainstream. The deployment of a mathematical method in the pursuit of laws of motion and causation, in static equilibrium situations, makes the introduction of the entrepreneur in the mainstream a virtually insurmountable task. In contrast, economists who conceptualise the entrepreneur as a conscious economic agent who can exercise judgement in uncertain, but time and place specific, situations have made significant positive contributions to our understanding of the entrepreneur. It is the works of Schumpeter, the Austrians, and more recently Choi and Harper that provide insightful contributions to entrepreneurship research in economics. Despite the profound differences between these scholars, they all adopt a perspective that is essentially organicist and evolutionary. We argue that such a conceptual framework offers a suggestive theoretical underpinning for the study of the entrepreneur in economics.

Notes

1 Thus, several aspects of the theoretical constructs created by economists, such as the rewards of the entrepreneur within a system of distribution, the long term prospects of entrepreneurship will be excluded from our review.

2 In fact, Cantillon spent considerable time analysing the entrepreneurial function of farmers (Schumpeter, 1954). The farmer pays out contractual incomes, which are therefore certain, to landlords and labourers, and sells at prices that are uncertain.

3 In fact, of all the literature reviews on entrepreneurship (and there have been many during the past 1980s and early 1990s) only Barreto (1989) discusses the work of Hawley.

4 A point forcefully stressed by scholars working in the Harvard Centre for Entrepreneurial History, and particularly Professor Cole (for a review see Chapter 3).

5 More specifically Knight (1921) argues that ends are modified in three ways. Firstly, the individual may be disappointed when achieving one end and he may decide to pursue another end. Secondly, a person may be so committed to the means he has adopted to achieve his end that the means become an end. This is part of a wider trend that ends recede in the process of attaining them. Man is committed to strive towards goals which recede more rapidly than he advances towards them. Lastly, to a significant extent man is the product of his environment.

6 For evidence of the exclusion of the entrepreneur from economics textbooks see, Kent (1989) and Kent and Rushing (1999).

7 Schumpeter (1954) was an early advocate of the thesis that it was the concept of natural law which was instrumental in defining awareness of economics as a distinct science.

8 The notion of the constitutive metaphor was developed by Stephen Pepper (1942). He identifies four such metaphors: formism, mechanism, organicism, and contextualism corresponding to the roots of similarity, machine, organism, and historic event.

9 Whilst elements of Cosgel's approach have been criticised by Fontaine (1998), it is undeniable that Cosgel adds an original contribution to the historiography of the entrepreneur.

10 For examples of the elevated status afforded to economics, in relation to ther social sciences, see Andreski (1972) and Hands (1987).

11 Because readers may not be accustomed to the Misesian use of the term 'human action' we deploy the term 'entrepreneurial action' to Mises' concept.

12 'Trial and error' is as the main instrument in the acquisition of new, entrepreneurial knowledge.

13 Indeed, our review of Kirzner draws heavily from his 1997 article which is a significant corrective to his earlier writings, and a return to basic premises of the Austrian tradition.

For those interested in reviews of his seminal works in the 1970s and 1980s see Barreto, 1989 and Ricketts, 1987.

14 This greater emphasis on uncertainty in the JEL article constitutes a significant change from earlier works of Kirzner.

15 These approaches are based on the notion that individuals chose between entrepreneurship, and uncertain returns, and paid employment on account of their abilities and the prevailing wage levels. This wage is therefore the opportunity cost of chosing to undertake the entrepreneurial function, and thus economic agents must be convinced that they can earn a residual income in excess of this wage (Glancey and McQuaid, 2001). If the wage rate falls then the opportunity cost to entrepreneurship will decline and less able individuals will be involved in entrepreneurial pursuits and vice versa. The key question within this context is what ability required to become an entrepreneur? Lucas (1978) identifies this ability as being one of managerial co-ordination, whilst Khilstrom and Laffont (1979) identify the ability to bear risk, which they take to mean uncertainty in the Knightian sense.

16 In fact, Baumol's work though squarely placed within mainstream economics is unlike that of most neo-classical economists. He sets out to address 'real' problems of the world of market economies, building bridges between theory, policy and practice. In that respects he is perceived as 'revolutionary from within in that he masters the tools of the trade and insists that they be used, as far as possible, to address real-life problems of great urgency' (Eliasson and Henrekson, 2004, p. 1).

17 The emphasis placed by Casson on the co-ordination of – rather than the allocation – of scarce resources emphasises the entrepreneurial capacity of improving economic efficiency. This point was discussed in considerable length by Leibenstein (1968 and 1987) who introduced the concept of X-efficiency to conceptualise the degree of inefficiency in the use of resources within the firm. X-efficiency arises because resources are not utilised in the optimum way. This is because: i) contracts are incomplete, ii) effort is discretionary, iii) the employee takes decisions on the basis of his/her own interest, and iv) the employee takes time to settle to a new routine. Leibenstain perceives entrepreneurship as the response to X-efficiency. Other people's lack of effort, and the consequent inefficiency of organisations that employ create opportunities for the entrepreneur.

18 Thomas Khun was undoubtedly the foremost influence in the work of Choi. Khun introduced paradigms as 'some accepted examples of actual scientific practice ... [that] provide models from which spring particular coherent traditions of scientific research' (Kuhn, 1970, p. 10).

19 Margolis (1987) uses the notion of 'pattern' to capture good or bad examples acquired through experience by individual agents, which provide guides for action, and are used in situations where there is an urgency to act.

20 Choi's notion of the future as a source of uncertainty appears to be narrower from that of the Mises-Hayek-Kirzner tradition, especially as he distinguishes the actions of other economic agents as a distinct source of uncertainty. Overall, however, the conceptualisation of uncertainty is broader in Choi than in the Austrian tradition.

21 For Popper the growth of human knowledge proceeds from our problems and from our attempts to solve them. These attempts involve the formulation of theories which, if they are to explain anomalies which exist with respect to earlier theories, must go beyond existing knowledge and therefore require a leap of the imagination. Therefore, Popper places special emphasis on the role played by the independent creative imagination in the formulation of theory. However, scientific theories, for Popper, are not inductively inferred from experience, nor is scientific experimentation carried out with a view to verifying or finally establishing the truth of theories. Instead, for him, all knowledge is provisional, conjectural,

hypothetical. As a consequence, we can never finally prove our scientific theories, we can merely (provisionally) confirm or (conclusively) refute them; hence at any given time we have to choose between the potentially infinite number of theories which will explain the set of phenomena under investigation. Faced with this choice, we can only eliminate those theories which are demonstrably false, and rationally choose between the remaining, unfalsified theories.

22 Interestingly, it is the work of, probably, the two most influential and competing philosophical perspectives, those of Popper and Kuhn, which underpinned the emergence of contemporary advances in the economic theory of the entrepreneur.

Chapter 3

The Sociology and Psychology
of the Entrepreneur

Introduction

More or less at the same time that Schumpeter and Knight led the revival of entrepreneurship research in economics, Weber turned his attention to the area of entrepreneurial studies. However, it was not until the post-war era that entrepreneurship research grew into prominence in disciplines outside economics. Research in this area has provided suggestive insights in the characteristics and attributes of the individuals who perform the entrepreneurial function. It is herein that the main contribution of non-economic approaches lies.

However, the impact of these theoretical constructs upon the advancement of entrepreneurial studies remained modest in relation to the accumulated body of knowledge. This is because entrepreneurship research from disciplines other than economics lacks even the tentative links identified in Chapter 2. More specifically, researchers invariably draw ideas from sources (journals, conferences etc.) specific to their discipline, and disseminate their own work in the same manner. Thus, traditional divides in terms of outlets of academic publication raise some real, practical difficulties in the cross-fertilisation of knowledge for the best part of the twentieth century. This has been combined with the late emergence of such outlets in the area of entrepreneurial studies[1]. Another reason behind the lack of continuity is the absence of current reviews of this body of literature. Indeed, there is hardly any attempt at exploring the theorisation of entrepreneurship in sociology and psychology since the positive contribution of Kilby in 1971, whilst most new theoretical contributions in economics begin with a review of the relevant literature within the discipline[2]. Lastly, some scholars from other disciplines often approached entrepreneurship as an exemplar of a discipline specific problem.

As a consequence, reviewing this voluminous body of literature is problematic. Conventional approaches based upon the discipline 'of origin' or chronology, alone, are probably less than adequate for the task at hand[3]. Instead, we focus upon theoretical constructs that address relatively distinct subject matters. Thus, we begin with the exploration of the sociology of the entrepreneur, which combines ideas derived from sociology, as well as economic history, and economic geography (see Table 3.1). Then we go on to explore approaches which examine the psychology of the entrepreneur, again not differentiating regarding the disciplinary origin of the approach. Lastly, we review a number of approaches that try to explore the interface between the context (sociology) and the agent (psychology). In all three instances, chronology is used as secondary element in our analytical framework.

Table 3.1 Non-economic Theories of the Entrepreneur

	Sociology of the Entrepreneur	Psychology of the Entrepreneur
Mono-causal constructs	Weber (1922) *Entrepreneurial History* • Cole (1949) • Cochran (1949) • Jenks (1949) *Social Marginality* • Hoselitz (1961) • Young (1971) *Evolutionary Approaches* • Hannah & Freeman (1977) • Thornton (1999) • Aldrich & Martinez (2001) • Stam (2002)	McClelland (1961) Hagen (1962) *Locus Control* • Rotter (1966) • Gilad (1982) Kets de Vries (1977)
On the interface between agent and context	*Situational Approaches* • Glade (1967) • Greenfield and Strickon (1981) Gardner (1985) *Social Constructionism* • Chell (2000)	

The Sociology of the Entrepreneur

The Pioneering Work of Max Weber

Max Weber's work on entrepreneurship is part of a wider research exploring the origins of economic consciousness and the specific contents of a religious faith. He worked in a totally different disciplinary context from early scholars (emanating more or less exclusively from economics) researching the entrepreneur, and thus introduced a very different research approach. Weber did not pursue the creation of theoretical constructs regarding the entrepreneur and his or her function in the market process. He did not attempt to formulate causal laws in a general theory of economic development but chose to identify certain correlations, and conditional relations between selected aspects of capitalism, and of verifying these correlations by drawing comparisons between capitalist and non-capitalist societies (Martinelli, 1994). Therein lies his main contribution: influencing subsequent generations as well as his contemporaries (including Schumpeter) studying the entrepreneur.

Weber (1922) distinguishes between the capitalist entrepreneur and his historical predecessors. The capitalist entrepreneur is involved in a rational and systematic pursuit of economic gain, his calculations are measured in relation to this economic criterion, he or she extends trust through credit, and subordinates consumption in the interest of capital accumulation. The rationalisation of every aspect of the entrepreneurial pursuit (defined as instrumental rationality) is what makes the capitalist entrepreneur different.

In addressing the question of what drives the capitalist entrepreneur, Weber points at the importance of exogenously supplied religious beliefs. He identifies the Protestant ethic as the key factor driving the capitalist entrepreneur: it stresses the inherent goodness of work. Within this context, an individual's work is regarded as a calling, in the very literal rendering of the concept of vocation. Moreover, the Protestant Ethic regards the financial rewards of ones work as a manifestation of God's blessing. At the same time, however, Protestant values called for self-restraint and the accumulation of productive assets (Weber, 1922). The transformation of the drive provided by the Protestant ethic into actual entrepreneurial ventures is on account of the development of experimental science, rational authority stemming from Roman law and rational government administrations (Kilby, 1971).

Weber's work constitutes the point of departure of a long tradition of sociological approaches in entrepreneurial studies. Whilst his actual argument has received sustained criticism, leading to serious questions about the robustness of the centrality attached to the Protestant Ethic, his intellectual legacy remains.

Entrepreneurial History and the Sociology of the Entrepreneur

Entrepreneurship research during the early post-war era was dominated by the works of economic historians working in or associated with the Harvard University Research Centre in Entrepreneurial History. Within this setting research was focused upon the development of an 'entrepreneurial approach to economic history'. A key research question involved the relationship between society – and especially social attitudes – and entrepreneurship. Work in this context was based upon a common (though not always identical) conceptualisation of the function performed by the entrepreneur. This is defined

> as the purposeful activity (including an integrated sequence of decision) of an individual or group of associated individuals, undertaken to initiate, maintain, or aggrandize profit-oriented business unit for the production or distribution of economic goods and services with pecuniary or other advantage the goal or measure of success, in interaction with ... the internal situation of the unit itself or with the economic, political, and

social circumstances ... of a period which allows an appreciable measure
of freedom of decision (Cole, 1949, p. 88).

A key element of this definition is the importance attached upon the business unit
as a distinct setting (from the socio-economic milieu) for the performance of the
entrepreneurial function.

Scholars working in or associated with the Harvard Centre were
influenced from two main intellectual quarters. The first involved the seminal
contribution of Schumpeter, who also worked at Harvard University at that time,
and remained closely linked with the Centre. The second influence revolved
around the theoretical structures created by Professor Talcott Parsons. This was in
response to the realisation of the importance of the position of the entrepreneur
within the community where he or she operated. This created the need for the
adoption of a rigorous and comprehensive sociological framework. One of the
most influential outputs to emerge from the Harvard Centre is the symposium
volume *Change and the Entrepreneur* published in 1949. In this volume Arthur
Cole (1949) attaches explicit significance to the degree of social approval which
the entrepreneur will receive in a given milieu. Thomas Cochran (1949) in the
same volume advances the notion of sanctions to encourage the deviant behaviour
of entrepreneurs[4]. However, it is the stimulating contribution of Leland Jenks
(1949), who concerns himself with theorisation of entrepreneurial roles, which
warrants more detailed consideration.

Jenks defines roles as probable action patterns of economic agents in
specific, recurrent social contexts. Thus, roles do not stand alone but are part of
systems of social interaction, where agents engage in relationships involving two or
more roles. The parameters which define the role(s) of individuals in interpersonal
relationships involve

> structure in terms of "positions"... that individuals who hold such
> positions or take such parts tend to behave in more or less consistent ways
> and that a degree of uniformity in the behavior of such individuals is
> observable; and ... that the persons with whom they interact ... manifest
> more or less uniform attitudes and expectations about the behavior of
> occupants of such positions (Jenks, 1949, p. 133).

"Position", the ensuing behaviour, and expectation of behaviour by others are
instrumental in defining roles. Thus, the actions of entrepreneurial economic
agents can not be adequately understood unless they are placed within the social
context. However, Jenks attempts to move a step beyond social determinism by
the dichotomy between personal and social roles and the possibility of discrepancy
between them.

No two personal roles are exactly the same, any more than any two
personalities are, mainly for the same reason. This is because of relatively stable
motivated pre-dispositions to act in certain ways. These pre-dispositions are
'learned' by the individual during childhood experiences and in the context of other

adult roles. Jenks (1949) goes on to identify four ways in which an economic agent learns a personal role. The first is the agent's perception of the expectation that other individuals have of him or her during the process of social interaction. The second involves learning by 'experiencing reward' for responses which are considered appropriate in certain circumstances and punishment for inappropriate ones. The third entails the adoption of 'role models', and the fourth the reorganisation of socially available roles into new combinations. It is the fourth of these learning processes which offers the scope for diversity and change, both between different personal roles as well as between personal and social roles. The solution in the latter situation may 'take the form of a distinctive phrasing of the role which, if socially accepted, may end in modification of the social role' (Jenks, 1949, p. 138). Thus, personal role variation emerges, in Jenks' analysis, as the major analytical tool for understanding the dynamics of social change.

The social role, in turn, is viewed by Jenks as a 'social fact', a collective representation which provides direction and defines the boundaries of individual behaviour. Social roles are the result of social communications within a social group, rather an individual or an unorganised group of individuals. Thus, the economic agent knows the social role through 'regularities in what people may say they do or should do ... [s]uch regularities will be called *sanction patterns*' (Jenks, 1949, p. 143). These sanction patterns may be formal or informal, external, in the sense that they are imposed on the individual in specific situations, or fully internalised: but they are the acts by which the expected behaviour is enforced.

Jenks, one among a group of individuals associated with the Harvard Centre, made a positive contribution in emphasising the importance of the socio-economic milieu in understanding entrepreneurship. Moreover, he placed considerable attention upon the processes by which entrepreneurial economic agents learn. However, his work occupies a position at the other extreme of some theoretical constructs created by economists and psychologists: focusing heavily upon the context, whilst allowing little room for the function of agency.

Social Marginality

The influence of social marginality upon the emergence of entrepreneurship has attracted considerable scholarly attention. Indeed, there is a long tradition of research that dates back to the work of Sombart (1916-1927)[5], which suggests that creativity and the ability to break traditional values, associated with entrepreneurship, is more frequent among marginal and minority groups than the population at large. Non-acceptance in the societies within which they live, enables individuals belonging in such groups to avoid, more easily than others, the traditional values and norms that regulate economic behaviour. Theoretical constructs in the context of social marginality, provided by Hoselitz and Young, focus squarely upon social groups rather than individual economic agents, and date back to the 1960s and 1970s. It was not until the 1980s and 1990s that a number of empirical studies provided empirical evidence to support this thesis.

Influenced by the work of Sombard, Hoselitz (1963) makes the observation that individuals belonging to marginal groups are particularly important in promoting economic development.   He uses the experiences of Jews and Greeks in early modern Europe, the Lebanese in West Africa, the Chinese in Southeast Asia, and the Indians in East Africa as examples of the case.   Economic agents from these marginal groupings, because of their ambiguous position, are better suited to make creative adjustments in situations of change than individuals belonging in the mainstream of the socio-economic milieu. This is because socially marginal economic agents, excluded from the dominant value system, are subjected to lesser sanctions for behaviour that diverges from the mainstream. The origins of Young's (1971) work differ from those of Hoselitz[6]. He complements Hoselitz's thesis by arguing that social marginality is not a sufficient condition for the emergence of entrepreneurial behaviour. Group solidarity and the resources at hand also influence the decision to act entrepreneurially. He suggests that a social group will become reactive, when two conditions coincide:

> a group is experiencing low status recognition and denial of access to important social networks, and it possesses a greater range of institutional resources than other groups in society at the same system level (Kilby, 1971, p. 13).

More recent research exploring the experiences of ethnic minorities entrepreneurs (Waldinger et al, 1985, 1990; Portes and Min Zhou, 1992; Ram, 1998), lend support to the social marginality approach. Within this context, empirical evidence suggests that group (ethnicity) specific resources constitute a significant source of advantage for entrepreneurs.

Evolutionary Approaches

During the past twenty-five years or so, entrepreneurship research conducted within business schools has become increasingly dominated by an evolutionary approach, originally known as population ecology (Hannan and Freeman, 1977).   This 'substantial research endeavor has focused on the presence, characteristics and changes in a population of organizations in an ecological context, provided by the host society' (Reynolds, 1991, p. 59).   Research in this context, influenced by Low and McMillan (1988), concentrated upon integrating the outcomes of entrepreneurship and the processes that lead up to these outcomes, and the social context within which entrepreneurship occurs. As a result of the former it diverged considerably from previous works in the field, which centred squarely upon the economic agent, towards the organisational structures created by entrepreneurs. Evolutionary approaches are often considered, by the very same scholars who develop and advance them[7], to fall within the confines of organisational theory. Thus, however suggestive the theoretical constructs derived within this context may be, they do not fit easily within the confines of our purposeful review of the literature. There are nonetheless, two, relatively recent, exceptions of scholars who use an evolutionary approach in the study of the entrepreneur: namely Patricia Thornton (1999), who uses population ecology to gain an understanding on entrepreneurship as a social class (group), and Erik Stam (2002) who sets out to explore the issue of the context within which the entrepreneur operates.

Thornton's point of departure is a concern - characteristic of evolutionary approaches - that supply side explanations (i.e. those exploring the availability of individuals suitably qualified to perform entrepreneurial roles) have been unable to provide robust grounds for theory building. Instead, she sets out to combine advances regarding demand-side explanations, and particularly the influence of firms and markets on how, where and why new ventures are founded. More specifically, she advances the idea that ecological and institutional analyses enable the development of multi-level models. This means that context can comprise of a number of (sub-) contexts: individual, spatial, temporal, organisational, and socio-cultural. In her analysis, she identifies four contextual levels: individual, organisational, market, and environmental. Then she goes on to argue that it is the combination of these four contexts which enables us to understand how individual behaviour is influenced by individual factors and social structure.

Stam's (2002) work focuses squarely upon individuals rather than groups. Moreover, evolutionary and institutional analyses are combined with time-geography - derived by economic geography. Whilst acknowledging considerations regarding the entrepreneurial personality (the dead end of scholarly pursuits according to Stam) and the creation of organisation (a much more straightforward pursuit), he examines entrepreneurship as a contextual phenomenon. This enables him to perceive entrepreneurs as individuals who act within certain social and physical contexts, living at certain concrete times and places.

Institutional analysis in his work is perceived very much along the lines of the New Institutionalist Economic of Williamson and North. Formal and informal institutions provide us with the tools needed to penetrate the maze of social relationships. In doing so he places emphasis upon institutionalising, as a process that imposes constraints upon entrepreneurial economic agents, who in turn possess the ability to implement change upon the institutional setting[8]. Evolutionary analysis offers the instruments for exploring change in systems. It makes possible the explanation of how forms of organisation and behaviour emerge and evolve in specific socio-economic milieus. He adopts an essentially Darwinian approach, which addresses human reflexivity and purposive action. Lastly, time-geography

> is an approach where time and space are not looked upon as a composition of two dimensions, but as a framework for analysis … The basic point of departure in time-geography (or 'geo-historical analysis' as it is sometimes called) is that "when, where and in what order something happens affects how it happens" (Stam, 2002, p.8).

The approach developed by Stam attempts to introduce unity between space, time and the process. Though only cursorily described at a brief paper it offers suggestive insights into the study of entrepreneurship.

One underlined problem that raises concerns about the explanatory power of the argument developed by both Thornton and Stam is that of agency. More specifically, to what extent and how economic agents can act independently of the context to which they operate. What are the factors and processes that enable purposive actions over social determinism? Under which circumstances is behaviour prescribed by the context or the free will of the economic agent? Aldrich (1999) efforts to explore variation in organisational behaviour on account of intentional actions of agents seeking solutions to actions offers a useful point of departure in this direction.

The Sociology of the Entrepreneur: Gerschenkron's Critique

Alexander Gerschenkron[9], going against the grain of the early post-war era, attempted to move beyond over-socialised perceptions of the entrepreneur associated with the work of economic historians. His contribution rests with the identification of the need to strike a new balance between the agent and his or her context[10]. Gerschenkron, influenced in part by the work of Schumpeter, was concerned with the deviant, in the sense of different from what is socially prescribed, behaviour of entrepreneurs. Deviance, he argues, is a defining influence of entrepreneurial behaviour, and it matters only because it occurs despite environmental resistance. Schumpeter's heroic innovating entrepreneur would seem somewhat pedestrian if he or she did not have to confront hostility and resistance to change. However, whilst deviant behaviour has often been taken-up by scholars involved in the study of the entrepreneur, it exists uncomfortably with the emphasis placed upon social roles, and the sanctioning acts by which behaviour is enforced. He goes on to argue that

> while it may make sense in certain historical situations to take a dominant system of social values for granted, it is much less satisfactory to accept the deviant behavior as given. ... But if suddenly deviant values make their entry upon the economic scene, the urge for further explanation is irresistible (Gerschenkron, 1954, p. 5).

Thus, the problem with which researchers in the field are left with is reconciling the deviant element of the entrepreneurial behaviour with the dominant and resistant to change context. His answer to the problem is less satisfactory, and of lesser importance, than the identification of the problem itself. He argues that social approval matters less than has been previously considered by academics.

In the same article Gerschenkron raises an issue that lies at the heart of the rationale that underpins our attempt to develop an institutionalist approach. He advances the notion that a

> ... rigid conceptual framework is no doubt useful in formulating questions, but at all times it evokes the peril that those questions will be mistaken for answers. There is a deep-seated yearning in social sciences for the

discovery of one general approach, one general law valid for all times and all climes. But these attitudes must be overgrown. They overestimate both the degree of simplicity of economic reality and the quality of scientific tools (Gerschenkron, 1954, p. 12).

Analytical schemata that cut across diverse socio-economic settings are not well equipped to understand entrepreneurship. This is probably because entrepreneurial studies require an understanding of human behaviour, which is influenced heavily by the specificities of the institutional regime.

The Psychology of the Entrepreneur

McClelland and the Need for Achievement

David McClelland published his seminal book *The Achieving Society* in 1961[11]. In that work he sets out to address the question of why are some societies more likely to produce more entrepreneurs than others. In doing so, he explores the influence of cultural attitudes in the process of early socialisation, which in turn influence entrepreneurial attitudes. In his work McClelland deploys a comparative methodology, spending considerable time and effort in examining the explanatory capabilities of other (competing) theoretical constructs. Thus, his work provides a good example of systematic hypothesis testing.

McClelland's work was influenced by the earlier writings of Max Weber (reviewed in the Section above). In fact *The Achieving Society* has often been conceived as an extension of the Weberian Protestant Ethic, in which an intermediating psychological dimension is introduced (Kilby, 1971). McClelland stresses the importance of middle childhood, as the formative period of entrepreneurial attributes (see Figure 3.1). He argues that this is achieved through

> reasonably high standards of excellence imposed at a time when the son (sic) can attain them, a willingness to let him (sic) attain them without interference, and real emotional pleasure in his (sic) achievements short of overprotection and indulgence (McClelland, 1961, p. 356).

The prime determinant in this process - according to McClelland - is the parent's beliefs. Other - lesser - influences include the father's occupation and living arrangements, as well as the climatic conditions[12].

As a result, he argues, childhood experiences create in certain individuals a particular psychological factor which he calls 'need for achievement'. This notion is used to denote characteristics such as little interest in performing routine tasks or in dealing with situations of high risk, keen interest in situations involving moderate risk where skill counts, and a desire for responsibility and a concrete measure of task performance (Kilby, 1971). He goes on to argue that high need for achievement is the 'particular psychological factor ... responsible for economic growth and decline' (McClelland, 1961, p. vii). In support of this thesis he produces evidence indicating that children in Western industrialised societies internalise attitudes and symbols that favour a higher need for achievement.

The high achievers in these societies have become entrepreneurs who have fostered economic growth. In contrast in underdeveloped countries McClelland finds fewer people with a high need for achievement. Besides this smaller number, most go into other fields than business and industry.

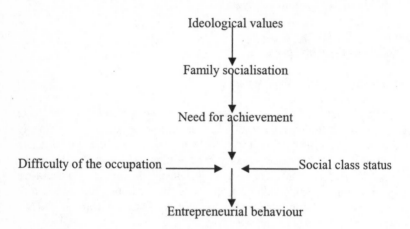

Source: Derived in part from Kilby (1971).

Figure 3.1 McClelland's Approach

McClelland also identifies the mechanism by which individuals with high need for achievement are directed towards entrepreneurial careers (see Figure 3.1). Occupational choice appears to be the function of the difficulty of the occupation and social class status. Business occupations hold a position somewhere in the middle - as far as difficulty is concerned - below the professions. Thus, entrepreneurial pursuits represent the desired moderate risk situations for individual, with high need for achievement, coming from lower and lower middle classes (McClelland, 1961).

In a later contribution, McClelland (1969) alters his position on the importance of child-rearing practices as the intrinsic determinant of the achievement motive. He emphasises the arousal of latent need for achievement among adults, typically associated with a new sense of superiority. This raises the prospect of training to enhance achievement-oriented behaviour.

McClelland's work, by virtue of its methodology has been influential in the area of entrepreneurial studies, fostering a large amount of empirical research (Martinelli, 1994). However, rather perversely, it is the empirical part of McClelland's work that failed academic scrutiny (McDonald, 1965; Kilby, 1971).

The Work of Hagen

The work of Hagen, which appeared more or less at the same time as that of McClelland also attempts to explain the incidence of entrepreneurship, however, his approach is significantly different. Whilst McClelland concentrates upon individuals in a specific socio-economic milieu, Hagen focuses squarely upon social groupings. Thus, Hagen also introduces the question: why do entrepreneurs come more often from certain social groupings than others (Martinelli, 1994). Hagen's work also stands out for another reason: although an economist by training, he develops a theory of mediating psychology (Kilby, 1971). Thus, concepts conventionally associated with economics (such as capital accumulation, opportunity recognition etc) are rarely mentioned in his work.

For Hagen the entrepreneur is an individual interested in solving practical or technical problems, and is driven by a duty to achieve. Entrepreneurs occupy the 'creative end' of a personality dichotomy, which is central to Hagen's work. The opposite end of the dichotomy is the authoritarian, non-innovative personality. The emergence of creative personalities is the result of historical processes that may go back several generations (see Figure 3.2). In Hagen's work, up-bringing in traditional authoritarian families merely reproduces non-innovative personalities. Withdrawal of status, is one of two exogenous variables which instigates changes in personality formation. Status withdrawal in Hagen's work 'is the perception on the part of members of some social group that their purposes and values in life are not respected by groups in the society whom they respect and whose esteem they value' (Hagen, 1962, p. 1985). The withdrawal of status is the result of four types of events: i) displacement by force; ii) denigration of valued (often religious) symbols; iii) inconsistency of status symbols within a changing distribution of economic power; and iv) non-acceptance of expected status on migration to a new society. Once status withdrawal has occurred, a sequence of change in personality formation is set in motion.

As a result of the loss of status by the group there is a breakdown in the authority of the family. The diminishing influence of the authoritarian influence of the father is combined with an increased influence of a nurturing and protective mother. The result is the emergence of individualism and self-reliance as key personality attributes, which in turn favour creativity and entrepreneurial activity. Hagen then goes on to identify the process by which such individuals become involved in entrepreneurial pursuits. Relative social blockage is an essential in this process. More specifically, Hagen argues that

> [i]f traditionally honored roles are not open to an individual or if prowess in them does not win him (sic) recognition because his (sic) other characteristics bar him (sic) from being honored, and if armed rebellion is impossible because of the preponderance of strength of the new dominant group or because of the growth of effective social sanctions against the use of force, and if migration is not a feasible solution, then the pressure of unsatisfiable values and frustrations may be expected over a number of

generations to inculcate new values. In short, the requisite for economic growth in a traditional society is not merely that upward social mobility by new means is possible but also that social mobility by traditional channels is not possible (Hagen, 1962, p. 242).

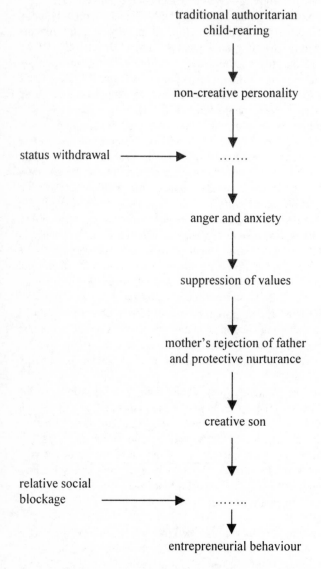

Source: Derived in part from Kilby (1971).

Figure 3.2 Hagen's Theoretical Construct

There is a significant body of literature which supports the thesis, advanced by Hagen, that entrepreneurs frequently belong to ethnic or religious minority groups[13]. The essence of his argument also influenced the work of Kets de Vries' psychodynamic model. However, considerable concerns have been raised about some of the assumptions that underpin his work. Does the authoritative-creative personality dichotomy approximate modal personalities in all contexts? And is there a necessary association between authoritarian personality and non-innovative behaviour?

Locus of Control

Another influential attempt at exploring the psychology of the entrepreneur derived from social learning theory. The assumptions that underpin this approach are well-suited to the study of the entrepreneurial personality. This is partly because social learning theory identifies as the main unit of analysis the interaction of the individual and his or her environment (Rotter, 1954). Thus, in order to deal with behaviour traits, situational parameters - both personal and environmental - must be examined. Moreover, social learning theory advances the notion that there is unity and purpose to personality: thus enabling the entrepreneur as an economic agent who though functioning within specific situations has the ability to choose.

Social choice theory is essentially an attempt to explore how individuals make choices from the variety of potential behaviours open to them (Phares, 1976). The task of prediction involves ordering the potential alternative behaviours in a manner so as to determine which is the strongest and therefore, most likely to occur. In doing so, social choice theory considers two parameters: i) reinforcement value, i.e. 'the degree of preference for any reinforcement to occur if the possibilities of their occurring were equal' (Rotter, 1954, p. 107); and ii) expectancy, which indicates the probability held by the individual that a reinforcement will occur in a specific situation. Thus social learning theory centres upon the complex interface between expectancies, reinforcement values, and specific situations. In addressing this complexity individuals resort to generalised expectancies: i.e. expectances (of success) rendered similar on account of past situations that have been resolved. Thus, behaviour is also dependent upon learned behaviour.

One such generalised expectancy, which is of particular importance in interpreting entrepreneurial behaviour is the degree to which economic agents believe in that what happens to them is dependent upon their own behaviour, and is thus controllable by their actions, or is contingent upon luck, powerful others etc. In order to capture this Rotter (1966) used the notion of locus of control. More specifically,

> when a reinforcement is perceived by the subject as following some actions of his own but not being entirely contingent upon his (sic) action, then, in our culture, it is typically perceived as the result of luck, chance, fate, as under the control of powerful others ... we have labelled this

belief in external control. If the person perceives that the event is contingent upon his (sic) own or his (sic) own relatively permanent characteristics, we have termed this a belief in internal control (Rotter, 1966, p. 1).

Empirical research, using social learning theory, in the areas of entrepreneurial studies supports the thesis that an individual's locus of control is a major factor determining his or her level of entrepreneurial alertness (Gilad, 1982). The argument goes, that, internal locus of control gives rise to heightened alertness, which is necessary for incidental learning (the recognition of opportunities) with spontaneous learning resulting into entrepreneurial behaviour. Moreover, since economic agents with an external locus of control believe that external factors influence events they are assumed to be less proactive in entrepreneurial ventures. Indeed, during the 1980s and 1990s there has been a number of studies (Begley and Boyed, 1987; Duchesnau and Gartner, 1990; Rauch and Frese, 2000) lending support to this thesis.

The concept of locus of control, and the evidence supporting this argument by a number of empirical studies, has grown to considerable prominence in the area of the psychology of the entrepreneur. Students in entrepreneurial studies soon become familiar with this notion (alongside the need for achievement).

The Psychodynamic Model of Kets de Vries

A more recent enquiry into the psyche of the entrepreneur was undertaken by Kets de Vries, who aspired to conceptualise the entrepreneurial personality and provide a convincing explanation to how it was formed. The origins of his work can be traced in the very same psychological perspective as that of McClelland's *Achieving Society* and Rotter's *Locus of Control* (discussed earlier in this Section). Kets de Vries profoundly different understanding of the entrepreneur, in relation to that of the two earlier psychologists exploring the entrepreneur, appear to be the result of substantial differences in the subject of his enquiry. Indeed, Kets de Vries himself recognises that there is no single entrepreneurial type. But this much having being acknowledged he focuses all his efforts in understanding one particular type: the deviant entrepreneur[14].

His point of departure is a near-Scumpeterian admiration for the entrepreneur. He argues that

> [w]e see that Prometheus and Odysseus have been replaced by that folk hero of the industrial world, the entrepreneur. He has become the last lone ranger, a bold individualist fighting the odds of the environment (Kets de Vries, 1977, p. 34).

However heroic, Kets de Vries' entrepreneur is a tormented individual scared by early childhood experiences. He describes the entrepreneur as a loner, existing in relative isolation from his or her context, a 'misfit' who feels displaced in his or her environment, a 'reject, a marginal man (Kets de Vries, 1977). The entrepreneur translates his or her feelings of anxiety, anger and rebelliousness into innovative activity. Thus, he conceptualises the entrepreneur as a highly complex individual bearing no resemblance to the 'economic man'[15].

Having identified, in a very detailed and restrictive (even by his own admission) manner, his subject of enquiry Kets de Vries provides an engrossing account about the process which leads to the formation of such entrepreneurial personalities (see Figure 3.3). He analyses the family dynamics of entrepreneurs in terms of two polarities: high control-low control, and acceptance-rejection, attitudes of the parents towards their children (Kets de Vries, 1977). The configuration of these polarities in the family of a potential entrepreneur

> gives the impression of a father as low on control and basically rejective (in the child's fantasy world remoteness easily becomes synonymous with rejection) while the mother will be perceived high on control and accepting. ... The lack of integration of these parental configurations, in addition to each parent's stand on these two personality dimensions leaves the child with a feeling of inconsistency, confusion and frustration (Kets de Vries, 1977, pp. 46-47).

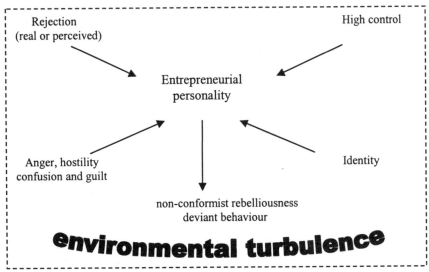

Source: Kets de Vries, 1977.

Figure 3.3 The Psychodynamic Model

The combination of the 'deserting' father and the nurturing though controlling mother can result in problems in identify formation. This combined with a feeling of unacceptability of role models, may lead the individual to rebellious activities. As a consequence, the entrepreneurial individual may enter a period 'drifting from one job to another' without apparent goals. To others he or she demonstrates 'deviant' behaviour in the sense of being unable to 'fit', provocative, and non-conformist. To the individual it is this non-conformist rebelliousness which becomes his or her way of dealing with an environment that he or she perceives as uncontrollable. Kets de Vries goes on to argue that, the entrepreneurial attributes of self-confidence and inner strength are manifestations of insecurity, ambition is an attempt to suppress feeling of inferiority, while hyperactivity covers up passive longings.

Some evidence supporting this approach came from Sarachek's research (1978). He identified a high incidence of poor relationship between the entrepreneur and his or her father, as well as loss of the father early on in life. The main difficulty of the psychodynamic model advanced by Kets de Vries[16] lies in an inconsistency between defining assumptions and outcomes. Thus, whilst the emphasis is placed upon one type of entrepreneurial behaviour, the outcomes are presented in terms of the conceptualisation of the entrepreneurial personality (as if a single type exists).

The Psychology of the Entrepreneur: A critique

There are growing concerns among scholars in the field of entrepreneurial studies regarding the value of attempts to delve into the psychology of the entrepreneur. Bygrave and Hoffer (1991), Bygrave and Willard (1995) and Stam (2002) raise the issue of the usefulness - or otherwise - of the pursuit of approaches which enable us to delve deeper into the economic agents who perform the entrepreneurial function, a suggestion that has acquired a position of prominence in the field. Within this context, it is argued that 'it may be useful to shift our focus from the "characteristics and functions of the entrepreneur" and the myriad of definitions of what constitutes an entrepreneur, and to focus, instead, on the nature and the characteristics of the "entrepreneurial process"' (Bygrave and Hoffer, 1991, p. 14). Indeed, it is very difficult to dispute the fact that research into the psychology of the entrepreneur has failed to advance a coherent and fairly robust theory. It is also, probably, the case that the insights gained in the psychology of the entrepreneur compare unfavourably with our understanding of the sociology of the entrepreneur, although, this argument may be disputed by some colleagues in the field.

However, it is unclear to what extent the productivity of research in the area of the psychology of the entrepreneur (measured through some illusive index of outcome to scholarly effort) has been lower than in other areas of entrepreneurial studies. Even if this was the case, and we suggest that there is no evidence that this is so, this would not be sufficient cause to justify a move away from research into the psychology of the entrepreneur. This is because, research into the entrepreneurial function more than any other economic function requires an element of agency: i.e. economic actors engaged in purposive action.

Moreover, the consequences of a shift of emphasis away from the entrepreneur towards the entrepreneurial process are considerable. An excellent parallel of these consequences can be drawn from the lecture delivered by R. H. Coase when he received his Alfred Nobel Memorial Prize in Economics regarding the state of the art in industrial organisation before New Institutional Economics. He argues that whereas mainstream economics have made considerable advances in understanding how prices co-ordinate economic activity in a market economy, very little is known about internal arrangements within organisations. Thus, 'what happens in between the purchase of factors of production and the sale of the goods produced by these factors is largely ignored ... The firm ... appear(s) by name but ... lack(s) substance ... The firm in mainstream economic theory has often been described as a "black box"' (Coase, 1971, p. 714). In a similar manner a shift in emphasis away from the entrepreneur would transform the economic agent at the centre of the entrepreneurial process, into the 'black box' of the new field of study. Whereas adopting a processual approach in understanding the entrepreneur may provide us with new insights into the agent and the interface between the individual and his or her context, focusing upon the process instead of the entrepreneur may significantly hamper the development of the field of entrepreneurial studies.

However suggestive sociological approaches may be they will always provide us with only part of the explanation. Not all Protestants engage in entrepreneurial pursuits, in the same manner that not all members of socially marginal groupings create entrepreneurial ventures. If not all entrepreneurs are the same (a point discussed in greater detail in the Section below), we would need some analytical instruments to understand why this was the case. Thus, research into the psychology of the entrepreneur is an essential element in any attempt to theorise in the areas of entrepreneurial studies. This is irrespective of the success or productivity of earlier attempts to do so. However, what this review of the literature indicates is that this needs to take place alongside an attempt to understand the sociology of the entrepreneur.

Between Agent and Context

The Situational Approach

Dissatisfaction with theoretical constructs exploring both the psychology and sociology of the entrepreneur led to the emergence of the situational approach. This approach dates back to Glade's (1967) critique of the works of McClelland and Hagen as instances of comparative statics. More specifically, he argues that entrepreneurial studies became embedded upon a set of assumptions that implied two contrasting types of system (one underdeveloped and the other developed), whilst providing few – if any – insights regarding the process of change from one state to the other. What is missing in the literature, according to Glade is a theory of change, 'which explains the transition from the state of affairs depicted by the undeveloped economy model to that represented by the developed economy model' (Glade, 1967, p. 246).

In addressing this gap, Glade advocates a shift in emphasis away from the entrepreneur himself or herself towards the behaviour of individual entrepreneurial agents. The changing focus towards the micro-level enables Glade to explore actors and their choices and decisions within specific social and cultural settings. He calls the circumstances confronting the entrepreneur opportunity structures, encompassing the general economic, social, technological and political conditions. As these conditions change over time, they provide new opportunities for the individual members of the society, some of whom may take advantage of them while, others may not. Thus, what emerge 'as integral features of any given situation are both an 'objective' structure of economic opportunity and a structure of differential advantage in the capacity of the system's participants to perceive and act upon such opportunities' (Glade, 1967, p. 251).

However, it is Greenfield and Strickon (1981) who, following upon the intellectual footsteps of Glade, provide the most coherent exposition of the situational approach. In order to provide an alternative conceptualisation of entrepreneurial behaviour they set out to identify the reason(s) behind the weaknesses of earlier theoretical constructs. Why is it that researchers in the field of entrepreneurial studies focus upon the conditions that produce entrepreneurs rather than what the entrepreneurial agents actually do? The answer to this question according to Greenfield and Strickon, is that it is the adoption of a structuralist/essentialist metaphor by social scientists in general and economists in particular that define the boundaries of scholarly inquiry. Within this context, reality is seen 'in terms of societies, institutions, classes, economies, kinship systems etc,; and the behavior of the individual is assumed to be explained by the higher-level institutional and societal phenomena' (Greenfield and Strickon, 1981, pp. 480-481). In response, Greenfield and Strickon (1981) advance a more radical solution than Glade, replacing the structuralist/essenitalist framework that underpins the bulk of research in entrepreneurial studies with a 'population model' based upon the ideas of Darwinian biology[17]. In Darwin's thinking whilst species are defined by the characteristics of an ideal representation, the actual animals that make up the several species may vary considerably from this ideal representation. This underpins a change in emphasis towards 'the uniqueness of everything in the organic world. What is true of the human species - that no two individuals are alike - is equally true of all other species ... Indeed, even the same individual changes continuously throughout its lifetime' (Mayr, 1976, pp. 27-28).

Greenfield and Strickon, drawing upon Darwin's populational model, perceive the world as composed of individuals who are goal oriented. These economic agents exist in communities, performing a variety of behaviours. Whilst

> the sum of total behaviors performed of a given kind may be averaged to produce a pattern ... It must be remembered, however, that for any regularities in behavior that we might refer to as "the pattern" there will in fact be a variety of behaviors actually performed by the individuals who make-up the community (Greenfield and Strickon, 1981, p. 487).

Thus, they shift the emphasis away from patterned regularities of behaviour (that they refer to as institutions) towards variation in behaviour performed by individuals.

Individual economic agents strive to achieve their goals, i.e. to obtain resources, within a given environment. In doing so they conceptualise a range of alternative possibilities in attaining their goals, and select the one that, in their best judgement and given the information they posses, most probably will enable them to obtain their goals. This process of identifying alternatives, and selecting the one most likely to obtain the desired end is defined by Greenfield and Strickon as decision-making.

The varying behaviours of economic agents enable some of them to obtain more resources, and subsequently achieve more of their goals, than others. These behaviours which lead to the attainment of more goals than other behaviours could be viewed as being more appropriate for the specific environmental setting. As a result, the most successful variants of behaviour are going to become increasingly common at later periods, as more economic agents adopt them. For Greenfield and Strickon the key instrument by which the selection of behaviours is attained is learning. Learning within this context is a continuous process present in individuals of all ages.

> Therefore, by learning we mean the continuous process through which new behaviors are added to the repertories of the individuals that constitute a population or a community; and, as new behaviors are learned and added, others previously performed may be discarded (Greenfield and Strickon, 1981, p. 488).

Thus, Greenfield and Strickon (1981) develop a theory based upon 'learning by doing'. Within this context, individuals learn that not all alternative actions will result in the desired outcomes. In many instances the individual may miscalculate, either on account of insufficient information or because he or she misjudged the situation. These actions which do not produce the desired results will not be selected again, and other actions will be tried until the economic agent obtains the goals he or she desires.

Given the importance of interaction and communication in their approach Greenfield and Strickon introduce the notion of 'symbols'. Symbols bring together communities: they are the definition and notions that are common to the agents who participate in the community. Symbolic ability, of which language is a good example, enables the economic agent to contemplate events and situations other than those he or she experienced directly.

In some ways, the approach developed by Greenfield and Strickon has come full circle. Starting from the rejection of institutions they introduce 'symbols' which look suspiciously like institutions. In attempting to move beyond over-socialised views they excise institutions only to re-invent them subsequently as the means which facilitate interaction and communication. More importantly, however, Greenfield and Strickon provide few - if any - details as to how economic agents develop alternatives and select the most appropriate ones. In exploring the question of how entrepreneurs behave, they overlook the key consideration of why entrepreneurs behave in this manner, a charge they themselves lay before economic theories of the entrepreneur. Whilst the solution is problematic the issue (over-socialised approaches) raised by Greenfield and Strickon is a valid one. Moreover, their construct provides suggestive insights into the process of entrepreneurial learning which have not been exploited sufficiently by other scholars in entrepreneurship research.

Gartner's Framework

Departing from an altogether different disciplinary setting Gartner, that of the rapidly advancing management studies, was also critical of mono-causal explanations developed in the areas of the psychology and the sociology of the entrepreneur. In a oft repeated statement, he argued that

> [t]he major thrust of most entrepreneurship research has been to prove that entrepreneurs are different from non-entrepreneurs ... The basic assumption underlying this research is that all entrepreneurs and their ventures are much the same (Gartner, 1985, p. 696).

Instead, Gartner contents, the differences among entrepreneurs are much greater than one might expect, arguably even larger than the differences between entrepreneurs and non-entrepreneurs.

Once this is point is acknowledged, Gartner (1985) argues, the emphasis shifts away from commonality towards patterns, whereby entrepreneurs are classified into groupings that share similar characteristics. In addressing this issue he sets out to organise the many, appropriate, variables that have been used in entrepreneurship research into a comprehensive framework. This comprises four dimensions (see Figure 3.4 below): the individual, the organisation, the environment and the process.

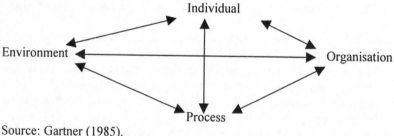

Source: Gartner (1985).

Figure 3.4 Gartner's Framework

Each of the elements of the framework are further dissected using a number of variables. Thus, differentiation of types of individuals engaged in entrepreneurial ventures can occur on account of need for achievement, locus of control, risk taking, as well as a number of 'demographic characteristics' (namely age, education, parental involvement in entrepreneurship, work experience, and job satisfaction). The process can be explored using six - stage-like - variables: the identification of the opportunity, the accumulation of resources, the creation of the organisation, production, marketing and responding to government and the society. The environment dimension comprises a number of variables which capture not only resource endowments (such as capital and skill availability, the knowledge infrastructure, the size, nature and accessibility of markets & sources of supply, the role of government and policy support) as well as social attitudes towards entrepreneurial ventures. The characteristics of the organisation are conceptualised as strategic choice variables.

The point raised by Gartner, regarding the diversity between entrepreneurial economic agents is a particularly useful one - which will be exemplified on the basis of empirical evidence in Chapter 6. In addressing this issue the need to create a framework that synthesises different approaches is also apparent. However, the framework created Gartner falls short of expectations. In an attempt to be inclusive, he remains agnostic of the relative importance as well as the interface between the variables under consideration.

Social Constructionism

Another very recent attempt to explore the interface between the individual and his or her context involves a shift in the philosophical paradigm that underpins entrepreneurship research towards social constructionism. Social constructionism has two principal disciplinary roots, social psychology and sociology, and is concerned with how individuals and groups create their reality and make sense of it. As such it about the process of constructing the personality of individuals (Hampson, 1982). Based upon this basic premise, a number of scholars in the field of entrepreneurial studies, such as Bouchikhi (1993), Chell (2000) and Fuller (2002) set out to explore the construction of the entrepreneruial personality. The most advanced and coherent attempt at theorisation, in our view, is provided by Elizabeth Chell. Thus, our review of social constructionism in entrepreneurial studies will focus upon her recent work.

Elizabeth Chell (2000) suggests that what distinguishes entrepreneurs from non-entrepreneurs is their motivation for wealth creation and capital accumulation, as well as their ability to recognise opportunities, and their judgement. In this context the future orientation of the entrepreneurial actions is readily acknowledged, as entrepreneurs 'envision a future and attempt to realize it' (Chell, 2000, p. 73). Thus, the problem raised by the Austrian tradition is also present in the context of social constructionism however, the solution is different from that offered by Mises, Knight and Shackle.

The social constructionist solution is concerned with how individuals create their reality and make sense of it. Within such a context, the entrepreneur emerges as an active economic agent who shapes and creates his or her own reality.

The entrepreneur is simultaneously the driver of the entrepreneurial process operating within a reality which sets limits on choice and action possibilities (Chell, 2000). Therefore,

> [t]he social construction reality is both subjective and objective. It is subjective in so far as the individual in the situation deals with it according to their perception and interpretation of its elements, and their creation and construction of what it means to them and could or should mean to others. It is objective in so far as people use a common language to interpret and convey the meaning of situations; they use "evidence" in support of the particular interpretation, which then becomes the accepted or dominant interpretation – the reality (Chell, 2000, p. 68).

Social constructionism attempts to combine agency and context: the individual exists as a distinct entity, energised by a specific set of motives, capable of envisaging or imagining the future, and exercising judgement. However, the entrepreneur is contextually embedded. Thus, the process is one of interaction (between agency and context) from which outcomes emerge.

The centrepiece of the social constructionism approach is the (social) process by which the subjective experiences of individuals become the shared reality of a defined socio-economic milieu, and consequently objective knowledge. The first step (from the individual to the shared reality) raises few grounds for concern. Indeed both old institutionalists and Greenfield and Strickon (discussed earlier in this Chapter) provide detailed accounts of this process. The second step (from the shared reality to the objective) is more problematic. The shared reality even of natural phenomena is invariably laden with social considerations. Moreover, the shared reality is influenced by the prevailing level of technological sophistication. Thus, there are many historical instances where the shared reality was different from the 'objective' reality as perceived by an outside observer. The implications of this upon the outcomes of entrepreneurial actions are profound. Moreover, the shared reality – objective or otherwise – is present oriented. As a result, it has very little to contribute in the entrepreneurial 'states of affair' (as conceived by the Austrians), simply because the future is unknowable.

Conclusions

The insights gained from the host of non-economic approaches to entrepreneurship are significantly different from those provided by economics. In the former case the entrepreneur acquires an element of realism that is absent from many theoretical constructs developed by economists. The entrepreneur operates in and is influenced by social and cultural factors. The entrepreneur is an individual who possesses psychological attributes that distinguish him or her from other economic agents[18]. Thus, psychological approaches offer us the scope of exploring diversity in agency. Whilst the importance of both agency and context is evident in the entirety of approaches discussed in this Chapter, it has been an onerous task to devise a theoretical construct that balances the conflicting demands of under- and over-socialised views.

Indeed, it is in the approaches examined in the Section which explores the interface between agency and context, that a wealth of suggestive insights of the entrepreneurial phenomenon are to be found. This, alongside other theoretical constructs in the sociology of the entrepreneur, appears to converge (though not agree) on three issues. The first issue is concerned with the usefulness of institutionalist analysis. It is becoming increasingly realised among scholars in the field that institutions not only matter, but also that institutional analysis enable us to gain an in-depth understanding of the context in relation to the individual. Thus, institutions are becoming increasingly important instruments of scholarly inquiry. The second issue is concerned with the adoption of an evolutionary approach. There is a large number of scholars who, though departing from different premises and dealing with entrepreneurship in somewhat different manner, utilise the insights of evolutionary analysis. The fact that institutional and evolutionary analyses can co-exist comfortably with each other, the former concentrating upon the prevailing state of affairs whilst the latter exploring change, only reinforces research in this direction. The final issue revolves around entrepreneurial learning. How entrepreneurs learn is an issue that has been addressed in different ways by a large number of scholars in the field. Jenks' interface between social and personal roles involve a strong element of learning – both social and individual. Greenfield and Strickon spent considerable time and effort in identifying and analysing manners in which individuals learn. This issue becomes increasingly important if placed alongside issues around information and the processing of information raised by economists.

Notes

1 During the first half of the twentieth century there were no journals or conferences dedicated to the field of entrepreneurial studies. In fact it was not until the 1970s and 1980s that some of the main journals in the field (such us *Entrepreneurship Theory and Practice, Small Business Economics, Journal of Business Venturing* and *Entrepreneurship and Regional Development*) came into being.

2 A good example of this is Casson's book published in 1982.

3 The main problem in using the 'discipline of origin' as the analytical framework for reviewing non-economic theories of the entrepreneur rests with the diversity of the key research question within each discipline. Moreover, scholars involved in the study of the entrepreneur, even the few reviewed here, emanate from a number of disciplinary settings offering the potential for further fragmentation of the field. As far as the use of chronology as the analytical framework for the review of the literature is concerned, we believe that though useful it is not on its own sufficient.

4 A notion subsequently criticised by Gerschenkron (1954).

5 The issue of social marginality has been examined by many scholars working in the field of entrepreneurial studies. However, there are considerable differences in the disciplinary

origin of these scholars: including sociology, economic history and psychology. In this sub-Section we focus upon the work emanating from the former two disciplinary settings, addressing the essentially psychological theory of Hagen later on in the Chapter.

6 The former is influenced by Durkheim and Levi-Strauss.

7 The work of Aldrich, who, probably, more than anyone else consistently advanced the evolutionary approach over a period of nearly twenty years, centres upon the organisation rather than the economic agent.

8 The institution changing function of the entrepreneur is linked to the Schumpeterian process of creative destruction.

9 Alexander Gerschenkron is primarily known for his comparative investigation of the economic development process among a handful of late developing countries. His ideas regarding the entrepreneur constitute part of this wider and undoubtedly ambitious research agenda.

10 In that respect he is the intellectual progenitor of a number of approaches attempting to redress the balance between agency and context. However, the link is not a direct one, as his work remained little known outside the group of academics exploring entrepreneurial histories. This could be attributed partly on the nature of his argument (i.e. more what the study of entrepreneurship should not be about rather than what it should be about) and partly on a 'heated' debate with David Landes regarding the nature and interpretation of the empirical evidence used by Gerschenkron.

11 McClelleand returned o entrepreneruship research in the late 1960s (together with Winter) and reviewed some of his original ideas. However, it is his 1961 work which has has been both pioneering and influential and constitutes the focus of our review here.

12 McClelland suggests that high climatic energy may influence the incidence of polygamy and subsequently child rearing practices.

13 For example see Ward et al, (1984); Waldinger et al, (1990).

14 This is in sharp contrast to the type of entrepreneur explored by McClelland and Rotter. In their case the entrepreneur is essentially the outcome of the prevailing social norms, individuals who have internalised the values of the context within which they operate rather than deviants.

15 Interesting in his criticism of the mainstream tradition in economics he misconstrues Veblen's celebrated caricature of 'the lightning calculator' as a cynical description of the entrepreneur.

16 More recent examples of the same approach (Chell, 1985), which attempt to discover the traits(s), that distinguish entrepreneurs from non-entrepreneurs remain rather unconvincing.

17 The ideas of Greenfield and Strickon, by virtue of their Darwinian origin, are by far the most akin to the approach of Veblen, and consequently the institutionalist approach developed here.

18 Admittedly, to date, too much attention has been paid upon the difference between entrepreneurs and non-entrepreneurs than between different entrepreneurial agents. This balance undoubtedly needs to be redressed in the literature.

Chapter 4

The Entrepreneur: Between Purpose and Context

Introduction

Past theoretical constructs in the field of entrepreneurial studies attempted to introduce an alternative conceptualisation of the entrepreneur. Psychologists concentrated upon the motivation and cognition of the agent, sociologists and anthropologists focused upon his or her relationship with the context, and economists explored aspects of cognition, and economic actions. For economists the magnitude of the task was augmented by the implications of 'success'. As discussed at length in Chapter 2 introducing the entrepreneur may result in considerable revision of the neo-classical experiment. This is a challenge that Veblen would have relished. It is his work, which provides us with the stimulus to explore the entrepreneurial economic agent as a unified being who exists within a specific setting, within which he or she takes decisions and implements actions.

Veblen and those following in his intellectual footsteps were unable to establish an integrated theoretical system (Hodgson, 1998). This lack of consistency is manifested in the development of diverging statements not only between individual scholars but also within the works of the same author (Veblen being a very good example of the case). Thus, in this Chapter we set out to revisit the two main concepts of old institutionalism (habits and instincts), with the aim of providing clear and consistent (though not new) definitions. We believe that an attempt to explain why one definition was adopted over others can not be undertaken here, save to note that it was not because of its dominance among old institutionalists. The primary reasons lie elsewhere: namely the pursuit of coherence and consistency and the ability to explain the entrepreneurial phenomenon. Later on in the Chapter we attempt to deploy habits and instincts in the development of theoretical propositions that enhance our understanding of the entrepreneurial process. The emphasis in this Chapter is upon the individual economic agent, i.e. how cognitive and motivational influences shape the entrepreneur in a specific socio-economic milieu. Central to this issue is the interaction between purpose and content. In Chapter 5 we will develop our approach further by focusing upon the decision-making process of the entrepreneur in the process of transacting. Before going any further we set out to discuss in some detail the definition of entrepreneurship for our purposes.

Entrepreneurship: A Definition

We think of the entrepreneur as the economic agent who puts together factors of production, as well as contracts with other entrepreneurs and other economic actors in a network of production and distribution. The entrepreneur, unlike the salaried manager, involves the ability to make judgemental decisions about the process in its entirety. Thus, the unit of analysis is commonly, though not exclusively, the individual. Indeed, other units of analysis (some of them emanating from pre-capitalist or non-capitalist milieus) may perform the entrepreneurial function.

Placed within the context of existing theoretical constructs, the definition used for the purposes of our investigation, follows on a lengthy tradition of functional conceptualisations of the entrepreneur emanating from economics. Within this context, the emphasis is placed on types of behaviour as opposed to structure (which is the remit of the theory of the firm). However, we do acknowledge that in many instances this distinction is blurred and apparent only in the eyes of the observer – especially in cases of micro-entrepreneurial ventures that take place within the confines of the family household unit.

There are two key elements to our conceptualisation of entrepreneurship. The first is concerned with the co-ordinating function of entrepreneurs, i.e. their ability to access and combine factors of production in the making of goods and the provision of services. Thus, it follows along the lines of the tradition initiated by Say. However, our definition expands the notion of combination and co-ordination beyond factors of production, to include contracts and personal as well as inter-organisational relationships (and the embodied information and knowledge) as key assets in economic activity. The importance of individual relationships as well as that of networking practices (coherent sets of relationships) has become increasingly apparent in the area of entrepreneurial studies, though not as yet explicitly introduced in the conceptualisation of the entrepreneur. The acknowledgement of the importance of 'relationships' can be attributed to the work of New Institutionalists (Williamson, 1985; 1993) - and the emphasis they place upon the costs of transacting and the introduction of 'hybrid' governance structures - as well as the Scandinavian network tradition (Johannisson, 1990 and 1995) - which explores the role of personalised social networks. As a consequence, the definition deployed here enables us to capture entrepreneurship in its entirety, comprising of decisions to compete as well as co-operate with other economic agents.

The second key element of our conceptualisation of entrepreneurship concerns the judgemental nature of entrepreneurial decision-making. This constitutes recognition of the influence of time upon entrepreneurial decision-making, a theme extensively discussed by advocates of the Austrian tradition (see Chapter 2). Thus, all combinations of factors of production and networks of relationships are developed at present but are oriented towards the future. As a consequence, there is an inherent uncertainty emanating from the inability to predict accurately the actions taken by other economic agents engaged in the process of market exchange. The impact of uncertainty is further augmented on account of the entrepreneur's limited and 'idiosyncratic' access to information regarding present markets and agents. As a consequence, judgement constitutes a defining element of entrepreneurial decision-making. The recognition that time matters in our understanding entrepreneurship however, does not mean an acceptance of Austrian subjectivism. Instead, we aspire to explore (mainly in Chapter 5) an institutionalist alternative that addresses this key consideration in entrepreneurship research.

Veblen on Entrepreneurs – A Parenthesis

Before proceeding in the exposition of an alternative approach in understanding the entrepreneur to that advocated by other scholars in the field, it is essential to examine how Veblen perceived entrepreneurship. The main reason behind the decision to explore, in some detail, Veblen's perception of the entrepreneur is that it exemplifies institutionalist thinking regarding the impact of institutions upon individual behaviour. In doing so, we attempt comparisons with other influential conceptualisations - and particularly that of Schumpeter - in order to establish a distinction between disparate understandings of the phenomenon from differences in approach.

Veblen worked more or less at the same time and place (early twentieth century United States) that Schumpeter and Knight led the revival of scholarly interest on the role of the entrepreneur, whilst his work was well known to both entrepreneurship scholars. Moreover, Veblen attempted to develop an alternative model of human agency, which, we contend, provides a suggestive instrument in understanding the entrepreneur. However, his conceptual schema remained detached from the area of entrepreneurial studies. To date there has been no attempt to use Veblen's approach in the study of the entrepreneur, whilst only one published paper compares his ideas with those of Joseph Schumpeter. This concludes that

> ... their visions of capitalism are fundamentally opposed ... Veblen ... held the system in contempt and was convinced that it operated contrary to the welfare of the community. His villain was the entrepreneur dedicated to realising profits at the expense of efficient production ... [Schumpeter] saw capitalism as a wonderfully productive system ... Entrepreneurship was central to the rapid advance of technology under competitive capitalism (O'Donnell, 1993, p. 201).

These remarks draw upon Veblen's critique of capitalism at the turn of the twentieth century (Hodgson, 1992). He suggests that the divorce between ownership and control led to the emergence of absentee-owners as a separate analytical category. Thus, the corporation financier became removed from the management problems of the enterprise, and grew ignorant of the technical industrial process. Ultimately, absentee-owners evolved into mere intermediaries between industrial experts and large financial concerns, creating trusts in an attempt to achieve excess profits at the expense of the public. This is attained through 'sabotage', a conscious withdrawal of efficiency with the sole aim of maintaining prices at levels above those that would prevail in a competitive system (O'Donnell, 1993). Such a conceptualisation stands in sharp contrast, to the theoretical constructs emanating from economics. For example Schumpeter (1942) explains the emergence of big business in terms of economic efficiency, as it facilitates a more rational and orderly way of introducing innovations. Moreover, advocates of the Austrian tradition attach an equilibrating function to the entrepreneur. Specifically, Kirzner (1979) argues that the entrepreneur identifies opportunities in the form of price differential and acts upon them.

Veblen's pitiless criticism of 'absentee-owners' stands in sharp contrast to his positive view of the early entrepreneurs - the craftsmen, the small businessmen and the merchants of the pre-industrial era. He identifies them, as the economic agents that performed the function of both the financier and the day-to-day manager of the enterprise. This enabled them to appreciate the conditions imposed by the existing level of technology upon the objects of their pursuit. Therefore, the early entrepreneur learned to combine tools in functional patterns, and his or her attention was habitually centred upon the causal forces at work as he or she applied skill, dexterity and judgement to the functioning of goods (Veblen, 1914). This view of pre-industrial craftsmen and merchants displays considerable similarities with the definition of the entrepreneur deployed by prominent scholars such as Say, Schumpeter and more importantly Casson, in the sense that it is production oriented. Nearly eighty years after the publication of the *Instinct of Workmanship and the State of Industrial Arts*, Casson defines the entrepreneur in strikingly similar terms.

Though in both instances (absentee-ownership and craftmanship) entrepreneurship is linked to the co-ordination of factors of production - using finance as the co-ordination mechanism in the case of absentee-owners and technology in early entrepreneurs, there is an apparent 'disparity' in the realisation of such behaviour. This disparity in motives and behaviours is indicative of the impact of the specific institutional setting on the interpretation of economic phenomena[1]. Cochran (1955) provides a suggestive, though controversial, depiction of the changing nature of entrepreneurship in the US. The heritage of the colonial era, where

> salaried positions in the Army and the Navy were held by the British... [and] Similarly the highest offices of government were of British appointment... (Cohran, 1955, p. 126),

transformed trade and manufacturing as the preferred avenues for social mobility. Geographical mobility (associated with the continuous move of the Western frontiers) encouraged self-help as opposed to help from the family; willingness to co-operate with relative strangers; and adjustment to alien and changeable conditions (Cochran, 1964). These combined with the loose integration of American culture have created an attitude of competitiveness that underpinned entrepreneurial pursuits. Within this context, and despite a level of technological knowledge below that of England, American entrepreneurs had introduced a more highly mechanised process of industrial growth[2]. This was an era associated with the emergence of the strong investment banks that deprived the entrepreneur of control and weakened his or her authority (Heilbroner, 1956). This was combined with the growing importance of professional managers coming through the ranks of large organisations (Newcomer, 1952). As a result there was a shift in emphasis towards reducing risk and pursuing speculative profit. The latter was attained through the rapid advancement of industrial combination and the formation of large holding companies. These purely financial bodies were created for the purpose of exercising control over the policies of previously competitive companies (Ashworth, 1975).

Late nineteenth and early twentieth century entrepreneurs in the United States operated in a very different cultural setting and responded to different motivations from their predecessors. The impact of the specific socio-economic context upon what is essentially the same (co-ordinating) function was so profound as to enable Veblen to identify two distinct types: crafsmen and absentee-owners. This is indicative of the influence that habits can have upon human - and more specifically - entrepreneurial decisions and actions.

Core Concepts: Habits, the Contextual Dimension

The role of habits has rarely featured in the process of entrepreneurial decision-making. This is not particularly unexpected, as it appears to stand in sharp contrast with many of the defining attributes of the entrepreneur. Entrepreneurs have the ability to innovate (see Schumpeter in Chapter 2), and imagine actions for an unknowable future (see Shackle in Chapter 2). Habits, however, involve 'establishment in our nature of a rule of action' (Peirce, 1958, p. 121). The essence of habit is repetition. Indeed, Hodgson provides a suggestive definition of habit

> ... as a largely non-deliberative and self-actuating propensity to engage in a previously adopted pattern of behaviour. A habit is a form of self-sustaining, nonreflective behavior that arises in repetitive situations (Hodgson, 1998, p. 178).

Thus, habitual behaviour - by virtue of its frequent occurrence - is automatic in its performance, in a manner reminiscent (though not identical), in the area of entrepreneurship research, of Casson's 'response to transitory change'[3] (see Chapter 2).

Habits perform two conflicting tasks: perpetuating traits that emanate from the past (frequently from many generations past), whilst increasing the efficiency of repetitive human behaviour and allowing individuals to address new or unique circumstances[4] (Veblen, 1899). More importantly however, for our purposes, habits are both social and individual phenomena. Drawing upon this distinction we set out to explore here the social dimensions of habits through the notions of institutions and technology, whilst their individual manifestations through the experiences of economic agents will be discussed in a later Section of this Chapter.

Institutions (or habits of thought) and technology are the two component elements of habits in institutionalist analysis. Institutions refer to the regular, patterned behaviour of individuals in a specific social setting, as well as the ideas and values associated with these regularities (Neale, 1994). They are defined as social constructs regarding the validity, expediency or merit of a given line of conduct or deliberation. According to Veblen they are 'settled habits of thought common to the generality of men' (Veblen, 1919, p. 239). Markets and specific sets of property rights are institutions, as is language, religious codes and beliefs, law courts with their formal and informal procedures and legal codes. Institutions are the embodiment of long-standing, widely accepted practice in the society. They are intangible but real. Evidence of their existence is the regularity of people's actions. Institutions emanate from the past, i.e. they are habits that have been formed and established in previous generations and have been passed down through learning to young individuals and subsequent generations as existing ideas and beliefs (Waller, 1988). Institutions are stable and resistant to change but not unchangeable (Veblen, 1899). Later on in this Chapter we will discuss how entrepreneurs in particular can instigate change in the institutional setting.

The second social dimension of habit is based on matter-of-fact knowledge, meaning mechanical cause and effect. Technology is the embodiment of matter-of-fact knowledge accumulated by previous generations. It is the cumulative body of knowledge which we (humans) have been using to transform the world. With technology we adapt the environment to our needs rather than adapting, through biological evolution, to the environment (de Gregori and Shepherd, 1994). This is attained through testing 'hypotheses' to see if they have 'linkages' with the accumulated body of technological knowledge. Those hypotheses judged to be correct are adopted, whilst all the others are discarded, a process not greatly dissimilar to that advanced by Greenfield and Strickon (see Chapter 3). This process of technological change is not only constant and ongoing but also cumulative (Waller, 1982). It is from the accumulated body of knowledge, which we have been using to transform the world, that we derive the building blocks for technological change. Within an institutional context, technology is a dynamic force in economic, societal and cultural transformation (de Gregori and Shepherd, 1994). Thus, technology is perceived as problem-solving as well as problem-creating. This means that technology does not only provide solutions for existing problems, but it influences the institutional setting in a manner that may redefine ends, or create new ends.

In our analysis technology emerges as the dynamic force in a socio-economic milieu, whereas institutions tend to be relatively static, a force of continuity between past, present and the future. More importantly however, institutions tend to reflect the prevailing technological development. Thus, 'states' of technology give rise to characteristic sets of property rights, social and economic structures and so on (Ekelund and Herbert, 1997). Institutions however, are not only the product of the prevailing state of technological development but also impinging upon technology, thwarting it or encouraging it as the case may be. Taken together institutions and technology perform a key function: preserving knowledge, including tacit knowledge, through time. Habits are the embodiment of everything we know about ourselves - as human beings - and about our environment

Core Concepts: Instincts, Introducing Purpose to Human Endeavour

Habits constitute the learned element of human behaviour. However, human behaviour is not prescribed by the prevailing institutional and technological milieu, and manifested in a fixed selection of actions. This is, in large part, on account of the influence of instincts. Instincts are the natural dispositions that are common to all economic agents: they provide direction and force to the process of human development. It is the complement of instincts that makes-up human nature (Jensen, 1987). Instincts could be defined as the

> various natural proclivities that ... have the characteristic in common that they all ... propose an objective end of endeavour (Veblen, 1914, p. 3).

Despite the universality of instincts, they are not rooted in the biological constitution of humans (Mitchell, 1937). Instead,

> it is a distinctive mark of mankind that the working-out of the instinctive proclivities of the race is guided by intelligence to a degree not approached by the other animals (Veblen, 1914, p. 10).

Thus, instincts are more than simple reflex reactions: they involve consciousness and intelligence (Jensen, 1987). Instincts do not prescribe the actual behaviour exhibited by an economic agent in response to any given stimulus. Instead, instincts define the anticipated (desired) outcome of whatever action takes place (Seckler, 1975). Instincts define ends: leaving the sequence of acts by which ends are to be achieved open to the influence of human intelligence and habits.

    The introduction of purpose or an end of human endeavour is not something new in the area of entrepreneurial studies. In fact, many scholars in the field (Knight) introduce notions that explore the 'ends' which drive the entrepreneur, whilst others (advocates of the Austrian tradition) emphasise a dissatisfaction with the present and the pursuit of a future that fulfils individual needs. Whilst essentially not particularly novel, instincts constitute a useful concept: universally present but contextual, driving human intelligence but not prescribing the behaviour of economic agents[5].

Our subsequent analysis of instincts (hereafter used interchangeably with purpose of human endeavour) draws heavily on the pioneering work of Veblen. This is because we perceive his original - and sometimes contradictory - model of human agency as particularly useful in the context of entrepreneurial studies. Our interpretation of his work is informed by insights provided by Dewey and Commons, as well as economic sociologists who drew directly from the institutionalist tradition (such as Polanyi and Granovetter) who enable us to gain greater insights into the works of the entrepreneur than Austrian theorisations. The outcome - we posit - is coherent but not novel. More importantly, however, we believe that it provides a more appropriate framework for understanding the entrepreneur than those provided by other scholars in the field.

For purposes of analytical convenience we provide a distinction between self-regarding and other regarding purposes of human endeavour. The former refer to instincts that focus on the self: the survival of the individual and the satisfaction of his or her needs, whereas the latter concentrate upon ends of human endeavour that can be satisfied only through participation in social groups. Idle curiosity is discussed separately, mainly on account of its importance in understanding the entrepreneur and his or her decision-making process.

Self-regarding Purpose of Human Endeavour

We can identify two main instincts that define the individual as a distinct entity from the social group. Together the desire to compete and the propensity to acquire are the most alert and persistent instincts that underpin self-preservation[6]. The desire to compete (predation in the writings of early institutionalists) links to the tendency towards aggression and conflict (O'Hara, 1999). The desire to compete drives the individual to prove his or her attributes and qualities in relation to others. Success (or failure) in competition provides more than the mere satisfaction (or not) of material needs that secure physical reproduction: it defines the individual's position within a specific context. The importance of the desire to compete is widely acknowledged in entrepreneurship research: Schumpeter presents this as the desire to prove one better than the others (Chapter 2), whilst McClelland defines it as the individual's need to achieve (Chapter 3). In both Schumpeter and McClelland, however, this concept becomes detached from the often intense and sometimes ruthless reality of competition and elevated to a higher level. In sharp contrast, Veblen is fully aware of the excesses of the desire to compete.

The second self-regarding instinct - the propensity to acquire - can be perceived as the social manifestation of success in competition. It is essentially a comparison of an individual's efficiency in the competitive game, using commonly accepted criteria of status and prestige. In later stages of economic development it gives rise to the institution of ownership. Thus, property emerges as 'the conventional basis for esteem the criterion for respectability, reputability and moral worth' (Mayberry, 1969, p.316)[7]. The propensity to acquire as evidence of one's respectability and moral worth has also been stressed by scholars who explored motivational influences in the entrepreneurial process. Thus, Schumpeter advances the importance of 'creating one's own empire' as a key driver of the entrepreneur (Chapter 2). This conceptualisation of the propensity to acquire within the context of a specific set of (private) property rights provides a challenging aletrnative to Demsetz' (1996) notion of acquisitivenes. In his attempt to link rationality and the evolution of intelligence, he argues that acquisitiveness means 'not only a preference for more wealth ... [but also] ... the realization that more wealth can be had' (Demsetz, 1996, p. 492).

Other-regarding Purpose of Human Endeavour

Within the context of our approach we are distinguishing between two main other-regarding instincts[8]: workmanship and a propensity to co-operate. The human aptitude for 'effective work and distaste for futile effort ... may be called the instinct of workmanship' (Veblen, 1899, p. 15). Workmanship is essentially the work ethic, the aptitude towards technological knowledge and material production[9]. Conceptual schemata in the area of entrepreneurial studies, with the notable exception of Weber's early contribution on the importance of the commitment to work associated by the Protestant ethic (Chapter 3), overlooked the importance of workmanship. Interestingly, practitioner focused manuals and textbooks (for examples see Kuratko and Hodgetts, 1994; Wickham, 2000; Kirkby, 2002) tend to emphasise the importance of the work ethic of entrepreneurs.

The second other-regarding purpose of human endeavour, the propensity to co-operate - broadly corresponding to what Veblen termed as the 'parental bent' - relates to the tendency of human beings to care for other people (O'Hara, 1999). Although this instinct is stronger regarding persons that the individual knows well, such as members of the family and friends, it also includes the society within which one operates. Thus, it is the instinct of co-operation that drives individuals to strive for social cohesion and the advancement of the collective. It is this propensity to co-operate which makes society possible. Interestingly, without the propensity to co-operate, and the ensuing set or property rights, neither the desire to compete, i.e. to prove better than 'others', nor the propensity to acquire criteria for respectability (by whom), would be possible. The importance of a propensity to co-operate in influencing entrepreneurial behaviour is not addressed and not even acknowledged in the bulk of scholarly enquiries. It is only in the work of Frank Knight that careful consideration is provided (Chapter 2).

Idle Curiosity

The one instinct that appears to 'be incorruptible by the exigencies of culture is idle curiosity' (Veblen, 1914, p. 9). Idle curiosity[10] is defined as the human propensity towards experimentation and creative innovation that could generate novelty in an ongoing manner (Veblen, 1914). This is a disposition not only to know about things but also to know the 'why' of things (Seckler, 1975). This explanatory capacity of the human mind, carries thought into the range of creative intelligence and could lead to new and improved ways of thinking and doing. Thus, idle curiosity[11] occurs in the realm of the psychological but drives the cognitive and is speculative in nature, i.e. it is activity for the sake of activity alone rather than the rewards that may result from the activity (a notion that bears some similarity with Knight's argument about the enjoyment derived from 'playing the competitive game' and Schumpeter's belief that entrepreneurs are driven by a desire to win 'for the sake of it'). The essence of the notion of 'idle curiosity' is not new to the area of entrepreneurial studies. Kirzner stressed the importance of entrepreneurial alertness to unknowable information, whilst Shackle emphasised the ability of entrepreneurs to imagine - in the sense of projecting to an uncertain future - actions and policies. 'Idle curiosity' though conceived in a totally different theoretical context, combines the incessant pursuit of information (alertness) with creative intelligence (imagination) in one instinct, present in all economic agents.

'Idle curiosity' exists alongside pragmatism, the former referring to innovation and knowledge whilst the latter on practical life. There is a trade-off between 'idle curiosity' and pragmatism. Thus, the former, though an instinct can function only within the scope left by the latter.

Between Purpose and Context

Previous Sections of this Chapter introduced the two core concepts of our approach in understanding entrepreneurship. On the one hand there are certain 'universal' instincts common to all men: they do not prescribe behaviour but define human purpose. On the other side there is the context (habits), which is variable among economic agents depending on time and place. Whereas instincts give direction and force to the process of human development, habits provide the specific content of the moment (see Figure 4.1). Here we attempt to explore the interface between instincts and habits in shaping the entrepreneurial agent.

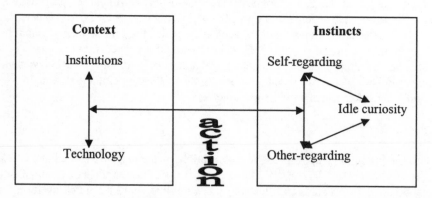

Figure 4.1 The Interface between Purpose and Context

In our analysis the purpose of human endeavour is natural to economic agents, i.e. it is present, both historically and biologically, prior to the formation and establishment of habits. However, instincts are also abstract drives that are meaningless outside a specific socio-economic milieu. Thus, although 'first in time' they are not primary in fact. This is because

> instincts may cancel one another through the sheer force of their contrary pull on the same body; or ... the institutional structure of society may suppress or encourage one class of instincts at the expense of another (Seckler, 1975, p. 59).

Thus, instincts do not prescribe the behaviour of entrepreneurs. At the same time however, the influence of institutions and technology upon individuals is not prescriptive. This means that individuals do not possess a thoroughly 'Institutionalized Mind' (Commons, 1959) in the sense of being conditioned to behave in accordance with the prevailing rules. This is partly on account of the function of instincts - and particularly idle curiosity.

Proposition 1: the actions of the entrepreneur are shaped by the interaction between purpose and context.

The Position of Individuals

The review of theoretical constructs in the area of entrepreneurial studies (Chapters 2 and 3) highlighted the significance of the interplay between actor and context. Entrepreneurs are economic agents who work in specific structural contexts. However, it is apparent from the literature that entrepreneurial socialisation may differ profoundly from case to case. Scholars like McClelland emphasise the importance of individuals internalising family and social beliefs regarding the importance of achieving high standards of excellence (see Chapter 3). Weber also seems to share this view in the case of the Protestant Ethic. This stands in sharp contrast to the thesis developed by Kets de Vries who perceives the entrepreneur as a reject, a 'misfit', who exists in relative isolation from his or her environment. The work of Hagen and Hoselitz offer an other variant of this thesis: distinguishing between the rejection of the individual from the 'mainstream' of the society, and his or her acceptance within a 'marginal' sub-group. Thus, the issue of how the entrepreneurial agents fits (or not) in the context within which he or she operates warrants careful consideration.

However, the contextualisation of the entrepreneur proved more than usually problematic. Earlier attempts to understand the entrepreneur were confronted with the issue of the relative importance of factors internal to the economic actor and those emanating from the external environment. Whilst the limitations of mono-causal explanations have been apparent for a considerable period of time, there has been little success in developing a meaningful synthesis. In that part of the literature emanating from economics this was manifested in a divide between those stressing the importance of the individual's free will versus those focusing upon the impact of the environment[12] (for a discussion see Seckler, 1975). A similar divide is also apparent in the broad and loosely defined area of business studies between those emphasising the freedom of the individual to take strategic decisions, and population ecology (for a review see Gardner 2001).

In order to resolve this apparent contradiction, we draw upon the insights provided by the concept of embeddedness. Polanyii (1944) used this concept to argue that economic behaviour in pre-market societies was heavily embedded in social relations. The development of industrial capitalism however, increasingly disconnected (disembedded) economic behaviour from the social structure. During the 1980s Granovetter (1985) used this concept in order to contextualise human hehaviour. In doing so, he advanced the thesis that

> ... [a]ctors do not behave or decide as atoms outside a social context, nor do they adhere slavishly to a script written for them by the particular intersection of social categories that they happen to occupy ... [t]heir attempts at purposive actions are instead embedded in concrete, ongoing systems of social relations (Granovetter, 1985, p. 487).

The concept of embeddedness precludes the atomisation of human behaviour, which is implicit in both under-socialised (neo-classical theory) and over-socialised (structural-functional sociology) conceptions. Instead, it enables us to understand economic agents as individuals with a purpose, who exist and function within concrete socio-economic milieu's. Thus, their actions are influenced but not prescribed by the context.

This raises two key issues that are instrumental in the development of an alternative model of human agency. The first revolves around the identification of the level or degree of embeddedness between members of the same milieu. This means that individuals who exist in the same context internalise the prevailing norms and customs to varying degrees. Diverse processes of early socialisation, the differential impact of learning, and a sense of belonging (or not) to distinct sub-groups may account for such disparities in the degree of embeddedness. The second focuses on the question: embeddedness to what? This means that individuals who function within the same geographical locality may be embedded in different contexts. For example, the context varies profoundly in the case of an entrepreneur who only recently moved to a locality but possesses experience and contacts in a specific industrial context, nationally or even internationally, from the case of another entrepreneur in the very same locality who was born and raised locally, and has rarely travelled or interacted with individuals from outside his or her immediate setting. This diversity in context would be apparent even if both entrepreneurs operated in the same industry[13]. The issue of embeddedness to what is particularly relevant in the case of multicultural societies, where different and interacting institutional settings exist within the same location. These two considerations (parameters) define the position of the individual in relation to his or her context[14].

Proposition 2: the interaction between purpose and context is influenced by the distinct (and in cases individual) positions that economic agents occupy in relation to their context.

Cognitive Frameworks and Learning

The interaction between an individual (who occupies a defined though not necessarily unique position) and his or her environment results in the formation of cognitive frameworks and the accumulation of knowledge and experience. More specifically, it is the context which imposes social coherence upon human activity, through the creation and of conceptual schemata and learned signs and meanings (Hodgson, 1998). Individual manifestations of institutions and technology, such as language, the ability to perform analytical skills, the capability of synthesising information, form the cognitive framework of individual economic agents. These cognitive frameworks are learned through social processes such as early socialisation, education and social interaction.

As a consequence, cognitive frameworks are essentially a shared (though by no means identical) view of the context within which individuals operate. The existence of a strong element of commonality in cognition within the same context, is a necessary condition for the interaction of economic agents within society. This is because when

> two agents communicate with each other, they have to receive and understand signals from the other. To communicate successfully, they have to consistently interpret signals which they receive. It is clear that it is difficult for communication to be successful when a sender and a receiver interpret the information according to their subjective frameworks. In such situations, the feasibility of transferring correct information seems to be reduced (Egashira and Hashimoto, 2001, p. 181).

The individual relies upon such cognitive frameworks before action is possible, because they are instrumental in the interpretation and the introduction of meaning to information (perceived here as sense-data). These lead us to conclude that economic agents, at any point in time, have an image of the world (cognitive framework), of what they believe to be true. It is this image that largely governs the agent's processes of making information 'speak'.

This cognitive framework can be added to or otherwise modified by incoming information. It is important to stress here, a point originally advanced by Boulding (1956), that there is a mutual interdependence between the cognitive framework and information. On the one hand, information can lead to the revision of the economic agent's cognitive framework, and thereby alter behaviour. On the other hand, information never reaches cognition in an original or 'pure' form, as it is always filtered and processed through of the existing framework.

Cognitive frameworks are used in the interpretation of information. We identify two such processes at work. The former refers to the agent's view of the context. For example information about laws of nature provide us with an understanding of how the world works. Individuals who have access to such information at any one point in time will form a broadly similar view of the laws of nature. This is because the accumulated information invariably constitutes the outcome of the labour of previous generations. Such information may be codified and learned through education, in the broadest sense of the term. Thus, knowledge appears to be the outcome of learning as a social process, in a manner similar to cognitive framework formation.

Whilst an agent's view of the context is attained through learning as a social process, as it essentially constitutes of repeated impressions of other human beings, experience is individual (Commons, 1959). This is because experience is not just the manifestation of the context upon individuals: it is the result of the interaction between the economic agent and the environment[15]. Indeed, the acquisition of experience is different from the creation of cognitive frameworks because it results from individual actions taken by the economic agents[16]. As the actions of the entrepreneurs may differ – either on account of the interface between instincts and context or by differences in the understanding of the situation – their outcomes may also differ. Of course, not all actions will result in the creation of new experiences. It is those actions which are the consequence of judgemental decision-making, one of the two elements that define entrepreneurship for our purposes, that result in new experiences. In that respect experience is the result of a learning process which is specific to the individual concerned[17].

Proposition 3: economic agents use cognitive frameworks in the process of learning (both as a social and as an individual process).

The Entrepreneurial Process

Individual entrepreneurs exist and are influenced by the context within which they operate. The impact of the social content is manifested in the development of a cognitive framework and knowledge about the world and how it works. The cognitive framework also constitutes the main instrument in interpreting information in the process of entrepreneurial decision-making. However, a key premise of our approach is that the totality of information possessed by an individual falls short of what a neo-classical economist would equate with perfect information[18].

Idle curiosity is instrumental in driving economic agents to access and interpret information (see Figure 4.2). One manifestation of idle curiosity is an inherent inquisitiveness, which enables individuals to acquire new information. It drives the individual towards discovering new data - through enquiring, probing, or even 'prying' in the activities of other economic agents. It involves searching for information in a speculative manner. The second manifestation of idle curiosity concerns with the interpretation of information. It facilitates both the review of existing information and the creation of new syntheses of existing data with the purpose of identifying solutions or problems. Thus, idle curiosity also questions, challenges and ultimately undermines the prevailing wisdom. As a consequence, idle curiosity is central to the process of judgemental decision-making (discussed in detail in Chapter 5). In this capacity idle curiosity is creative intelligence, i.e. the ability of individual economic agents to generate - on the basis of existing information - images of future states of affairs.

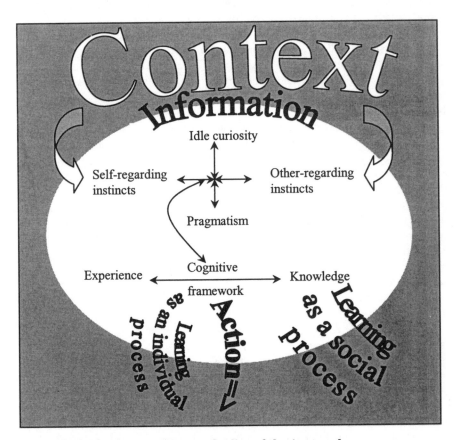

Figure 4.2 The Entrepreneur: An Outline of the Approach

However, whilst idle curiosity is present among all economic agents, its impact differs both in the case of economic agents active in different socio-economic milieus, as well as those individuals within the same setting. This is because idle curiosity exists alongside pragmatism, and its emphasis on use-value. The scope for judgemental decision-making (which is influenced by the trade-off between idle curiosity and pragmatism) is influenced both by the context and the individual's position in relation to his or her environment: manifested through the pervasive role of knowledge and experience.

As a consequence the incidence of entrepreneurship is expected to be greater in settings that encourage idle curiosity rather than those embracing pragmatism. In the former type of setting entrepreneurial roles are likely to be performed by those economic agents who are embedded in the milieu, and thus have internalised the prevailing moral values. In contrast, in contexts advancing pragmatism, entrepreneurship is frequently associated with individuals who are not well embedded - disembedded for the absence of a better word - from the context. This is because such persons are able to take actions or engage in activities which are not valued or are even openly disapproved by society at large.

This thesis enables us to reconcile the diverging arguments developed around the issue of influence of legitimation upon the incidence of entrepreneurial ventures. Research, dating back to the works of Max Weber (1922), points to the significance of legitimation and social recognition as a key influence in the emergence of entrepreneurial talent[19]. Similarly, research carried out by members of the Harvard Centre for Entrepreneurial History during the early post-war period explained differences in the economic development of industrialised countries in terms of the degree of legitimation of entrepreneurship (Cochran, 1949). In a comparison between France and the United States, Landes (1951) argues that the delay with which the former country attained economic growth and structural transformation was due to its feudal heritage and a tradition unfavourable to entrepreneurial behaviour. In contrast, in the United States the absence of a feudal past had allowed the formation of an institutional setting that was receptive to innovation and entrepreneurship[20]. It is in settings like this that processes of early socialisation lead to the creation of a need for achievement among individuals who subsequently perform entrepreneurial roles (McClelland, 1961). In contrast, in settings which do not encourage or attach considerable status to enterprise ventures entrepreneurs are to be found among socially marginal groupings or those experiencing status withdrawal. Hoselitz (1963) points at the greater propensity to entrepreneurship of marginal (for religious or ethnic reasons) groups, such as the Greeks, the Armenians and the Jews in medieval Europe, a context where entrepreneurial pursuits were spurned in the mainstream. Hagen (1962) also argues that entrepreneurs tend to come from groups who suffered from withdrawal of status, i.e. groups which believe that their values in life are not respected by groups in the society whom they respect and whose esteem they value. This prompts those individuals excluded from the mainstream to undertake entrepreneurial ventures.

The practices and organisational structures created by entrepreneurs in the entrepreneurial process are influenced by the interplay between self-regarding and other-regarding instincts in the specific context (see Figure 4.2). Self-regarding instincts prompt individuals to co-ordinate their activities through competition, namely the vertical integration of activities within firms who compete with each other in the marketplace, or the establishment of hierarchical sub-contracting. In this context, competitive advantage is gained through exclusive access to resources, whilst co-ordination and intensity of effort are attained through power. Other-regarding instincts, however, promote solutions which are based upon co-operation. These include the establishment of community-based initiatives, as well as (non-hierarchical) inter-organisation networks. In this case sharing of resources is a considerable strength for all those involved, whilst trust underpins co-ordination. Of course in many instances the choice is not either (self-regarding instincts driven) or (other-regarding instinct driven) but a combination of the two: hybrid co-ordination mechanisms, or governance structures (the term deployed by Williamson in other New Institutionalists).

Entrepreneurial actions, and their impact on the marketplace, result in the accumulation of experience (see Figure 4.2). This is because the actions of economic agents who behave entrepreneurially may lead to a multiplicity of outcomes: ranging from the successful attainment of objectives to outright failure. In some instances, entrepreneurial actions may result in partial realisation of the original objectives, raising the questions of either what actions are needed to achieve the original objectives or whether the objectives themselves need to be reviewed. In other cases, entrepreneurial actions may initiate reactions from other economic agents, which have not been anticipated in the first place, raising the need to implement corrective action. Actions leading to the attainment of more goals than others could be viewed as more appropriate for the specific environmental setting. At the same time, actions which are not producing the desired effects will be discarded.

Entrepreneurial actions may also result in the emergence of new information - that the entrepreneur was unaware of prior to taking the action. New information has to be interpreted in the light of existing knowledge and individual experiences and fed into the entrepreneurial decision-making process. Thus, new information may prompt idle curiosity to generate ideas about opportunities, or lead to a review and re-interpretation of data, resulting in new syntheses in the short-term.

Entrepreneurial Actions and Institutional Change

This Chapter has focused heavily upon the influence of institutions upon entrepreneurial decision-making. However, entrepreneurs do not merely engage in a process of continuous adaptation to environmental influences. Entrepreneurs, alongside other individuals, are able to influence their environment. In fact, a conceptual approach drawing upon the works of old institutionalists, and especially Veblen suggests that entrepreneurs are among the most influential agents of change in the socio-economic milieu. This issue, though not central to the argument developed here, merits some consideration. Entrepreneurs may influence institutional change through the process of technological change (which constitutes the focus of this Section).

Our point of departure is the diverse nature of institutions and technology: the former is relatively static whilst the latter is the dynamic force in society (as shown in the second section of this Chapter). More importantly, however, the institutional setting is defined by the prevailing state of industrial arts (technology) over that period (Ekelund and Herbert, 1997). This is because,

> the technological mode of the moment imposes a unique discipline on the behaviour of those most closely associated with it. From this disciplined behaviour emerges the characteristic habits of thought of the next stage (Seckler, 1975, p. 61).

Veblen (1914) spends considerable time and effort explaining how technology shaped institutions in different historical eras. For example[21], the pre-historic era of 'savagery' was defined by very low level of technological development, forcing economic agents to spend the bulk of their time on productive activities in order to ensure their physical reproduction. The scope for predatory activities was limited by the sheer effort required to meet essential needs, and the inability to accumulate resources which could offer an incentive for acquisition. Thus, the era of savagery was peaceful, characterised by the intensive application of labour upon low sophistication technologies.

In this context, idle curiosity is instrumental in instigating the process of technological change. It is the generation of new information and the application of creative intelligence, which result in actions that further the state of industrial arts. Even in instances where actions may not succeed in instigating change, they (actions) result in new data and experiences, through learning, which inform subsequent decisions. Within this context, entrepreneurs are of paramount importance, as it is they whose idle curiosity puts together factors of production and contracts with other entrepreneurs in a network of production and distribution. Thus, entrepreneurs are instrumental in advancing the state of industrial arts, and subsequently the institutional setting.

Conclusions

The institutionalist approach in understanding the motivational and cognitive in the entrepreneurial process has been presented here in a, more or less, stage-by-stage manner. This is for purposes of analytical convenience only. Real entrepreneurial processes are much more complex than this. For example, idle curiosity may be driven by data provided derived from previous actions, structures may be already present so that the practicalities of the implementation may be already known, and individuals may be embedded in more than one context, as is often the case with second generation ethnic entrepreneurs.

What conclusions can we draw regarding the behaviour of individual entrepreneurial agents, using an institutionalist perspective? The individual presented here is not the 'fairly rational' person who seeks to achieve maximum satisfaction in perfectly competitive markets. Instead s/he is a multidimensional economic agent who is *active* and *unified* in *specific contexts*. The entrepreneur within the institutionalist approach is not the

> lightning calculator of pleasures and pains, who oscillates like a homogeneous globule of desire and happiness under the impulse of stimuli that shift him about the area, but leave him intact (Veblen, 1898, pp. 73-74)

of the mainstream tradition in economics. S/he has purpose (instincts), which enables the combination of learned knowledge and individual experiences in purposeful action. Moreover, entrepreneurial behaviour encompasses the whole person – rather than either mainly the motivational or primarily the cognitive – in every act. Although it may make sense for purposes of analytical convenience to distinguish between the two (motivational and cognitive) these are not separate faculties. Thus, understanding the entrepreneur entails the acquisition of knowledge regarding both, as well as the interaction between them. Lastly, the actions of the entrepreneur are influenced – in large part – by the context. That is to say, entrepreneurial conduct is socially conditioned, whether we perceive the fact or not. However, what makes-up the context may vary, even among entrepreneurs who exist and function within close geographical proximity of one another. The degree of embeddedness of individuals upon their context may also vary, alongside individual experiences of the same phenomena. As a consequence, the context may influence or even condition but does not prescribe entrepreneurial behaviour. Methodologically one would describe our institutionalist approach as organicist: in the sense that it acknowledges that the individual qualities of an entrepreneur do not exist independently of his or her relationships with the environment. However, this organicism is compatible with individualism (i.e. that individuals are important analytical units), and the existence of real agency in individuals.

In this Chapter we have introduced the two key concepts and the three main propositions of our approach. We have subsequently deployed these instruments in understanding the entrepreneurial process. However, we did not explore how entrepreneurs are able to take decisions that involve judgement. This is the main problem addressed in the following Chapter.

Notes

1 Contradictory or diverging statements are not uncommon in Veblen's writings – as will be shown in subsequent Sections. However, he never really set out to define entrepreneurship. The impact of institutions upon business enterprise was however, of considerable importance for his work, thus, the disparity in the notion of entrepreneurial behaviour.

2 Cochran (1964) emphasises the importance of cultural reasons behind the rapid adoption of machinery in early nineteenth century United States. Another, not necessarily competing,

interpretation points at labour shortages in the US and the ensuing need to introduce labour saving devices (Habakkuk, 1962).

3 The role of habitual behaviour in facilitating entrepreneurial decision-making, as a suggestive alternative to Casson's work will be discussed extensively in Chapter 5.

4 In a more recent contribution Waller (1988) formalises this dual function by defining the former (conservative) function as ritualised habit, and the latter (progressive) one as routine.

5 Instincts, by definition, make economic action teleological, in the sense that the economic agent always and everywhere seeks to accomplish some concrete end (Hodgson, 2003). Whilst an individual actions is viewed here as teleological, in terms of aiming to achieve personal ends, this teleological character is itself the outcome of a non-teleological process of interacting instincts and habits, resulting in evolving needs.

6 The manifestation of self-regarding instincts in economic activity is 'power': an all-pervasive element, which can occur in different forms and aspects (Martin, 1977). As a consequence, there is a multitude of definitions of power, ranging from Weber's clear and simple description of power as the ability of a person to bring about desired consequences even against the resistance of others, to highly sophisticated game-theoretical mathematical treatments (Rothschild, 1971). In the markets of the 'real world' certain economic agents possess the power to define the terms of or conditions of exchange. Similarly the propensity to acquire and the ensuing property rights constitute a form of empowering certain individuals. Ownership defines whom may do what to whom, with what and under what conditions (Schmid, 1987).

7 The difference in approach is indicative of the broader divergence between old and new institutionalist approaches. The latter attempt to explain the emergence of institutions by reference to a model of rational individual behaviour. In contrast, old institutionalists in general, and Veblen in particular, explore how individual actions may shape institutions, as well as how the specificities of the institutional setting may influence individual purposes and preferences (Hodgson, 1998).

8 The manifestation of other-regarding instincts in economic activity is trust. Trust amounts to an expectation that the other party to an exchange will stick to the terms of an agreement, even if circumstances change. Such a commitment, which may result in lower than expected gains (pecuniary or otherwise), arises from the sense of duty associated with the propensity to co-operate, rather than from altruism, beneficence and justice (Khalil, 1994). The concept of trust has been increasingly deployed by economists and other social scientists in order to understand how economic agents react in complex situations. In such contexts it is often perceived as a type of tacit knowledge, used by decision-makers as a replacement for explicit knowledge, which is absent (Dibben, 2000).

9 Interestingly the instinct of workmanship may - in specific institutional settings - give rise to the propensity to acquire: i.e. an other-regarding instinct reinforcing a self-regarding instinct, providing evidence to the non-mechanistic function of instincts.

10 Although idle curiosity is instrumental in the entrepreneurial process it is not exclusive to it. Scientists and artists are also driven by idle curiosity.

11 This notion facilitates the incorporation of an element of choosing in the institutionalist approach.

12 Veblen was aware of the issue of attaining a balance between free will and context, however, he was not successful in formulating a consistent approach.

13 For a detailed discussion of the influence of origin on embeddedness, in the case of the Greek clothing industry, see Kalantaridis, 1997.

14 It is important to stress here that the conceptualisation of 'position' here differs profoundly with advanced by Leland Jenks and discussed in some detail in Chapter 3. In our case, the notion of position enables us to contextualise agency but move beyond the

excesses of social determinism. It facilitates an understanding of the individual as belonging, but belonging to multiple contexts and to varying degrees.

15 Although it is undeniable that people interact with their natural environment, to a very large extent even the manner in which individuals respond to physical conditions is influenced by their institutional setting (Jensen, 1987).

16 This raises the question, why would economic agents who share broadly similar cognitive processes act differently? This is on account of the defining influence of idle curiosity, which will be discussed in considerable detail in the following Section.

17 An outline of such a learning process is provided by Grenfield and Strickon (Chapter 3). This will be developed further later on in Chapter 4.

18 This is partly because an individual's position in relation to his or her context influences access to sources of information, and subsequently the quantity and nature of information at his or her disposal[18]. Access to information may also be restricted on account of the prevailing institutional setting. Indeed, institutions may facilitate (hinder) the flow of information within the milieu, or, enable (prevent) access to information selectively. The information used by an individual in his or her decision-making may also be restricted on account of the profound limitations in human ability to process data, Simon's (1982) bounded rationality. More importantly however, access to information is imperfect on account of the unpredictability of decisions made by other economic agents. These issues form the core of Chapter 5.

19 He identifies the positive contribution of the Protestant Ethic, alongside experimental science, rational authority and government administration in enabling entrepreneurial ventures.

20 Landes broader argument however, came under considerable criticism by Gerschenkron (1954) who questioned the appropriateness of the comparison between France and the USA. The essence of Gerschenkron's argument was not so much whether the legitimacy afforded to entrepreneurship affected the propensity to initiate entrepreneurial ventures, but that there was little evidence to suggest that the former was a necessary and sufficient condition for economic advancement.

21 Example drawn from Veblen's *The Instinct of Workmanship and the State of Industrial Arts*.

Chapter 5

Entrepreneurial Decision-making: Information and Cognition

Introduction

Economic theories of the entrepreneur - especially those derived using the intellectual toolkit of the Austrian tradition - provide an insightful conceptualisation of the problem confronting the entrepreneurs in their decision-making process. This is defined by two dimensions: information, or to be more precise the lack of it, and the information processing capabilities of the entrepreneur. Within the entrepreneurship literature there is widespread agreement, that entrepreneurial decision-making occurs in circumstances of less than perfect – in the neo-classical sense of the term - information. However, the nature and degree of information gaps confronting the entrepreneur vary considerably between different scholars in the field. At the same time, there has been some discussion of cognition as well as the ability of entrepreneurs to compute optimum solutions. The availability of information and the entrepreneurial capability to make sense of it are particularly important in contexts where more than one entrepreneurs engage in economic transactions. Thus, in this Chapter we turn our attention to the investigation of these two key issues upon entrepreneurial behaviour. In doing so, we combine the institutionalist approach developed in Chapter 4, with some suggestive arguments developed in the literature using the same theoretical underpinning. Thus, particular emphasis is placed throughout this Chapter in the consistency of the analytical instruments deployed.

Although for purposes of analytical convenience we explore issues around cognition separate from imperfect information, information and cognitive frameworks can not fundamentally be separated. This is because, the meaning of information is decided in accordance with the relationship between information and the cognitive framework, whilst means and modes of cognition are formed through the analysis and interpretation of information (Hodgson, 1998).

Information and Entrepreneurial Decision-making

Access to information is a key parameter influencing entrepreneurial behaviour. Attempts at relaxing the neo-classical assumption regarding perfect information followed two distinct lines of enquiry. The first, best illustrated by Casson, explores the implications of information, which is present but not freely available to all economic agents.   This perspective, which is influenced by the New Institutionalists, centres upon the issue of how the cost of acquiring information prompts entrepreneurs to take decisions with only partial information.   The second, and distinctly Austrian line of enquiry, attempts to explore entrepreneurial decision-making regarding an unknowable future.   In this case, information regarding the future actions of economic agents is simply not there.   Therefore, entrepreneurial economic agents have to foresee or imagine future state of affairs.

The distinctiveness of these two lines of enquiry, can be conceptualised through distinguishing between the notions of ambiguity and fundamental uncertainty.   The former can be defined as '... uncertainty about probability, created by missing information that is relevant and could be known' (Camerer and Weber, 1992, p. 330).   The work of Casson centres squarely upon addressing the effects of ambiguity upon entrepreneurial decision-making.   Fundamental uncertainty however,

> ... can not be anticipated ... because the future is yet to be created. Surprises may occur, both as intended and as unintended consequences of human action.... This means that some relevant information cannot be known, not even in principle, at the time of making many important decisions (Dequech, 2001, p. 8).

Old institutionalism can make a significant positive contribution in our understanding of entrepreneurial behaviour in conditions of ambiguity and fundamental uncertainty. This Section concentrates upon two key considerations: the conceptualisation of institutions as channels of information flows (contributing in our understanding of ambiguity), and the role of institutions in facilitating social interaction (the point of departure of a novel treatise of fundamental uncertainty).

Information in Context

The issue of information that is relevant, and could be known, and the ensuing ambiguity in entrepreneurial decision-making has attracted considerable attention in mainstream analysis. The most sophisticated attempt to deal with ambiguity involved the commoditisation of information, and was provided by George Stiglitz (1961). The argument goes that markets for information will arise as a result of the cost associated with searching for information, as well as the very real benefits emanating from 'knowing'. However, the treatment of information as a commodity is somewhat problematic, on account of attributes specific to information: namely indivisibility and inappropriability.   Babe (1998), building upon the work of institutionalists such as Veblen and Boulding, illustrates convincingly why these attributes distinguish information from other 'conventional' commodities. Information indivisibility can be expressed in terms of an infinite regress inherent in deciding whether it is worthwhile to seek information concerning whether it is worthwhile to seek information. Or putting it another way, the actual value of information is not known until the information has already been received, making purchase unnecessary. The inappropriability of information has best been expressed by Boulding's remarks that 'when a teacher instructs a class, at the end of the hour presumably the student knows more and the teacher does not know any less ... What the student gains the teacher does not lose' (Boulding, 1961, p. 35). Thus, information acquired by an economic agent is - more or less by definition - shared with the individual who provided this information. This means that the returns to information are not fully appropriable.

The issue of the inability of economic actors to realise the full returns of information enables us to illustrate the influence of the context upon the flow of information in a specific socio-economic setting. Indeed, the decision to supply or acquire information is conditioned by the degree to which individuals can realise the returns emanating from information. This requires a complete (or nearly complete) rigidity of contractual arrangements and property rights associated with the flow of information (Newman, 1976). In contexts, where appropriability is very low, there will be an under-supply of information in relation to contexts where appropriability is modest. At the same time however, attempts to introduce near complete rigidity of contractual arrangement and property rights (through copyright, patents, etc) may also cause difficulties in the flow of information.

Institutions also perform another function in the flow of information and the accumulation of knowledge: they could be perceived as channels of communication. Institutions such as the market, the business organisation, the educational system - to take but a few - are instrumental in the process of communicating information between economic agents. Scholars of the Austrian tradition, and more important among them Hayek, explored the function of prices as the main communication mechanism in the marketplace. Business organisations themselves have systems (formal or informal) for communicating information internally. Indeed, the issue of communication within organisations is becoming increasingly important in the context of business studies. The educational system is dedicated to the transfer of information that has been acquired and interpreted as codified knowledge by generations past. Moreover, there are institutions focusing exclusively upon the task of facilitating communication: language being a prime example of the case. Thus, it is seems safe to assume that the specificities of the institutional setting determine the efficiency or otherwise of information flows. This function of institutions does not mean egalitarian communication of information to all economic agents. Indeed, communication may be discriminatory on account of the position (Proposition 2) of the individual in relation to the institution.

The level of technological advancement may also influence the ease (or difficulty) of information flows within a specific socio-economic setting. This is an issue that has received relatively modest attention in the field of entrepreneurial studies, despite the fact that recent advances in communication technologies have impacted significantly upon the availability of information. For example, the introduction and development of the electronic means of communication during the past twenty years or so, has reduced significance the impact of geographical distance upon the flow of information in rural areas located in advanced industrialised countries. Although not all individuals located in rural locales have access to new technologies there is a growing body of evidence supporting the thesis that new technologies emerge as key channels of communicating information (Grimes, 2000; Kalantaridis and Bika, 2003).

Economic Interaction in Context

Institutions and technology are not only instrumental in defining the degree and nature of ambiguity but also enhance the ability of entrepreneurs to deal with fundamental uncertainty. Before going any further it would be useful to trace the origins of fundamental uncertainty in the context of market exchange. Dequech (2001) suggests that

> [f]undamental uncertainty exists in any society, but assumes a particular economic form under capitalism. The institutional arrangements are such that competition stimulates decision-makers to innovate in search for extra profits, which introduces an endogenous pressure for something that causes fundamental uncertainty (Dequech, 2001, p. 8).

Thus, it is new, in the sense of being different from those that preceded them, actions of entrepreneurs, aiming to influence future states of affairs, which are the source of fundamental uncertainty. If entrepreneurs continuously reproduced actions implemented in the past, fundamental uncertainty would be nearly non-existent. This is because change in future states of affairs would occur only as a result of external shocks – which can be very effectively addressed using sophisticated analytical instruments from mainstream economics. However, in circumstances where fundamental uncertainty is present, we need to deploy analytical instruments developed by alternative approaches.

The origins (entrepreneurial actions) of fundamental uncertainty constitute the point of departure of our approach. Dealing with fundamental uncertainty involves nothing short of predicting new (future oriented) actions of other economic agents. The magnitude of the task at hand prompted many economists in the field to stress the unique qualities of the entrepreneur, leading to the introduction of the concept of foresight by Cantillon and Knight. Shackle in turn attributes to entrepreneurs an ability to imagine future state of affairs. In both cases however, the essence of these entrepreneurial attributes remains vague, as it falls outside the confines of economic science.

The nature of the task of attempting to second-guess the actions of other economic agents vary significantly on account of social interaction. Indeed, the processes at work differ considerably between instances where the entrepreneur is familiar or even knows those economic agents whose actions he or she tries to predict, and cases where the entrepreneur is totally unaware of who the economic agents are and what are their characteristics. In the former case, the entrepreneur possesses valuable information regarding the characteristics of the economic agents concerned, and may have personal experience of their actions in past situations. Thus, the entrepreneur may be aware of the ability of other economic agents to identify and pursue new actions. Whilst admittedly 'past performance is not necessarily a guide of future performance' of other economic agents it undoubtedly influences the decision of the entrepreneur. Moreover, the entrepreneur may be able – on account of his or her ability to interact with these economic agents – to influence their actions.

Institutions are of particular importance in this case as they define the context of economic interaction. More specifically,

> institutions provide social knowledge which may be needed for interaction with other individual decision makers. Specifically, all interactive decision-making involves the actor's knowledge of other individuals' knowledge (Boland, 1979, pp. 963-964).

Thus, economic agents occupy institutionally defined positions, and enact, and expect others to enact, a set of rights, duties, and protocols of interaction. Of course, the degree of compliance with these rights, duties and protocols may vary from individual to individual, leading to criticism or even punitive measures. These rules that define social interaction are often taken for granted by economic agents. Against this background every situation will present a terrain of options, and it is upon this terrain that each economic agent will pursue his or her own strategies. An illustration of the defining influence of institutions upon social interaction comes from the function of price in the process of market exchange. Let us consider a process of market exchange without prices: where some economic agents (buyers) have to communicate – in a meaningful manner – their level of desire to acquire a product to those economic agents (sellers) who try to communicate the cost (in terms of time, intensity of effort, material and equipment) of making the same product. In such circumstances the information provided the buyers is complex and described in terms (or language) different from that used by sellers. Social interaction in a setting where price has not emerged as a commonly accepted means of communicating demand and supply will be very different from a setting where it did.

Whilst the insights gained in the behaviour of other economic agents, through economic interaction, are useful to the entrepreneur they are undoubtedly limited. This is because in many instances these are restricted to a group of economic agents in the immediate (not exclusively in the spatial sense of the term) vicinity of the entrepreneur. This is because the amount of time available at the disposal of the entrepreneur, prior to taking and implementing the decision, is limited by the threat (real or perceived) of other economic agents introducing either similar actions or actions that cancel the circumstances which enable the entrepreneurial decision. At the same time, the entrepreneur is unaware not only of the characteristics but also of the mere presence of other economic agents whose actions may have a bearing on future state of affairs.

How do entrepreneurs deal with fundamental uncertainty in such circumstances? Using a metaphor, we can draw parallels between the entrepreneur dealing with fundamental uncertainty and the mainstream economist engaging in theory-building. Referring to the latter

> Ely Devons, an English economist, once said at a meeting, if economists wished to study the horse, they wouldn't go and look at horses. They'd sit in their studies and say to themselves "What would I do if I were a horse" (Boettke et al, 2001, p. 2).

In the case of economists the shift away from the complexities of the real world, towards the experiences of the self maybe somewhat troublesome as it often leads to the development of sophisticated responses to imaginary problems. This is not the case regarding the entrepreneur confronted with fundamental uncertainty. In this case, exploring the potential actions of other economic agents would be both costly and result in a problem of considerable complexity (an issue discussed in considerable detail in the following Section). Even if the entrepreneur was to bear the cost of accumulating the voluminous body of relevant information, and possessed the exceptional computational capabilities needed to process this information, it would still provide him or her with insights drawn from past performance. Tapping into the accumulated experiences of the entrepreneur, by addressing the question of 'what would I do if ...' constitutes a more realistic alternative[1].

In both instances (when the entrepreneur knows those economic agents whose actions he or she tries to predict and when he or she is totally unaware of who these economic agents are and what are their characteristics) institutions also perform another key function: establishing the boundaries of human behaviour. It was stated earlier that institutions embody a long list of rights, duties, and protocols of interaction. Failure to make oneself intelligible in this context will bring requests for clarification, requests to behave oneself, criticism or worse. Thus, institutions provide the parameters within which the behaviour of other economic agents is likely to occur. As a consequence of this function of institutions some degree of predictability of behaviour is possible, even in circumstances of fundamental uncertainty (Hodgson, 1993). However, this is far from providing reliable information regarding the likely actions of others. This is partly because the boundaries of institutionally acceptable human behaviour may offer economic agents a large number of options, and partly due to the fact that behaviour outside these boundaries though reproachable is still possible. Nonetheless, the options available within the boundaries provided by the prevailing institutions are undoubtedly fewer than those that would have existed if no institutions were present.

In most instances an entrepreneur attempts to deal with fundamental uncertainty using a combination of both social interaction and his or her own experiences. This gives rise to a key 'tactical' problem confronting the transacting entrepreneur: to what extent and under which circumstances should the entrepreneur opt for social interaction as an instrument in dealing with fundamental uncertainty?

Cognitive Frameworks and Capabilities

In the Section above we have explored the implications of the availability, or otherwise, of information. Possessing information, however, is only part of the story. This is because for information to acquire meaning it must be processed by the entrepreneur. This raises two key considerations: the role of cognitive frameworks and the ability of the entrepreneur to process large and complex bodies of data.

Making Sense of Information

The approach advanced here supports an alternative to positivistic treatments of information, as an undifferentiated element that flows effortlessly from human senses to the mind. Our basic premise is that information 'does not speak for itself'. A cognitive framework is required to handle and process information. The attribution of meaning to the vast amount of sense data that economic agents receive from their environment requires the use of established concepts, symbols, rules and signs (Babe, 1994). Moreover, individuals have to interact with each other in order to develop cognitive skills, to form judgements about the world and to acquire guidelines for action. At a very elementary level the use of a common language is essential in order to achieve effective communication of information. The learned environment, which provides common instruments to the generality of human agents, is instrumental in the conversion of information into a form that has a meaningful content for an economic agent. The learned environment imposes form and coherence upon human activity through the creation and evolution of cognitive frameworks, signs and meanings.

    Cognitive worlds may vary between socio-economic settings. In this case, cognitive worlds may vary significantly on account of diverse institutional settings as well as differences in the prevailing states of industrial art. This was underlined by Lavoie (1991) who argues that any individual interpretative process is embedded to culture and is meaningful only in relation to culture. However, some difference may also be apparent within cultures since each economic agent's experiences are unique. This is because economic agents occupy different positions in relation to the learned environment. An important corollary of this is that understanding the same reality has an actor specific peculiarity. The implication is that economic agents understanding can not be perceived merely in terms of how many bits of information they have acquired but is contextualised within particular cognitive worlds[2].

    We would like to emphasise here that there is a profound difference in the degree of diversity of cognitive frameworks between different learned environments on the one side, and within the same setting on the other. In the former case communication between individual economic agents may be difficult or even impossible. For example, individuals in an advanced industrial economy such as the UK, are familiar with banking, will fill-out a check, use cash-points and credit cards, and queue orderly inside the bank, whereas immigrants from elsewhere in the world may need instruction in order to familiarise themselves with the institution. In contrast, differences in the cognitive frameworks of individuals from the same learned environment are modest. This is because, effective communication between two agents in the same setting is essential for social interaction. If cognitive frameworks were significantly different communication between economic agents would be problematic, as the receiver of the information may interpret it differently from the sender (Egashira and Hasimoto, 2001). In such circumstances the feasibility of transferring information would be reduced hampering economic activity.

Bounded Rationality and Beyond

One of the key considerations regarding entrepreneurial decision-making during the process of transacting revolves around the information processing limitations of economic agents in computing optimum solutions. Simon (1959; 1982) captured the essence of the problem in the notion of bounded rationality. This could be described as follows: if nothing is defined at the outset, the computational requirements for choice confronting the economic agent appear overwhelming. In such circumstances, 'far from being able to handle all the information that might be relevant to a problem, the boundedly rational decision maker will be stretched in terms of short-term memory capacity' (Earl, 1994, p. 285).

There are a number of alternative arguments addressing the computational limitations of economic agents. Indeed, as early as the 1930s Keynes argued that institutionally established rules of thumb are essential for decision-making. More specifically,

> [K]nowing that our own individual judgement is worthless we endeavour to fall back on the judgement of the rest of the world, which is perhaps better informed. That is, we endeavour to conform with the behaviour of the majority or average. The psychology of a society of individuals each of whom is endeavouring to copy the others leads to what we may strictly term a conventional judgement (Keynes, 1937, p. 214).

Simon himself developed the notion of 'satisficing' in order to illustrate how decision-makers systematically restrict the use and acquisition of information compared to that potentially available (Simon, 1959). When 'satisficing' economic agents set themselves targets regarding the situation they want to find themselves in the future. Then they use rules of thumb or behavioural routines to explore and evaluate ways of attaining the desired target. Once they have discovered an appropriate option, they select it unless other rules lead them to believe that further research could be worthwhile. As a consequence, economic agents may arrive at decisions ignoring altogether possible trade-offs that a detached observer may consider relevant to the problem at hand (Earl, 1994). More recently, Mark Casson, working within the broad area of entrepreneurial studies, developed an approach that builds upon a distinction between transitory and persistent change (for a more detailed discussion see Chapter 2).

Ronald Heiner (1983), drawing upon the institutionalist perspective, offers an alternative. He sets out to examine the mechanisms that restrict the flexibility to choose potential actions, which result in observed regularity of behaviour. Rather disappointingly his work, published in the *American Economic Review*, failed to inform contemporary entrepreneurship research[3]. In this Section we attempt to introduce Heiner's work on the origins of predictable behaviour in our approach aspiring to understand entrepreneurial behaviour.

The point of departure of Hainer's analysis is the matching of the 'competence' of an agent with the 'difficulty' in selecting most preferred alternatives. The presence of a gap between the agent's competence and the difficulty of the decision problem (hereafter referred to as a 'C-D' gap) introduces 'uncertainty in selecting most preferred alternatives, which will tend to produce errors and surprises' (Heiner, 1983, p. 562). The degree of the uncertainty resulting from a 'C-D' gap is determined by two sets of variables.

> The first are environmental variables (denoted by e) which determine the complexity of the decision problem to be solved by an agent … The second are perceptual variables (denoted p) which characterize an agent's competence in deciphering relationships between its behaviour and the environment. … In general, there is greater uncertainty as either an agent's perceptual abilities become less reliable or the environment becomes more complex (Heiner, 1983, pp. 564-565).

Using a metaphor from biology we can draw a parallel between p variables and the sensory and cognitive mechanism of an organism, and between e variables and the structure and stability of ecological relationships.

The theoretical construct developed in Chapter 4, exploring the interface between purposes of human endeavour and the learned environment, enable us to decipher in greater details the perceptual (p) and the environmental (e) variables. More specifically, a key element of the p variables is the balance between idle curiosity and pragmatism. As shown in Chapter 4, the balance between idle curiosity and pragmatism may differ significantly from one economic agent to the other even within the same socio-economic milieu. This means that economic agents possess varying degrees of inquisitiveness and different creative intelligence abilities. Thus, an agent's competence in deciphering relationships between his or her behaviour and the learned environment may differ from that of another economic actor in exactly the same context. Moreover, the perceptual variables are also influenced by the agent's ability to acquire and internalise the learned environment, and the ensuing cognitive frameworks. Whilst these processes may vary from one economic agent to the other leading to somewhat different cognitive frameworks, we argue that these differentials will be modest in instances of individual entrepreneurs operating in the same institutional setting.

The environmental (e) variables, capturing the difficulty of the situation, confronting the entrepreneur, comprise of two different dimensions - discussed earlier in this Chapter: the degrees of ambiguity and fundamental uncertainty. Ambiguity is defined by the availability (or not) of information in the local setting. The availability of information is influenced under the pervasive influence of institutions, and the degree to which they enable the diffusion of information. Thus, the greater the ease of information flows and sharing the lower the degree of ambiguity experienced by the entrepreneur regarding the present parameters of the situation. Institutions are also of some importance in conceptualising fundamental uncertainty, through their ability to define the boundaries of the behaviour of other economic agents. Though the number of options - within these boundaries - is considerable, it is undoubtedly smaller than instances where the behaviour of other economic agents is not constrained by institutions. Another e variable, focused upon fundamental uncertainty is the choice of instances of social interaction. Social interaction provides the entrepreneur in question with a greater ability to second-guess the actions of other economic agents, and thus, reduces fundamental uncertainty. The different positions that individuals occupy in relation to their setting, constitutes another element of the e variables. Indeed, the position of the entrepreneur influences his or her access to information, and consequently the degree of ambiguity associated with the situation. The degree of embeddedness of an economic agent, which could be differential between distinct elements of the socio-economic milieu, influences to a considerable degree his or her access to information. Thus, two entrepreneurs confronted, in the eyes of a detached observer, with the same situation may perceive it differently from each other on account of partial and selective access to sources of information.

In response to the uncertainty generated by the 'C-D' gap, the economic agent involved in decision-making can either tap into a finite and fixed 'repertoire of actions', i.e. solutions that have been used in the past in similar or different circumstances and currently form part of the accumulated experiences of the individual, or select an additional, and new, action. Before going any further it is worth exploring in some greater detail the concept 'repertoire of actions', and its origins.

In our approach the repertoire of actions are the part of an individual's experiences regarding the process of economic transacting. Thus, the repertoire of actions is the result of the interaction between an individual (who occupies a defined though not necessarily unique position) and other economic agents in his or her environment. In the context of entrepreneurship research the repertoire of actions is of particular importance in the process of removing doubt, and the discomfort associated with it, and the establishment of belief. They 'conserve intellectual effort and increase efficiency by allowing individuals to concentrate their efforts on new or unique circumstances' (Waller, 1988, p. 114). Thus, the repertoire of actions enables the economic agent to carry out essential, but often complex, tasks in the process of transacting very easily. Thus the economic agent often works at developing and expanding his or her repertoire of actions in order to increase the scope of activities that he or she can accomplish with little thought and effort. These range from very simple activities, like dealing with the consequences of employee holiday or sickness, to complex behaviour, such as confronting a period of recession.

The repertoire of actions is derived from the past, in the sense that it draws upon actions and their effects under certain circumstances, at specific points in time. However, the entrepreneur uses the repertoire of actions in order to influence events in the future. Thus, mistakes, errors and surprises may occur even in instances where the entrepreneur uses the repertoire of actions, rather than developing and enacting something new. One reason behind this is differences – even modest - in the circumstances between the past (when the actions was also used) and the present. Another reason why errors may occur even in instances where the entrepreneurs taps into his or her repertoire of actions is the introduction of a new action by another economic agent.

Under conditions of uncertainty the agent is unaware, *ex-ante*, whether the new action is appropriate in the specific context (the 'right time' to select the new action) or not (the 'wrong time' to select the new action). Thus, the agent will not necessarily select the new action when it is the right time to do so, resulting in errors and surprises. 'Such mistakes are by their nature unpredictable and erratic' (Heiner, 1983, p. 562).

This raises the question of when is an economic agent going to select a new action, over existing ones. In order to address this question, a reliability condition that specifies when to allow or prohibit the choice of new actions is developed by Heiner. This suggests that the selection of a new action occurs when the chances of correctly responding under the right circumstances relative to the probability of responding mistakenly under the wrong circumstances exceeds the minimum required reliability to improve performance (Heiner, 1983). The latter is determined by whether the gains from selecting the action under the right conditions will cumulate faster than the losses from selecting it under the wrong conditions (Heiner, 1983).

Table 5.1 below attempts to illustrate the anticipated gains and losses of selecting a new action. For purposes of analytical convenience, we concentrate on two extreme positions, described as high and low, regarding 'competence' and 'difficulty'. In the first row of the Table, where there is only a limited degree of difficulty associated with the situation, the cumulative gains-losses are expected to be only modest, as a number of entrepreneurs are likely to possess the competence to deal successfully with the situation. The competence of the entrepreneur (low or high) will determine whether he or she will be able to select the right action at the right time. In instances where the degree of difficulty is high the cumulative gains and losses are expected to be high as only a small number of entrepreneurs are likely to possess the competence to deal successfully with the situation. However, it is the competence of the entrepreneur (low or high) which will determine whether he or she will be able to select the right action.

Table 5.1 The 'C-D' Gap and Outcomes from the Adoption of a Novel Action

	Low C	High C
Low D	In circumstances of low difficulty cumulative gains-losses are expected to be low. The chances of selecting the right (new) action at the right time are low.	In such circumstances of low difficulty cumulative gains-losses are expected to be low. The chances of selecting the right (new) action at the right time are high.
High D	In circumstances of high difficulty cumulative gains-losses are expected to be high. The chances of selecting the right (new) action at the right time are low.	In circumstances of high difficulty cumulative gains-losses are expected to be high. The chances of selecting the right (new) action at the right time are high.

This lead us to conclude that a significant 'C-D' gap – resulting mainly on account of the degree of ambiguity and fundamental uncertainty (**e** variables) – will:

> ... both reduce the chance of recognizing the right situation to select an action, and increase the chance of not recognizing the wrong situation for selecting it. ... Therefore, ...[it] ... will cause rule-governed behavior to exhibit increasing predictable regularities, so that uncertainty becomes the basic source of predictable behaviour (Heiner, 1983, p. 570).

Thus, entrepreneurs confronted with a large 'C-D' gap may be obliged to rely heavily on already known actions.

Conclusions

The arguments developed in this Chapter provide us with an illustration of entrepreneurial decision-making in contexts of exchange (i.e. where more than one entrepreneurs interact with each other). Entrepreneurs in such contexts are confronted both with ambiguity (on account of less than perfect information regarding the present state of affairs) as well as fundamental uncertainty. Thus, the difficulty associated with taking judgemental decisions is considerable. However, these are not the only constraining influences upon entrepreneurial behaviour. Even if an entrepreneur possessed perfect information regarding the present, his or her ability to exploit the ensuing large body of data would be limited by his or her computational capabilities. Therefore, it seems safe to conclude that the solution to the difficulties associated with ambiguity and fundamental uncertainty is not to be found in an incessant pursuit of information.

So how do entrepreneurs take decisions in such circumstances? The main instruments at the disposal of entrepreneurial economic agents are their idle curiosity, their position in relation to their learned environment, and their accumulated body of experiences. This set of instruments is specific to individual entrepreneurs. At the same time, entrepreneurs operate in institutional settings, which define the flow of information and the processes of economic interaction, provide the boundaries of acceptable behaviour, as well as influence to a considerable degree individual cognitive frameworks. This set of factors is broadly similar among all economic agents operating within the same socio-economic setting.

It is appropriate here to explore the interaction between the entrepreneurial instruments and the context in the decision-making process. The economic agent has access to information regarding past situations and the present state of affairs that defines the level of ambiguity. However, even within the same context (where the institutions and technology which facilitate the flow of information are common) the information available may vary from one individual to the other. This is on account of the agent's position in relation to the context and his or her idle curiosity. The former may enable (or prevent) the individual to access sources of information available in a discriminatory manner, whilst the latter prompts the economic agents to actively pursue the acquisition of information. However, the advantage of ever increasing amount of information begins to diminish from some point on account of the limited computational capabilities of the human mind. What is important in this case is the ability of the economic agent to tap into already existing solutions from his or her repertoire of actions (which themselves are part of the experiences of the actor), that will enable the individual to concentrate upon new and complex problems. As a result of differences in the availability of information and the ability to focus upon new challenges, the perception of present situations may vary considerably between economic agents.

This may enable certain individuals - using the interpretative function of idle curiosity - to alter future states of affairs. This confronts the economic agent with the issue of whether to act upon the decision immediatedly at some point in the future or not. Acting early enables the entrepreneurial agent to influence adversely the level of fundamental uncertainty confronting other (competing) individuals. Reverting to solutions already present in his or her repertoire of actions encourages the economic agent from implementing the new decision. In a situation where the future actions of other individuals are predictable reaching a decision will be relatively easy. However, this is not often the case. Thus, the entrepreneurial agent has to attempt to 'predict' the future actions of other economic agents. The institutional setting provides the boundaries of human behaviour, thus restricting the number of options open to other individuals. For example, *ceteris paribus*, competing individuals in a setting where property rights are poorly defined possess a greater number of options to react to the introduction of a radically new (and say patentable) product, than in a setting where property rights are well defined. The establishment of relationships with some economic agents, whose actions may be important in the success or failure of the action taken by the entrepreneur, enables further reduction in the levels of fundamental uncertainty. The last instrument open to the entrepreneurial agent is to tap into his or her own experiences and consider his or her own reactions to a comparable situation. The outcome of this exercise may enable the reduction - but by no means elimination - of the level of fundamental uncertainty. The result may be a reduction of the 'C-D' to levels acceptable to the agent. If the entrepreneur acts upon a new decision a new process of accumulating experiences is instigated[4].

Thus, the entrepreneur, although surrounded by ambiguity and fundamental uncertainty, concentrates upon the factors the he or she can influence. Utilising his position to tap into restricted information, eliminating those behaviours that social sanction is likely to discourage, tapping into himself or herself for experiences, and building selective and differential relationships with other economic agents. Participating in the socio-economic collective as a distinct, though embedded, entity.

Notes

1 We should emphasise here that tapping into the accumulated experiences of the entrepreneur is useful in attempting to second-guess the actions of other economic agents. This is different from the search of information regarding the current state of affairs, associated with the identification of opportunities that underpins entrepreneurial planning.

2 This idea bears some resemblance to Hayek's work discussed in (Chapter 2), and constitutes a viable alternative to Harper's (1996) attempt to develop a growth of knowledge model which sets outs to explain how entrepreneurs learn from the market, how they may retain some part of their systems of knowledge and how they may even devise entirely new systems.

3 This is despite the fact that Heiner himself was familiar with the Austrian contribution to entrepreneurship research, and utilised the notion of alertness in his work.

4 The degree of attainment of the objectives sought when the decision was made will enable the economic agent *to learn* from his or her actions. In instances where the original objectives were achieved (wholly or to a considerable extent) the new decision will be learned and added to the repertoire of actions. In this case previously performed learned actions may be discarded from the agent's repertoire. In many cases the decision may not achieve the desired objectives. This may lead – in the light of the information provided by the feedback mechanism – to a revision of the decision, or the total abandonment of the decision.

Chapter 6

Understanding the Entrepreneur: Some Evidence from Russia

Introduction

Earlier on in the book we explored a multitude of theoretical constructs in the area of entrepreneurial studies, focusing upon the key issues under consideration for the advancement of the field. We then went on and developed an approach that draws from the work of scholars falling within the broad – and loosely defined – confines of old institutionalism. In doing so, the proposed approach has been placed within the context of the existing literature. Having completed the task of conceptual development, we return to the underlying aim of our venture: understanding the entrepreneur. More specifically, to what extent does the approach advanced here enables us to gain insights in the entrepreneurial process. In this Chapter we set out to examine the explanatory power of our approach, by focusing upon the case of Russian entrepreneurs. Our paramount objective is to deploy the institutionalist approach developed in Chapter 4 in order to understand entrepreneurship in post-socialist Russia. Given the specificity of the context, i.e. the changes in the institutional setting, the adoption of an institutionalist approach seems *a priori* suggestive.

Before going any further it is worth explaining briefly the rationale behind the decision to concentrate on Russia, and the emphasis placed upon the entrepreneur rather than the entrepreneurial decision-making: what may seem unlikely choices in the first instance. As far as the former decision is concerned, the diversity of the country, both geographical and ethnic, as well as the limited tradition of entrepreneurship research - in relation to advanced industrialised regimes - provide fertile grounds for scepticism. The profound changes associated with the process of post-socialist transformation increase the complexity of the task at hand. Lastly, the distinctiveness of Russia in relation to industrial market economies, the place of origin of old institutionalism, in terms of the prevailing socio-economic milieu (Ageev et al 1995), raise concerns about the appropriateness of transferring existing theoretical constructs[1]. However, diversity alongside attempts to impose 'new' upon 'existing' institutions are the very same factors that attracted the attention of a small army of western and native researchers, to the case of Russian entrepreneurship. Moreover, one of the assumptions behind old institutionalism is that it is well equipped to allow for differences in context, as it offers some general principles, which could be combined with data regarding specific historical settings - such as post-socialist Russia. As far as the choice of the specific topic under consideration, this was mainly data driven. Scholarly efforts over the past decade or so, resulted in a large, and growing, body of literature. One of the questions which attracted the bulk of academic attention is 'where do entrepreneurs come from, and what are their motivations'? The abundance of data combined with the multidisciplinary and disparate nature of research on Russian entrepreneurship, provides us with a wide spectrum of approaches. Thus, accessing, collating and interpreting the results of these studies is an exciting and worthwhile venture on its own right. However, the diverse methodologies and conceptual approaches underpinning earlier research raise the issue of the comparability of the data, which will be addressed in the following Section.

The Data

The multidisciplinary nature of research exploring the origins of entrepreneurship in Russia creates difficulties in identifying and accessing sources of data, a feature common to the field of entrepreneurial studies the world over. This is particularly the case for research published during the past ten years or, the period when entrepreneurial studies in Russia grew into considerable prominence. Therefore, it is useful to review the main sources of information in the field[2].

Sources of Data

Attempts to understand the entrepreneur in Russia can draw upon five groups of sources, although the degree to which each source was used for the purposes of our study, varied significantly.   The first source of data comprises of archives and travellers narratives which provide insights in the life and works of entrepreneurs in pre-revolutionary Russia.   Other sources regarding this era include books by Russian historians, documents and papers on industrial development as well as company records of the late nineteenth and early twentieth century.

The second, and by far the poorest source of information, comprises of the scholarly literature developed within the USSR.   However, entrepreneurship received marginal attention during the Socialist era, on account of two factors. Firstly, entrepreneurial ventures existed in the shadows, outside the prevailing legal framework, which identified the public sector (in all its different guises) as the sole agent of economic activity. Thus, illegal entrepreneurial pursuits were not perceived as warranting scholarly attention. Secondly, in the context of a tightly controlled political and cultural setting, entrepreneurial individuals offered a model of behaviour that differed - or even competed - with the Socialist mainstream. Thus, it was not until the 1980s that a handful of publications emerged within the then Soviet Union.

At the same time however, outside the USSR, there were a number of academics who researched the nature and conduct of entrepreneurs in Imperial

Russia (Gerschenkron, 1954; Blackwell, 1970; Owen, 1981), the ingenuity of Soviet managers in overcoming persistent and pervasive shortages of material (Berliner, 1957 and 1976; Granick, 1960 and 1972; Gregory and Stuart, 1981; Conygham, 1982), and entrepreneurial individuals who operated in the twilight of semi-illegality (Grossman, 1976; Kateleinboingen, 1977). This culminated in the publication of a collaborative volume (Guroff and Carstensen, 1983) of leading US and Russian researchers, exploring Russian entrepreneurship from the sixteenth century up to the New Economic Policy (hereafter NEP) of the 1920s.

The fourth source of data comprises of contemporary literature and data focusing on the experiences of Russian entrepreneurs during the post-socialist era. The process of economic transformation provided the intellectual stimuli for the conduct of a large number of studies exploring contemporary entrepreneurship in Russia. Two apparent trends in contemporary entrepreneurship research include the emphasis placed in understanding the fundamentals of this phenomenon, such as characteristics and motives of entrepreneurs, as well as the examination of this phenomenon within a global context. Apart from research in the mainstream of entrepreneurial studies, suggestive insights are provided by sociological research exploring crime as well as the changing composition of elites, and particularly the business elite, in Russia, ethnographic studies of family survival strategies, and research from other business studies disciplines such as leadership and innovation management.

The final source of data, specific to our work, comprises of the empirical findings of a recently completed INTAS funded project[3] on rural entrepreneurship. This study involved fieldwork investigation in rural areas of the Republic of Bashkortostan and the Novosibirsk Region[4]. The definition of the rural has been problematic in the context of Russia. This was the result of the adoption of administrative, rather than substantive, definitions in both countries. The difficulties associated with a radical review of existing administrative notions of rurality, especially in accessing secondary data, prevented us from introducing wholesale change. Instead, we introduced population density as a second defining criterion. Thus, the rural comprised those administrative units that were officially termed as rural, but also had population density of less than 150 persons per square kilometre (the OECD measure). Within the areas under investigation, a population survey was conducted. Criteria used in the stratification of the sample included age and gender. For the purpose of the survey a structured questionnaire was devised[5]. In order to overcome the villagers' reluctance to participate in the survey the instrument was delivered on a face-to-face basis. Interviewers stressed the academic nature of the research and provided evidence of their credentials. Some 300 questionnaires were completed in the rural areas of each of the two regions (total 600). The second element of the research methodology comprised of a survey of a stratified random sample of entrepreneurs in the same villages where the population survey took place. During the earlier stages of the research the intention was to stratify the sample using criteria such as the number of years since the formation of the venture, the gender and the socio-economic grouping of the entrepreneur. However, the small numbers of practising entrepreneurs in the countryside of all three regions meant that more or less everyone who fell within the boundaries of our working definition, and were willing to participate in the study, was interviewed. A semi-structured schedule was developed for the purposes of the survey. Considerable effort was expended in the harmonisation of a large part of the instrument in order to ensure the comparability of the data. Existing networks of contact and snowballing techniques were used in order to engage entrepreneurs who operated in the twilight world of semi-illegality. Again the academic nature of the research and the credentials of the interviewers assisted in this process. Questions regarding finances and the legality - or otherwise - of the ventures were not included in the instrument in order to secure participation. Some 100 in-depth interviews with entrepreneurs were conducted in each of the regions (total 200).

Some Limitations

Before the analysis and interpretation of the data some important limitations must be discussed. These are associated with the fact that the evidence presented here is not the result of a dedicated study, deploying an institutionalist perspective but a collection of outputs, derived using diverse definitions and methodologies. Only the INTAS funded study was defined by the institutionalist perspective developed here, though the focus of the work was exploratory, i.e. what are the features and characteristics of entrepreneurship in rural areas. Thus, careful consideration has been placed on the impact of methodological and conceptual differences upon the findings of individual studies.

Many previous studies concentrated upon 'entrepreneurs that are economically significant', i.e. individuals responsible for the creation of relatively large number of salaried/wage jobs (Ageev et al, 1995; Shulus, 1996), or business elites (Kukolev, 1997). As a consequence 'marginal' entrepreneurial ventures have received much less attention in the main body of the accumulated literature. Some other researchers introduced other restrictive criteria regarding the age of the firm (Smallbone and Welter, 2001) or the origin of the entrepreneur (Khotin, 1996), that undoubtedly influence results[6].

Another factor that may influence the results of empirical research on post-socialist entrepreneurship is time. More specifically, the fieldwork research of previous published works was conducted between 1989-2000, a very long and diverse period in the framework of Russia, where change in the external environment is rapid and multidirectional. Thus, our attempt to use data from different studies in order to understand the entrepreneur in post-socialist Russia will be cautious, and will acknowledge the impact of time.

A third key consideration when exploring entrepreneurship in post-socialist transformation is the considerable variation between spatial and regional contexts with dissimilar historical trajectories, which undoubtedly influence the incidence and characteristics of entrepreneurs (Rona-Tas and Lengyel, 1998; Smallbone and Welter, 2001). However, whilst diversity in the national level is rightly acknowledged, regional and local differentiation is rarely addressed (a point also raised by Radaev, 2001). Thus, our attempt to compare the experience of entrepreneurs in different contexts has been hampered by the absence of an explicit recognition of spatial or geographical variables in many earlier studies of entrepreneurship[7].

A final consideration regarding the conceptualisation of entrepreneurship has to do with diversity in perspective. Specifically, preconceptions or theoretical schemata of the academic carrying out the research influence heavily the interpretation of the findings. A suggestive example of this can be drawn through the comparison of Khotin's (1996) and Kukolev's (1997) understanding of 'red directors' - i.e. entrepreneurs drawn from the ranks of the most senior managers of formerly state enterprises. The former scholar perceives them as responsive, hard working and responsible: a pillar underpinning the social infrastructure. He argues that :

> directors on the whole had a highly developed sense of social responsibility ... [and] according to the respondents' evaluation, the vast majority of directors ... possessed the following qualities: good knowledge of production, ability to get along with subordinates, fairness (strict but fair) sensitivity to employee needs, loyalty to enterprise ... workaholism and absence of racial prejudice (Khotin, 1996, p. 50).

In sharp contrast Kukolev portrays the 'red directors' in a very negative light. He suggests that:

> the process of creation of joint stock companies enabled them to gain control of a considerable portion of the shares of their own enterprises ... they have been actively engaged in shady commercial activity ... workers at their enterprises are often placed on forced leave and receive no wages for several months, while the management buys property abroad and immerses itself in luxury, creating the image of the 'new Russians' (Kukolev, 1997, p. 66).

Similar differences of perception among scholars are to be found in the interpretation of evidence regarding 'new wave entrepreneurs'[8]. Although this apparent influence of individual perspectives upon the interpretation of evidence is neither particularly unexpected nor unique to Russia, in the highly ideological nature of the debate, it necessitates the adoption of a critical view.

An altogether different set of limitations derives from the fact that the data were generated, and analysed in order to enhance scholarly understanding of the origin and process of entrepreneurship. As a consequence, there was an emphasis in clustering the processes at work either into a small number of groupings, or even into a single prototype which is based upon typical or average characteristics. The problem with the adoption of such an approach is that it tends to diminish diversity and stress factors of commonality. More importantly, however, it prevents us from exploring individual entrepreneurial decision-making processes, which lie at the heart of the approach advanced in earlier Chapters of the book. In the absence of empirical findings derived in order to explore the explanatory power of the approach advanced here, we will build upon the multitude of group processes, and wherever possible, illuminate them further through material derived from individual case studies.

The Context in Post-Socialist Russia

The Process of Post-Socialist Transformation

Understanding the process of post-socialist transformation from an institutionalist perspective is more than usually problematic. Feige, drawing from a new-institutionalist perspective, graphically captures the essence of the difficulty, stressing that from

> ... the perspective of economic history, the institutional change that shapes the evolution of societies is seen as "overwhelmingly incremental" and highly "path dependent". How are we to reconcile this "glacial" view of institutional change with the radical transformations now under way in Central and Eastern Europe and in the New Independent States? (Feige, 1998, p. 19).

The answer to this question is that the transformations reported in Russia are less revolutionary and less discontinuous than they appear at first sight. This is partly because change is not introduced in a vacuum, and partly due to the fact that change was instigated from within, in response to the shortcomings of the previous regime. These two theses, though not strictly within the confines of our investigation, merit further consideration.

The first thesis, i.e. that changes are introduced upon - and consequently influenced or even shaped by - the old is less controversial. Indeed, there is a growing body of scholarly opinion advancing the idea that 'post-community society does not appear on an empty space ... within [an] uninhabited planet "tabula rasa"' (Kusnezova, 1999, p. 61). Thus, individuals act within a milieu that combines very concrete and real remnants of the past, alongside elements of the new (Ageev et al, 1995). As a consequence, scholars adopt a historical perspective exploring the influence of the socialist as well as the pre-revolutionary era upon entrepreneurial decision-making during the post-socialist era. Entrepreneurship in Russia is influenced by the distinct philosophical underpinnings of Eastern - in relation to Western - Christianity (Kusnezova, 1999), the pervasive influence of strong state control throughout Russian and Soviet history (Volkov, 1998), the heritage of exchanging favours of access to scarce goods and commodities (Ledeeva, 1998) and the tradition of rule evasion emanating from the days of central planning (Leitzel, 1998)[9], and the increased emphasis placed on nuclear families and individuals during the post-war era (McMylor et al, 2000). Sorensen and Popova (2002) take this argument even further by suggesting that

> the literature in transition economies leaves the impression that "markets" were handed down by Government in replacement of the central plan ... nothing could be more wrong. What existed in Russia ... in 1991 was a population of state enterprises that interacted, or better, that were co-ordinated under a central planning regime. What existed in 1992 was a liberal governance regime (Sorensen and Popova, 2002, p. 2).

Within this context the natural choice for Russian managers was the reformation of existing networks in an evolving context. Thus, it seems safe to argue that continuity exists alongside discontinuity even in the context of what appears to be a radical event (the collapse of the Soviet Union and the introduction of market reforms)[10].

The second thesis, i.e. that post-socialist transformation is the consequence of friction between institutions and the prevailing state of industrial arts, is highly controversial. Indeed, to date there has been a number of interpretations regarding the demise of the Soviet Union. Some of them emphasise the importance of external influences such as the pressures imposed upon the Soviet economy by the arms race of the Cold War (Hough, 1986), or the role of improved communications technologies in projecting western consumerism on USSR citizens. An alternative set of explanations draws from events within the old regime: including the rise of nationalism (Strayer, 2001), the desertion of the system by large numbers of the old elite (Kotz and Weir, 1997), and a failure to remain at the forefront of technological change. Another interpretation within the latter context, centres upon the failure of the planning system during the 1970s and 1980s, a point advocated by second generation Austrian economists[11]. The argument goes that technological advancement as well as the greater use of technology in the production process of the early Soviet era resulted in levels of economic advancement that the planning system was ill-equipped t ɔ manage. Thus, in the case of the Soviet Union of the Brezhnev era, the institutions governing economic activity acted as a constraint in the advancement of the state of industrial arts. The evolution of these institutions was prevented by the prevailing political institutions, which themselves were dependent upon the perpetuation of economic institution (Dorn, 1991). As a result, the changes in the former Soviet Union appeared to be radical and discontinuous.

The Context: An Outline

In order to gain insights .into the learned environment within which the entrepreneurial processes described and discussed in the following two Sections occur, we adopt a two-stage approach. In this Section we identify some elements common to Russia as a whole. In subsequent Sections, we attempt to introduce features and characteristics of the local socio-economic milieus within which entrepreneurial processes take place. Our aim is not to be exhaustive but focus upon those factors which may influence the entrepreneur.

During the early 1990s, wholesale changes in the rules that govern the relationships between the State and the private sector, and between firms and individuals were implemented in Russia (Johnson et al, 2000). Private property rights were introduced - though they remained poorly defined; there was a liberalisation in the economic actions of individuals and a parallel decline in the direct involvement of the State in the network of production and distribution; and a host of new - and in many cases alien - institutions were established (Swain and Hardy, 1998). All these changes aspired to engineer a shift in emphasis away from collectiveness towards individualism. However, the introduction of change was arduous and idiosyncratic. The elite of the Soviet era did not disappear into oblivion, but became a key agent influencing both the pace and direction of change (Kryshtanovskaya and White, 1996; Hughes, 1997). This led Khanin (2000) to argue that such individuals have a vested interested in the preservation of the process of post-socialist transformation[12]. As a result, the emerging markets are imperfect, the definition of private property rights weak and their enforcement problematic whilst the regulatory system burdensome.

One characteristic of the post-socialist era, widely acknowledged by scholars in the field, is the relative weakness of the State. Volkov (2000) develops a convincing argument about the importance of the State as the cohesive force in the evolution of Imperial, Soviet and contemporary Russia. He argues that the fragility of the civil society in Russia means that there is no alternative to strong State control. Thus, in periods where the State is weakened, phenomena such as widespread rule evasion (Leitzel, 1998) and a prevalence of predatory behaviour (Feige, 1998) become commonplace.

Two other elements of the institutional setting which have attracted widespread attention are the balance between the collective and the individual, and social attitudes towards entrepreneurs. The former consideration has been explored widely by advocates of the Populist tradition during the late nineteenth and early twentieth century. They developed convincing arguments about the central role of households and communities in the day-to-day life of the Russian peasantry (for a detailed review see Kitching, 1989). Within this context, the concept of *obshchina* or *mir* was used to describe communities in which arable land was in hereditary holding and pastures and forests were held in common. In a setting where the family household was the basic production and consumption unit, members were jointly responsible for taxes, whilst there were also instances of egalitarian repartition of arable land. Peasant structures were profoundly affected by the civil war, and the radical social ideas of the Soviets. Socialist ideology encouraged independence from parental control (Geiger, 1968), female emancipation, and the detachment of families by residence resulting in the 'privatization' of the nuclear family (Shlapentokh, 1989). At the same time there was an increasing attachment of individuals to the state and collective enterprises which were responsible for the provision of elements of the social infrastructure. This distinct and evolving relationship between the collective and the individual lead to the conceptualisation of Russian collectivism as a voluntary union of people which combine the pursuit of common goals with the self-emancipation of the individual (Kusnezova, 1999).

Historically social attitudes towards entrepreneurs appeared to be negative. In Imperial Russia entrepreneurial activities remained largely at odds with the dominant system of values. In rural areas, which accounted for the large majority of the population in Russia as a whole, steeped in a combination of archaic and Orthodox traditions

> the Good Life which God intended for man to lead implied tilling the land, which belonged to God, and receiving the divine blessing of its fruit. The Good Life certainly did not mean craving for riches, did not mean laying up treasures on earth where moth and rust both corrupt (Gerschenkron, 1954, p. 7).

At the same time the predominance of Populist ideals among the intelligentsia espoused the values of the peasantry and derided the 'acquisitive class'. The nobility also had nothing but contempt for any entrepreneurial venture except of its own (Gerschenkron, 1954). Knowing that by accepted standards their life was a 'sinful' one entrepreneurs in Imperial Russia tried to make amends by donations to the Church (Kusnezova, 1999). Negative social attitudes towards entrepreneurship however, did not result in the absence of enterprising ventures. Entrepreneurs - such as S. Morozov, L. Knopp and P. Ryabushinski - emerged and grew in late nineteenth and early twentieth century Russia (Ageev et al, 1995). At the same time rural enterprises became increasingly associated with ethnic groupings such as the Jews, the Armenians etc. Entrepreneurial ventures did not end altogether after the October Revolution. Lenin's introduction of the NEP during the Spring of 1921, encouraged individual entrepreneurs to lead economic growth (Boettke and Butkevich, 2001). Entrepreneurs of the NEP also operated in a setting which strongly disapproved of their activities (Boettke, 1993). Entrepreneurial ventures, not necessarily in the form of conventional private enterprise but, within state enterprises and the shadow economy re-emerged during the 1960s. The fact that these ventures existed in the twilight of semi-illegality often reinforced negative social stereotypes regarding entrepreneurs (Mugler, 2000). Empirical studies of social attitudes across Russia report relative positive attitudes towards entrepreneurship but ambivalent perceptions towards entrepreneurs (OECD, 1998). Recent research into parts of the Russian countryside also indicates the prevalence of sceptical perceptions of entrepreneurial ventures (Kalugina et al, 2001).

Entrepreneurial Characteristics: Exploring Convergence

Previous research on the origins of entrepreneurship in the Russian Federation followed a two-stage approach: identifying some common characteristics among the majority of practising entrepreneurs, and exploring diversity by focusing upon diverse entrepreneurial processes.   In this Section we will review empirical evidence regarding the characteristics shared by many Russian entrepreneurs.

Indeed, there is considerable agreement among researchers regarding the characteristics and motivation of entrepreneurs in Russia. Shulus, in a study of 500 Russian entrepreneurs, conducted in early 1994, argues that the average entrepreneur is 'a man aged between 30 and 40 with a university degree' (Shulus 1996, p. 105).   He goes on to suggest that entrepreneurs in Russia are driven either by opportunism, i.e. a desire to accumulate wealth quickly at any cost, or more 'mainstream' business objectives – adopting a long-term perspective on the development of the venture. Drawing from a study of 32 successful Moscowite entrepreneurs Ageev et al (1995) claim that

> the majority of the entrepreneurs (84%) were male with an average age of 34.1 years ... [S]ixty-six percent had a college degree and the remainder the equivalent of a high school degree or some college (Ageev et al, 1995, pp. 371-372).

For Ageev et al (1995), like Shulus, pull factors provide the main incentive behind the decision to start a business. Push factors, such as necessity are reported only by 16% of what is admittedly a small sample. More or less at the same time, Green et al (1996) posit that 79% of 'new generation' entrepreneurs in Moscow were males, whilst their mean age was 30 years, and nearly 60% possessed a higher education qualification (sample size = 108). They go on to argue that internal locus for control and need for achievement are the main drives of entrepreneurs.   In an influential study of Russian entrepreneurship, the OECD (1998) reports that most entrepreneurs are males aged between 36-45 years old. This is despite the growing involvement of females and younger individuals in the process of business enterprise during the latter stages of reform.   As far as educational attainment is concerned, 80% of Russian entrepreneurs hold university diplomas, whilst one in ten have doctoral degrees (OECD 1998).

More recently, Kalantaridis and Labrianidis (2004) argue that some of the findings regarding the demographic characteristics of Russian entrepreneurs may be on account of the sampling criteria deployed and/or the definitions used.   Thus, the desire to focus upon entrepreneurs who are economically significant, in terms of employment and income generation, may be responsible for some of the reported gender divides.   Indeed, Kalantaridis and Labrianidis (2004), in a study which pursues representativeness, identify higher rates of female entrepreneurial ventures than those reported in the literature. Not unexpectedly, female entrepreneurs are engaged heavily in marginal ventures, which were excluded more or less by definition by earlier studies.   This supports the thesis, developed by Izyyumov and Razumova (2000), that the explosion of unemployment has pushed many women in Russia into the ranks of micro-entrepreneurs. Burawoy et al (2001) graphically illustrate a number of excellent examples of entrepreneurial strategies deployed at the margins.

This, combined with the diverse methodologies deployed, raises concerns about the validity and usefulness of all embracing generalisations such as those discussed in this Section. More importantly however, arguments about typical entrepreneurial attributes tend to conceal profound differences between individual entrepreneurs. Thus approaches which place greater emphasis upon the specific characteristics of the processes at work, and explore and interpret diversity are both more robust and suggestive.

Entrepreneurial Processes: Identifying Divergence

The Entrepreneurial Transformation of Directors of the Socialist Era

The changing role of directors of state or collectively owned enterprises during the process of post-socialist transformation, has attracted widespread attention in the literature (see Gimpelson and Schultz, 1994; Khotin, 1996; Kukolev, 1997; Kusnezova, 1999).   This is partly because of the relative importance of such individuals in the process of economic development and partly due to their ability to re-invent themselves within the changing institutional setting. As a result, there is a large body of evidence exploring the origins of such individuals.

Those falling in the broad and loosely defined confines of this entrepreneurial process were more often males than females who have risen from low level duties to senior managerial positions in enterprises of the Socialist era (Khotin[13], 1996). They acquired higher technical education, frequently later on in life through evening or distance learning courses (Kukolev[14], 1997).

Even before the introduction of reforms, during the late Brezhnev era, directors of enterprises performed increasingly entrepreneurial functions. The rigidities of the planning system resulted in bottle-necks both in sourcing material and distributing outputs.   As a result, the fulfilment of the plan, as well as the obligations of the enterprise to its employees and their families demanded a considerable degree of ingenuity (Kusnezova, 1999). Thus, enterprise directors became flexible and responsive to opportunities emanating from the old system. Thus, during the early 1990s, they were well positioned - both in terms of skills and a network of contacts, as well as their role of authority within organisations - to benefit from privatisation.

At least three different entrepreneurial processes, associated with directors of the socialist era, are reported in the literature.   The first process dates back to the late 1980s, when Soviet law allowed small and micro-scale enterprises to function. This allowed directors to set-up new ventures, which were invariably situated on the premises of the enterprises they managed, use the machinery and equipment of the existing enterprise virtually free of charge, and hire its best workers (Khotin, 1996). Thus, the new venture - subsidised by the old - would become a source of personal wealth for the director. Another entrepreneurial process associated with directors was instigated with the privatisation of existing enterprises[15].   Already in a position of authority, they were able to gain effective control of reorganised collectives and closed joint stock companies. They went on to encourage further re-organisation into open joint stock companies, which enabled directors of the Soviet era to transform control into outright ownership (Gimpelson and Schultz, 1994; Khotin, 1996; Shulus, 1996; Kusnezova, 1999). More recently, directors of large agricultural enterprises in prosperous farming regions have accumulated land – either through purchase or rental – into very large private concerns (Makhmutov, 2002). The example used here to explore the origins of directors from the Soviet era falls in the latter process, and is drawn from the rural areas of the Republic of Bashkortostan.

The Republic of Bashkortostan constitutes one of the autonomous republics of the Russian Federation that enjoy a greater degree of control in economic policy than the regions. The Republic occupies a position in the semi-periphery of the Russian Federation[16], however it possesses a diverse industrial structure even in rural areas. In the countryside, the prevailing agrarian structure is still dominated by a small number of very large organisations, however, large-scale private commercial agriculture is also present in the region. Indeed, as late as in 2001 a total of 1,047 large farms occupied 5.8 million hectares, some 81% of all agricultural land (Makhmutov, 2002). Household production occupied some 212 thousand hectares, 3% of the total, whilst the remaining 15% of the land was in the hands of 3,286 private farmers, making the Bashkir countryside relatively advanced in terms of the development of private commercial agriculture. Interestingly, this is despite the fact that the introduction of private property rights remained incomplete due to the introduction of a moratorium in the sale of land in Russia for nearly a decade (Kalantaridis and Labrianidis, 2004). Moreover, rural areas offer a number of other employment opportunities outside agriculture. Indeed, the processing of agricultural products, forestry, the repair and service of machinery, the production of construction material, and the construction industry are present in the countryside of the Republic of Bashkortostan[17] (Makhmutov, 2002).

In this setting Nikolai Dementev, lived with his family in a small hamlet of just eighteen houses. He acquired technical educational qualifications, and gradually rose to the position of the director of the local collective farm. As a result of the reorganisation of the collective he received 'twenty one hectares of arable land, eleven hectares of grassland, one tractor, four cows, one horse, and twelve sheep' (Makhmutov, 2002, 27). His previous role as the director of the collective placed him in a much stronger position than other local farmers. Apart from technical knowledge regarding the cultivation of land, he had an understanding of areas of business such as finance, the management of human resources, capital and material, as well as experience of dealing in the markets. He had a strong network of contacts with other directors and individuals in prominent positions in the banking sector, which enabled him to get credit from the bank (Makhmutov, 2002). At the same time, he enjoyed the respect of the population in the hamlet where he lived and the surrounding villages, from his involvement in the collective. It is his position (embeddedness) in multiple contexts - local as well as professional from the Socialist era - which were instrumental in his entrepreneurial venture, as they afforded him not only access to information but leverage of resources. Thus, he occupied a pivotal position between the local and the regional/national context: able to tap into local resources, as well as the networks which enable the exploitation of these resources.

His favourable position in the local milieu, alongside his previous experience of managing an agricultural enterprise enabled him to form a new joint stock company bringing together

> inhabitants from seven out of the eighteen households ... [as well as the] ... share of local retirees ... [a total of] 326 hectares of land, three tractors, two trucks, one combine harvester ... a grain store with a capacity of 500 tonnes, 150 pigs, nine cows and 20 beehives (Makhmutov, 2002, p. 27).

The concept underpinning the new venture, is a projection of the old upon the new. Thus, the introduction of both private property rights and market exchange forced Mr Dementev to consider new organisation structures, as well as avenues of distributing the final products. However, the main source of competitive advantage derives from his experiences during the Socialist era: namely, economies of scale attained through co-operation, productivity gains achieved through mechanisation and the ability to store the main cash crop (the grain) rather than sell it soon after harvesting.

Self-regarding instincts were important influences in the entrepreneurial experience of Mr Dementev: success in competition with other enterprises, as well as the attainment of satisfactory living standards. Thus, he was careful to portray an image of moderate comfort, fit for someone who leads a growing venture. However, in the 'intimate' rural context, he refrained from the worst excesses of the 'New Russians'. This was partly on account of his desire to maintain social cohesion, and partly because he did not want to attract the attention of the criminal fraternity. In fact elements of his behaviour appear to be influenced somewhat by other regarding instincts: namely his commitment to hard work and the perpetuation of his role as investor/patron of the local social infrastructure by 'helping his countrymen, particularly retirees from the hamlet' (Makhmutov, 2002, p. 27). In this respect he appears to follow a long tradition of Russian entrepreneurs of the Imperial era, and Soviet directors who returned some of their entrepreneurial gains to the church (the former) or the community (both).

Nomenklatura Entrepreneurship

A prominent entrepreneurial process during the early stages of reform comprised of state and regional party officials. Individuals of this kind, quickly realised that the Socialist regime began to change, under the impact of the reforms introduced by Mikhail Gorbachev, and so too did the patterns of advantage which placed them at the top of the old social structure (Kryshtanovskaya and White, 1996). As political positions became a less secure guarantee of individual advantage, the emphasis was shifted to private property. Although not significant in terms of numbers, nomenklatura entrepreneurs are very important in terms of the size of the ventures they lead, and subsequently their contribution to the economy as a whole (OECD, 1998).

Kukolev (1997) provides a profile of the nomenklatura entrepreneurs. These were predominantly males, who were invariably educated to degree level or above. They had experience of working primarily in political settings, and to a lesser degree production activities. Their decision to become involved in entrepreneurial ventures is taken earlier on in life (mean age) and very early in the process of transformation (most starting-up in the mid-1980s).

Kryshtanovskaya and White[18] (1996) shed light in the processes of nomenklatura entrepreneurship. They suggest that the origins of nomenklatura entrepreneurs are to be traced back to the decision (in 1987) to establish a network of Komsomol scientific and technical centres which would operate on commercial principles. Soon the scope of these centres expanded to include the manufacture of consumer goods, establish relationships with foreign firms, and convert paper assets into liquid cash. Within these centres there was a multitude of opportunities for the development of early Russian entrepreneurship. Thus, the members of the nomenklatura, by virtue of their ability to travel outside the Soviet Union, found themselves performing the role of intermediaries between western companies and Russian enterprises. The ability to interact with foreigners also enabled the nomenklatura to engage in import-export operations. During the perestroika years, they were also involved in the

> conversion of assets into cash … Money, at this time, was of two kinds: cash (nalichnye) and nominal (beznalichnye). Only cash was money in the real sense; bank credits were necessary for purely paper transactions between state organisations (Kryshtanovskaya and White, 1996, p. 715).

Not a single state enterprise had the right to convert assets into cash. Thus, the Komsomol centres were able to charge a rate of up to 30% on the profits that arose from such transactions. Later on in the 1980s, the nomenklatura became involved in property dealings as well as the privatisation of state enterprises. They benefited from the divestiture of state assets (in the form of ministries and government industries), state banks, the distribution system, and profitable enterprises (Cox, 2000). Kryshtanovskaya (1995) provides a typical example of the processes at work:

> a minister would retire or become a consultant to the former ministry, while a deputy minister became president of the new concern. Acquiring the status of a shareholding company, the leadership of the ministry became the shareholders of the new privatized organization, as well as state enterprises that were under the jurisdiction of the former ministry. The leadership at the head of the ministry was in effect not only privatizing the concern, but privatizing it for themselves (Krystanoskaya, 1995, p. 15).

The example used here to illustrate the process of enterprising science is drawn from Moscow.   The capital of the Soviet Union, and subsequently of the Russian Federation has been the cradle of political power, with a concentration of large numbers of the nomenklatura. At the same time however, Moscow has been at the forefront of the process of post-socialist transformation. Changes here were probably faster and more profound than in most other parts of Russia. This was partly on account of the fact that Moscow constituted the obvious point of entry of foreign investment in the country.   Lastly, there were a number of research institutions employing thousands of scientists offering fertile ground for innovative thinking and the development of new ideas.

Vladimir Potanin[19] was born into a family with close relationships with the foreign trade executive of the Soviet Union.   Indeed, his father was Soviet economic representative in Indonesia during the 1950s, then head of the 'Vostokintorg' foreign trade association (Coulloudon, 2000).   Vladimir himself studied in the Moscow Institute of International Relations and worked for eight years in the Foreign Trade Ministry.   Thus, he was well placed to take advantage of the opportunities emanating during the process of post-socialist transformation as

> Potanin himself, as well as his father had always been in the circle of foreign trade executives … [I]n such an environment one had to be in the know before being recruited and all the economists from the Soviet/Russian government, who have not dealt with exports, were considered to be strangers, members of the "outside" world (Coulloudin, 2000, p. 72).

In 1991, Vladimir Potanin, aged thirty-three, was appointed head of a new bank - the United Export Bank (OneksimBank) which was soon authorised to manage the hard currency accounts of Russia's foreign trade organisations.   The bank - a private venture - was essentially an expression of the private interests of the top executives in the Foreign Trade Ministry.   This afforded Potanin an opportunity to access key policy decision-makers which enabled him to secure a number of financial deals.   For example, in 1995, the Bank was authorised to manage the funds allocated for the reconstruction of the Republic of Chechnya.   By 1999, the bank had become one of the most powerful in Russia, whilst Potanin became known as one of the oligarchs.

In the case of Vladimir Potanin, as in that of Mr Dementev, embeddedness in the old regime was instrumental in the establishment and expansion of the entrepreneurial venture. However, neither he nor his father occupied positions in the highest echelons of the Soviet Foreign Trade Ministry.   Thus, he was chosen partly because he was an insider and partly on account of his ability to grasp the information available and translate it into opportunities in a changing context. Unlike Mr Dementev he did not rely on his experiences of enterprise strategies from the Socialist era - as he did not possess any.   Instead, he was able to combine information not widely available in the exploitation of market opportunities.   In doing so, he was driven predominantly by self-regarding instincts: namely the desire to compete and the propensity to acquire. Consideration for others was restricted only to those individuals (former patrons of the Soviet era), who were responsible for his appointment as director of the OneksimBank, and maintained shareholdings in the venture.

The Process of Enterprising Science

A third, distinct, entrepreneurial process involves individuals who remained detached from the Socialist regime. These entrepreneurs - also called 'new wave entrepreneurs' or 'physicists' - have attracted widespread attention in the accumulated literature (Gimpelson and Schultz, 1994; Ageev et al, 1995; Kukolev, 1997; Kusnezova, 1999), and have been often hailed as the champions of the new era.

Kusnezova (1999) describes them as

> high-qualified, well-educated specialists who are bored to death with the system of research and scientific centres... [M]athematicians, physisists and engineers are involved in this group ... [T]he average age of this strata is 30-40, a lot of them has PhD degree, high qualification, non-standard intellect, ... [and] is ready to take reasonable risk (Kusnezova 1999, pp. 64-65).

Gimpelson and Schulz (1994), drawing upon a number of in-depth qualitative interviews, also describe such individuals as 'competent specialists' in their thirties and forties, who are tired of the stagnant state system of research. Kukolev (1997) stresses that enterprising scientists are not only well educated themselves, but are also born and brought-up into families involved in scientific occupations (often university professors). Very few have any experience of working in political structures, whilst even the minority of them who were members of the Communist Party left its ranks even before the process of transformation. Enterprising scientists are by profession individuals with developed curiosity and creative intelligence, relatively free of ideological blinders. Thus, they are well placed to identify opportunities for private enterprise and take calculated risks.

The process of enterprising science is invariably associated with venturing in information technologies and applied sciences, often incubated within research centres in renowned higher educational institutions or other State research facilities (Kusnezova, 1999). This has profound implications upon the geography of the process of enterprising science: concentrated in cities like Moscow and Novosibirsk (with strong science research), as well as a number of formerly closed cities. In these settings enterprising scientists create new organisations, compete intensively with each other and privatised ventures and search for innovations, reflecting the new economic thinking.

The example[20] used here to illustrate the process of enterprising science is drawn from Moscow (the local context has been discussed earlier). The process of post-socialist transformation found Stepan Pachikov in the position of senior researcher in the Academy of Sciences, earning no more than $60 per month (Ito, 1997). However, it was not the poor and irregular pay alongside the absence of resources for research, that were symptomatic of early post-socialist Russia, that were the main reasons behind his decision to set-up an entrepreneurial venture. Stepan Pachikov appears to be a visionary on the 'Schumpeterian' mould aspiring - in his own words - to 'create something like Bell labs but with a commercial bent, to capitalize on the brains of the Soviet Academy of Science' (interview with Meier, 2002, p1). Thus, the mission of the enterprise was to 'enable people to build their own worlds' (Ad, 1997, p. 22). He is an individual, who is, by profession, instinctively curious and creative. Indeed, his success during the Socialist regime was associated with his ability to advance scientific knowledge through creative intelligence rather than conformism.

In sharp contrast to the experience of the two entrepreneurial processes discussed above, Pachikov remained outside the economic and political mainstream of the Soviet era. In fact, in '1968 he was ousted from Novosibirsk State University after he scrawled graffiti on a wall protesting the Soviet invasion in Czechoslovakia ...' (Ito, 1997, p. 53). The process of rehabilitation to the regime was protracted, but accomplished when he was allowed to complete his post-graduate studies at Moscow State University. Nonetheless, throughout the following twenty years or so, he remained detached from the Soviet economic and political elite.

His education, BSc from Tbilisi University, MSc from Moscow State University, and PhD in the development of a language to communicate with robots from the Soviet Academy of Sciences, was instrumental in his entrepreneurial venture (Ageev et al, 1995). This is because it placed him at the cutting edge of technological advancement of the late twentieth century. More importantly however, technological change in information technologies offered a wealth of entrepreneurial opportunities. Whilst working at the Academy of Sciences, Pachikov created a cross-discipline seminar on computer related problems, with computer specialists, psychologists and other experts. As a result, he was able to establish contacts with other leading researchers in the Soviet Union, individuals who would subsequently be instrumental in the success of his venture. His interest on computers also brought him together with Garry Kasparov, the Russian chess champion, who provided financial support for Pachikov's venture (Ito, 1997). Thus, Stepan's position involved embeddedness in the context of the intellectual elite of Moscow and relative disembeddedness from the system.

Thus, in 1989 Stepan Pachikov, together with his brother and Garry Kasparov, set out to create ParaGraph. The enterprise tapped into scientific expertise of the Moscow Academy of Sciences in developing handwriting recognition technology. In 1994 the company moved internationally not by merely exporting software, but by exporting Russian programmers who set-up shop in California. ParaGraph was successful in gaining big contracts with Disney and Apple, making it a celebrated case of Russian entrepreneurship in the mid 1990s. In 1997, Silicon Graphics bought ParaGraph for $50 million (Meier, 2002).

The experience of Stepan Pachikov does not only exemplify the process of enterprising science, but also lends support to the thesis that embeddedness to the learned environment may be differential. Thus, the individual may internalise only selectively behaviours prescribed by the institutional setting.   In this case, this could be attributed - at least in part - to the pervasive influence of idle curiosity. Indeed, Mr Pachikov appears to be an individual who incessantly pursues the acquisition of information and intensely utilises creative intelligence in his decision-making process[21].   Although not particularly well off during the early period of post-socialist transformation, he was not pushed into entrepreneurship. Instead he was drawn into business venturing as a process of continuous discovery, where he, and individuals like him, could fulfil their creative intelligence.   As a consequence, he is not burdened by any traditions of supporting the social infrastructure - as is the case with Mr Demendev.   Other regarding instincts are manifested in his work ethic, as well as his desire to co-operate with other Russian intellectuals.   However, self-regarding instincts appear to be of paramount importance: a desire to compete, and achieve excellence, as well as a propensity to acquire.

Capitalist Entrepreneurship in Agriculture

In urban settings enterprising scientists have often been heralded as the pioneers of a new wave of entrepreneurship.   This is partly on account of their origin, as outsiders of the old regime, and partly due to their ability to create ventures which employ significant numbers of employees.   Recent research into the rural areas of Russia has enabled us to identify an entrepreneurial process, which appears to perform a similar function.

However, capitalist entrepreneurs in agriculture differ profoundly from the urban-based enterprising scientists. The bulk of the accumulated literature, from the main conurbations of Russia, portrays the latter as young and well-qualified individuals who perceive entrepreneurship as an outlet for their creative capabilities (an issue discussed in the Section above).   However, in the Novosibirsk region, where capitalist entrepreneurs in agriculture are present, an area where agricultural land constitutes the main rural resource, they are invariably older individuals – with an age structure similar to that of the nomenklatura entrepreneurs[22].   They are more or less exclusively males, and are not as well educated as those in other groupings. Only 23% of them have a university degree.   However, they appear to have an ability to identify opportunities that is not directly linked to a specific entrepreneurial characteristic.   This may be linked to the adoption of a more co-operative stance that affords them access to information about markets and resources. All of them employ a number of wage employees, whilst a minority (4%) have expanded considerably and employ more than thirty persons (Kalantaridis and Larianidis, 2004).   In most cases their ventures are relatively recent, dating back to the late 1990s.

Informal Entrepreneurial Processes

Informal entrepreneurial activity is a widespread phenomenon in post-Socialist regimes, and not only, Russia. It ranges from a state of quasi-legality, i.e. evasion of taxes and other social security contributions, to outright illegal activities, namely theft, racketeering, drug trafficking etc. The former processes (hereafter referred to as shadow entrepreneurship) has been historically associated with the *tsekhoviki* however, it is not exclusive to them. Tax evasion is widespread among all entrepreneurial processes discussed in this Chapter. At the same time, there are entrepreneurial ventures associated with individuals or groups of individuals who operate outside the legal and moral framework of the socio-economic milieu (hereafter referred to as criminal entrepreneurship). The distinction between the two processes is useful for analytical purposes, however, the boundaries are often blurred, especially as shadow entrepreneurs invariably use the services of their criminal counterparts (often in the form of protection). Moreover, there is mobility within each grouping with a number of celebrated cases of entrepreneurial individuals who acquired fortunes through racketeering or rule evasion and gaining legitimacy through the pursuit of formalised enterprising pursuits.

The phenomenon of shadow entrepreneurial activity in Russia is not new. Indeed, numerous studies in the area of entrepreneurial studies (Ageev et al, 1995; Khotin, 1996; Schulus, 1996; Kusnezova, 1999) highlight their importance during the 1970s and 1980s. This period has been characterised by increased deficiencies in the production of consumer goods, alongside increasing incomes resulting in a burgeoning black market (Frisby, 1998). Within this context, shadow entrepreneurs became involved in the production of goods made with stolen state resources, and trade. Shadow entrepreneurs of this era were well placed to take advantage of opportunities created by *perestroika*: possessing both appropriate skills and some capital from their earlier ventures. Thus, it comes as no surprise that by the mid 1990s 40 out of the 100 richest Moscow entrepreneurs were drawn from the shadow economy (Khotin, 1996).

In sharp contrast to the limited published material regarding shadow entrepreneurship, there is a significant body of literature[23], mainly from a sociological perspective, regarding criminal entrepreneurs. This literature suggests the origins of the criminal fraternity, the world of thieves (*vorovskoi mir*), dates back to the end of the civil war, when crime was a survival strategy among the weakest elements of the population (Frisby, 1998). The world of thieves became a powerful informal organisation based upon

> a complex set of mores and prohibitions that regulate relationships with one another, with authorities and with outsiders. The central element of the world of thieves is the so-called obschack, the communal fund which accumulates the money acquired by theft and other illegal methods. Having donated the money to the obschack, the thieve then receives from it his share … [B]ut the bulk of the obschack is used to support those who serve their prison term (Volkov, 1998, p. 10).

During the Stalinist era, a large number of imprisoned criminals were instrumental in maintaining order in the labour camps (Volkov, 2000), whilst in the Brezhnev era, they began to turn to blackmail, extortion and the protection racket directed at the shadow entrepreneurs (Frisby, 1998).

In a number of recent contributions Vadim Volkov exploring the process of violent entrepreneurship[24] in post-socialist Russia, identifies its origins back to mid 1980s. He suggests that violent entrepreneurship, which is relatively recent phenomenon, is distinct from other historical precedents of criminal ventures (the *vorovskoi mir*). This new process grew into prominence during the early 1990s and often rose to positions of dominance in the local context. An interesting case of this process, presented by Volkov (2000), is drawn from Uralmashevskaya a working class district in the Ural city of Ekaterinburg. The founders of the gang in this district were

> brothers Grigorri and Konstantin Tsyganov, the wrestler Sergei Vorobiev, the skier Alexander Khabarov, and boxers Sergei Terentiev and Sergei Kurdiumov. They all grew-up in the same neighbourhood ... [and] ... were trained in the sports club (Volkov, 2000, p. 734).

It was in the district's co-operative market that these former sportsmen discovered the way their fighting skills, willpower and discipline could be turned into money, by offering protection. Soon the protection racket was expanded to private shops, whilst they begun the illegal production of alcohol. Their big break came in late 1991, when the main local state enterprise, a machine building factory,

> was hit by a cash deficit ... [T]he plant had difficulties in selling its products ... and was unable to pay wages to its employees. The leaders of the gang offered the management help with cash in exchange for a number of premises belonging to the factory, including the massive building of the factory club. The latter became the office of Intersport, the sportswear company founded by T. Tsyganov (Volkov, 2000, p. 735).

Subsequently, they decided to create an investment company, in order to invest the profits from the protection racket and increase their control locally. As a result of two successful turf wars with other gangs in the city, they were able to expand into the copper industry, energy and communications, whilst enhancing their public image through charity campaigns and support for the social infrastructure (Volkov, 2000).

The entrepreneurial process of the small group of individuals who formed the Uralsmashevskaya gang is fascinating. Born and brought-up locally they were well embedded in the local context. During the socialist era, they demonstrated an interest in sports but otherwise they were 'unremarkable' individuals: neither advancing through the hierarchical structures of the old regime nor excelling educationally. For these individuals the process of post-socialist transformation was manifested in the decline of the 'old certainties', such as the decline of the main local employer, and the emergence of a host of entrepreneurial opportunities. In a context (the *perestroika* era) where property rights were uncertain, insecure, and costly to protect, considerable resources must be employed for the protection of wealth and resources (Feige, 1998). It is in this context that the leaders of the gang identified the opportunity to become enforcers of private property rights - a personalised manifestation of the cost of transacting - in the district's co-operative market. In their venture they were driven by self-regarding instincts: the desire to compete (Veblen's predatory instinct) and the propensity to acquire. Other regarding instincts, such as the propensity to co-operate, were only apparent, though particularly strong, in the relationships with other members of their gang. Unlike their *voroskoi mir* counterparts, as well as other gangs in the city the group of individuals who led the Uralsmashevskaya gang were aware of the changing environment around them. This prompted them to adopt a strategy of continuous expansion into new, and increasingly legitimate, ventures. Part of their strategy was the increased emphasis on charity work and the support of the social infrastructure.

'Reluctant' Petty Entrepreneurship

This entrepreneurial process has received very little attention in the existing body of literature, despite the fact that it is probably significant in terms of the numbers involved[25]. The main reason behind this is the perceived marginal economic development potential of reluctant petty entrepreneurs, which prompted some scholars to question the extent to which they can be defined as entrepreneurs. Scase best articulates this argument by drawing upon Weber's distinction between entrepreneurship and proprietorship. The former term refers to the pursuit of capital accumulation and business growth, often at the expense of personal consumption. Proprietorship refers to

> ownership of property and other assets such that, can be but not necessarily, used for trading purposes and therefore to realise profits, are not utilised for the purpose of longer term process of capital accumulation (Scase 1997, p. 14).

The argument goes that, large numbers of individuals involved in starting and or running a business fall in the latter grouping. However, the fact that not all entrepreneurs aim to grow is not a characteristic confined to post-socialist regimes (as emphasised by Smallbone and Welter 2001). Moreover, motivations and aspirations do not remain the same throughout an individual's life. Thus, economic agents aspiring to survival rather than capital accumulation during the early period of transformation may alter their behaviour in response to either changes in their environment or the influence of their accumulated experiences. Lastly, these individuals appear to conform with the definition of entrepreneurship adopted for the purposes of our investigation.

Previous research either merely acknowledges the existence of this entrepreneurial process (Ageev et al, 1995) or provides a brief overview. Drawing from the experience of rural areas around Novosibirsk, Kalantaridis and Labrianidis (2004) argue that reluctant petty entrepreneurs have become involved in entrepreneurial pursuits mainly in response to unemployment or in order to avoid poverty and destitution. They invariably employ one to five persons, and the overwhelming majority is involved in trading activities, with others concentrated in the repair and service of machinery. Those falling in this grouping are predominantly females, and are younger than the average population for the region[26]. Reluctant petty entrepreneurs are very poorly educated[27]. Moreover, nearly two thirds of those falling within this cluster have lived in an urban environment.

The example[28] used here in order to illustrate reluctant petty entrepreneurship at work is drawn from the same region. The Novosibirsk region, located some 3,200 kilometres to the East of Moscow, is dominated by the city of Novosibirsk, a production centre for the military-industrial complex and a key transportation hub, and the university town of Academgorodock (McMylor et al, 2000). Outside these adjoining urban centres population density is very low (less than five persons per square kilometre), and there is precious little economic activity beyond agriculture and petty trade (Kalantaridis and Labrianidis, 2004). Moreover, there is a strong collective tradition, reinforced by the hostile climatic conditions. Thus, formerly collective or state farms, re-invented in the early 1990s as joint stock agricultural companies, are instrumental in the provision of social infrastructure in small communities that exist in a particularly harsh environment (Kalugina et al, 2001). Activities such as keeping the roads open during the winter, maintaining the inflow of basic goods to the rural population, and even the provision of some educational facilities are provided by the large joint stock farming organisations. These organisations exist alongside subsistence agriculture, providing the machinery and equipment needed in order to cultivate the household plots, and benefiting from subsidies (in the form of private agricultural produce for self-consumption) in the cost of physical reproduction of their workforce[29]. In this context, private entrepreneurial ventures are perceived with concern not only on historical grounds, but also they may undermine the viability of the joint stock companies, which underwrite the social fabric of the countryside.

In this environment the Karamanov family set-up its entrepreneurial venture, in early 1992. They were a

> young married couple with children who were compelled to migrate from Kazakhstan. In Novosibirsk they failed to get jobs in their trade (both have technical education). They went to a rural place, bought a house ... and opened a private business (trade) (Kalugina et al, 2001, p. 18).

During the early period of transformation, the collapse of the distribution channels of the socialist era offered a wealth of opportunities for trade. Such ventures required little or no capital for start-up, offered quick turnaround times, and - at that time - precious little accountability for bad debt or breach of contract, as business laws and courts were not yet in place (Buss and Yanser, 1999). In this context, access to information regarding both market demand as well as sources of supply conferred competitive advantage to economic agents. Thus, individuals embedded upon a defined local milieu were at a disadvantage when compared to actors who bridged geographical or industrial settings. The Karamanov's, who moved from Kazakhstan to Novosibirsk and subsequently to a large village in the surrounding countryside, fell in the latter grouping. They were equipped with information, but lacked salaried or wage employment opportunities, which could dissuade them from initiating their entrepreneurial venture. In such circumstances, where the option of guaranteed returns for their labour is not available and the need to make ends meet is acute, the constraints imposed by pragmatism upon the creative function of idle curiosity diminish. Setting-up a venture which combines knowledge about markets and sources of supply is the result of this process.

The decision to pursue the opportunity was influenced by the Karamanovs position in relation to their context. Indeed, in a socio-economic milieu which was at best sceptical and at worst outright hostile towards private entrepreneurship the Karamanovs were 'outsiders'. They were unemployed, and did not possess a household plot. Thus, their dependence upon the local, large agricultural organisation was virtually non-existent. This stands in sharp contrast to individuals who were born and brought-up locally, who were employees of the company and enjoyed a host of fringe benefits. Thus, whilst setting-up in direct competition with the retail outlet of the agricultural joint-stock company was a deterrent for the local populace, this was not the case for the Karamanovs. This illustrates the differential impact of the changing system of incentives and sanctions, upon individuals during the process of replacing the mechanisms of central planning and state ownership with market allocations and private property rights[30].

In the process of realising their entrepreneurial venture the Karamanovs were able to secure own and family resources. Thus,

> The starting capital consisted of own savings and financial aid from relatives, which allowed them later to acquire two shops. They have a personal car and truck vehicles. Keep four employees who work on a permanent basis and for the busy season hire a temporary worker (Kalugina et al, 2001, p. 18).

The case of the Karamanov family – a suggestive illustration of a push driven entrepreneurial process – lends support to the thesis that what drives individuals is not immutable. The interface between instincts and learned environment, and the ensuing sequence of actions aiming to achieve specific ends, may change over time. This could be on account of satisfactions of the purpose driving earlier actions, changes in the learned environment, or new information and experiences gained by the individual. In the case study examined here, there is a gradual shift of emphasis away from a desire to compete in order to ensure the means of physical reproduction to a propensity to acquire ownership of property (shops and trucks), evidence to the Karamanovs' success and a condition for further expansion. Thus, Scase's (1997) dismissal of 'proprietors' as 'real but relatively unimportant' needs to be revisited critically.   A shift in emphasis towards the conditions and processes that may transform the interface between purpose and content, and subsequently the actions, of an individual may provide a promising line of scholarly investigation.

Opportunity Driven Petty Entrepreneurship

The need-driven decision of the Karamanov family to start a new venture does not constitute the only process associated with petty entrepreneurship. The pursuit of opportunity, though admittedly at the micro (in terms of size) level, underpins an alternative petty entrepreneurial process.   Evidence drawn from the countryside of the Republic of Bashkortstan (described in considerable detail earlier in this Chapter) lends support in this direction.

In this context, there is also a number of individuals - some one in five of the total entrepreneurs - who start micro-level enterprises that employ predominantly family labour. Like their reluctant counterparts in rural Novosibirsk petty entrepreneurs are invariably engaged in the construction industry and financial services – activities involving relatively modest capital outlays at start-up. Females also dominate this grouping, as is the case of reluctant petty entrepreneurs. However, this is where similarities between the two types of petty entrepreneurship end. Opportunity driven petty entrepreneurs in the Republic of Bashkortostan are relatively better-educated individuals (both in absolute terms and in relation to the population at large in the study area): nearly half of them have a university degree. Moreover, their decision to become involved in the process of business enterprise was influenced by the identification and the desire to pursue an opportunity.

The characteristics of the learned environment as well as the individuals concerned may explain why petty entrepreneurship in this context, differs from that in the rural areas around Novosibirsk.   The Republic of Bashkortostan is a resource munificent area, with natural resources as well as a number of manufacturing and tertiary activities.   This is combined with the fact that employment in existing enterprises did not decline as dramatically as elsewhere in Russia[31].   As a consequence, unemployment or the threat of unemployment, as a factor forcing individuals into entrepreneurship, was never as profound in this context, as elsewhere in Russia. A lower degree of instability in the context, than that experienced by the Karamanov family, also characterises opportunity driven petty entrepreneurs. This is not only because of the slow pace of reform, but also because this process is initiated during the late 1990s, after the 1997 crisis, and the advancement of post-socialist transformation.

The ethnic make-up of the individuals engaged in the process of petty entrepreneurship may also explain why individuals pursuing opportunities fall in this grouping. In the study area as a whole Tartars make up the single largest ethnic grouping, followed by the indigenous Bashkirs and Russians (Makhmutov, 2002). However, Tartars do not feature prominently among the Republic's political elite and are under-represented among entrepreneurs, where Russians and the Bashkirs dominate. The only entrepreneurial grouping, with a significant representation of Tartars - even higher than that for the population as a whole - is that of petty entrepreneurs. Detachment (disembeddedness) from the political and economic mainstream, and the all-important networks of contacts, may divert the entrepreneurial talent of ethnic Tartars to entrepreneurship. However, the very same factor (isolation from networks of contact and information) may influence adversely the ability of their ventures to expand significantly. This raises the issue of ethnicity and its influence upon individual perceptions of the learned environment. Rather unexpectedly, given the multi-ethnic character of Russia this is an issue which has attracted only marginal attention[32].

Entrepreneurial Processes Among the Russian Diaspora

Another entrepreneurial process involves individuals from outside Russia, and especially returnees of the Russian Diaspora. A number of studies (Ageev et al, 1995; Kukolev, 1997) report the incidence of such individuals, however, to date there has been virtually no published information regarding their characteristics or the processes at work in the broad area of entrepreneurial studies[33]. McCarthy et al (1997) report the experience of the leadership qualities of Olga Kirova: a female entrepreneur with a bicultural Russian and American background. Drawing upon her experience, we set out to shed some light in what is an entrepreneurial process which remains at the shadows of the more enigmatic 'red directors', and the more heroic process of enterprising science.

Olga Kirova was born and brought-up in St Petersburg, to a family of engineers, where she received a fine education. When she was eighteen, she and her parents left St Petersburg for Chicago, where she studied industrial engineering at Northwestern University (McCarthy et al, 1996). She went on to study for an MBA degree at the University of Chicago, and a PhD in Management at Moscow State University, after she returned to Russia.

Thus, during the mid 1990s Olga Kirova occupied a pivotal position in the local context. She was a native Russian speaker with a couple of years working experience in Moscow. She was able to understand the nuances of the culture and the prevailing business practices, but without much of the adverse influences of the Socialist milieu. At the same time she was fluent in English with considerable experience of working in US companies. Thus, she had

> one foot in Western management and the other in Russian management. She understood well the American way of doing business, but also knew Russia's differences and how to adapt to them. Her bilingual skills allowed her to deal with Russians and Americans ... [M]oreover, her knowledge of both cultures allowed her to be effective in dealing with most other parties ... (McCarthy et al, 1997, p. 288).

Early 1994 found Olga Kirova completing her doctoral studies and in search for a new challenge. She had already experience in developing a Russian subsidiary for a US financial software company, as well as contacts in the Russian market. Thus, she set out to acquire exclusive distribution rights for Sterling Software Corporation, a developer of integrated financial software. Together with her American husband she invested $100,000 in the creation of Sterling Russia. The idea behind the new venture was straightforward: using Olga's extensive knowledge of the market and Russian culture, localise and market the sophisticated products developed by Sterling Software Corporation in the US for the needs of the rapidly expanding Russian market. By 1996, the company had established five offices in major cities around Russia and employed 150 employees (McCarthy et al, 1997).

The issue of the position of the individual in relation to her context is again of paramount importance in the experience of Olga Kirova: a Russian by birth but very much an American in terms of attitudes towards entrepreneurship and management style[34]. Thus she was able to occupy a pivotal position between US companies and the Russian market. In a manner reminiscent of the key activity of Sterling Russia, Olga Kirova localised the entrepreneurial venture: in the sense of contextualising Sterling Software Corporation to its Russian customers and interpreting Russia to American executives. In doing so, she was not influenced by the Russian entrepreneurial heritage of other-regarding purposes of human behaviour. Instead, co-operation was restricted only to the key managers of the organisation. Self-regarding instincts, and particularly the desire to compete aggressively, were pervasive in shaping her experience of entrepreneurship.

Change Through Time

Earlier in this Chapter, the issue of the influence of the passage of time upon the findings of scholarly research in Russia was raised. It is worth returning to this issue on the basis of the empirical findings presented here. Indeed, in the evolving context of post-socialist Russia the origins of entrepreneurship change significantly through time (see Figure 6.1). Thus, changes in the learned environment may prompt some entrepreneurial individuals to re-invent themselves or face extinction. Those who were deeply embedded in the old milieu offer good examples to these processes. Enterprising directors of the Soviet era identified three pathways to private entrepreneurship, defined by changes in the institutional setting. It is also important to note, that large numbers of such individuals, Kusnezova (1999) suggests as many as two thirds of the total, were unable to adapt to the changing context, and lost their position altogether. Moreover, during the period of transformation new entrepreneurial processes emerge. Thus, during the late 1980s and early 1990s enterprising scientists and violent entrepreneurs become increasingly important: the former a manifestation of the human potential of Russia, whilst the latter a symptom of post-socialist transformation. The difficulties of the early 1990s pushed many individuals into petty entrepreneurship, whilst from the mid 1990s onwards (even allowing for the 1997 crisis) the pursuit of opportunity (by the Russian Diaspora, petty as well as agricultural entrepreneurs) became increasingly important.   Therefore, at the dawn of the new millennium entrepreneurship in post-socialist Russia is significantly more pluralistic and diverse than during the *perestroika* era.

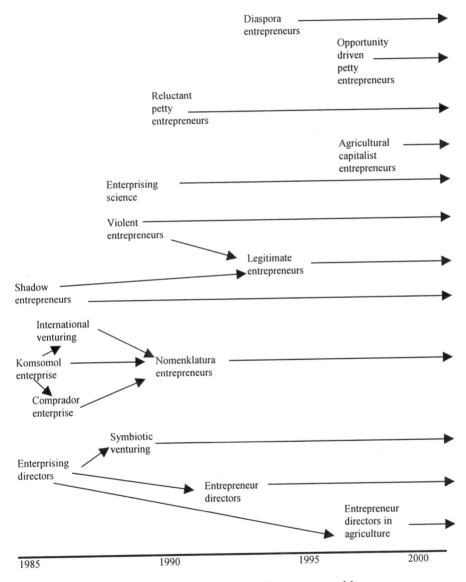

Figure 6.1 The Evolving Origins of Russian Entrepreneurship

Discussion

The institutionalist approach developed in Chapter 4 enabled us to decipher the evidence regarding Russian entrepreneurship. The entrepreneurial processes discussed in this Chapter, emphasise the importance of factors such as geography and ethnicity in influencing the context. A comparison between the experiences of Olga Kirova and Mr Dementev provides an excellent illustration of regional diversity in setting. The former lives and works in Moscow: where large numbers of enterprising intellectuals and scientists, exist alongside growing numbers of foreign investors. This combined with the advancement and embeddedness of institutions which facilitate market exchange, increase the incidence of entrepreneurial ventures. As a result, social attitudes are becoming increasingly supportive of individual ventures. This stands in sharp contrast, with the conservative and personalised setting of a small village in the Republic of Bashkortostan. The delay in the establishment of well defined private property rights in agriculture, an important resource in a rural context, and the importance of former collectives in supporting the social infrastructure, perpetuate sceptical views of entrepreneurial pursuits. In the case of the Republic of Bashkortostan ethnicity further complicates matters. This is partly because there are institutions which are ethnicity specific, and partly because of differential access to resources, as the example of the Tartars indicates. As a consequence, exclusive reliance upon over-arching and all-embracing conceptualisation of a single (pan-Russian) learned environment may be inappropriate.

However, diversity in context goes beyond geography and ethnicity. One outcome of our analysis is the identification of the centrality of the distinct and often individual position of the entrepreneurial agents under consideration, in relation to their context. This, is nowhere more apparent than in the cases of Vladimir Potanin and Stepan Pachikov. They are both males of similar age (born within six years of each other), who were well educated, lived the best part of their adult lives in Moscow, and became entrepreneurs within a relatively short time period of each other (the first in 1991 and the second in 1989). However, their position is profoundly different. Vladimir Potanin is embedded upon the Soviet network of political power. This is instrumental in defining the nature and scope of entrepreneurial opportunity in his case. Mr Pachikov is defined by his membership of the scientific elite. This does not only offer opportunities but also influences his view of the world and subsequently his actions. Thus, one could justifiably raise the question of whether these two entrepreneurs operate in the same context despite their geographical proximity.

The institutionalist approach developed in Chapter 4 also provided us with insights into how the position of the individual influences manifestation of idle curiosity. In the case of Mr Dementev, embeddedness on the old institutional setting strengthened the constraining influence of pragmatism – manifested in the adoption of tried and tested enterprise strategies. Thus, the scope for the function of idle curiosity was relatively modest, including the adaptation of these strategies in the new context. This stands in sharp contrast to the experience of the

Karamanov family.   They were forced to move away from Kazakhstan, and eventually settled in a village in the Novosibirsk region, where they have very little to lose - in the sense of employment, incomes, social relationships etc.   Thus, they are actively exploring their environment for entrepreneurial ideas.   Different from both these cases is the experience of Stepan Pachikov.   In his case idle curiosity is not only an instinct defining his behaviour but also it influences his experiences of the socio-economic milieu.   It is his inherent inquisitiveness and creative intelligence which influence his detachment from the old milieu.   Unfortunately, the case study material contains precious few data on the reasons why this was the case. In this instance information regarding the processes of early socialisation would be useful in enhancing our understanding of the entrepreneur.

Position also appears to influence the balance between self and other regarding instincts.   The diverse demonstration of self-regarding purpose is evident in the cases of Olga Kirova and the founders of the Uralsmashevskaya gang.   The former, undoubtedly influenced by her life and education in the US, demonstrates a desire to compete, which is broadly similar with that reported in the case of her American counterparts.   In contrast, the manifestation of the desire to compete in the latter case is predatory in nature.   As a consequence of the strong influence of self-regarding instincts in defining entrepreneurs the propensity to co-operate appears to be only of secondary importance.   Indeed, in most of the entrepreneurial process explored in this Chapter, this is restricted to those persons in the immediate environment of the entrepreneur (the communist patrons of Vladimir Potanin, other scientists in the case of Stepan Pacikov, members of the family in the case of the Karamanovs, and a senior managers of her business in the case of Olga Kirova). There are only two exceptions of behaviours which appear to be influenced by a broader interpretation of co-operation: Mr Dementev and the leaders of the Uralsmashevskaya gang.   In both cases, support of the social infrastructure is essentially driven by a desire to legitimise the activities of the entrepreneurial individual, a pursuit of commonly accepted criteria of status and prestige.   These are contemporary illustrations of the 'forced' assumption of social responsibility exhibited both by entrepreneurs during the Imperial era, and directors of the Soviet period.

The deployment of the approach developed earlier in this book identifies a number of issues for future research into the origins of entrepreneurship in post-socialist Russia. The first issue that warrants detailed consideration is the position that individuals occupy in relation to their context: the pace of institutional change alongside the resilience exhibited by some of the old institutions mean that embeddedness or disembeddedness is a key consideration in the entrepreneurial process. The second issue is the complex balance between self and other-regarding instincts in the entrepreneurial process. In a country where collectivism has strong and enduring roots whilst the legitimacy of entrepreneurship is at best moderate other-regarding instincts may be of importance even if underpinned by expediency. The third issue that merits careful consideration is that of the units of analysis. Indeed, the bulk of scholarly research in post-socialist Russia focuses upon the individual.   We suggest that the use of alternative entrepreneurial units (such as the family in the case of he Karamanov family and a social group in the case of the Uralmashevskaya gang) may be of importance in broadening and deepening our understanding of entrepreneurship. The final issue that requires scholarly attention is that of the influence of entrepreneurs upon the context. This spans across the range from local contexts (where individuals like Mr Dementev are central) to the national one (and the prominent position of oligarchs such as Vladimir Potanin).

Conclusions

So, has the institutionalist approach developed in this book furthered our understanding of Russian entrepreneurship? In addressing this issue it have decided to compare the explanatory power of the approach advanced in this book with that of competing theoretical constructs singled out in Chapters 2 and 3 for their ability to provide suggestive insights in the study of the entrepreneur. The theoretical constructs concerned were those developed by Schumpeter, the Austrians, Choi and Harper (in economics), and Gartner, and Social Constructionism[35]. Our comparisons centre upon two key considerations: i) the definition of entrepreneurship and its implications in a Russian setting, and the ii) the interface between agency and context.

The approach advanced here provides a fairly inclusive conceptualisation of Russian entrepreneurship. This stands in sharp contrast with the very narrow view of entrepreneurship adopted by Schumpeter. Indeed, using a Schumpeterian definition we would be hard pressed to identify more than two entrepreneurial individuals (Stepan Pachikov and Olga Kirova) among the cases presented in this Chapter. Such a restrictive view of who is an entrepreneur has significant implications upon the direction of research and public policy decision-making. The definition provided by Harper, with his emphasis upon entrepreneurship as a profit-seeking activity would also lead to the exclusion of marginal individuals such as the reluctant petty entrepreneurs and, maybe, shadow entrepreneurs, who simply aspire to make ends meets[36]. Moreover, the approach adopted here is the only one, apart from that advanced by Gartner, that enables us to perceive Russian entrepreneurship as a non-homogeneous phenomenon and explore diversity between entrepreneurs. This move away from entrepreneurship as an 'ideal type' is instrumental in understanding Russian entrepreneurs.

As far as the interface between the context and the individual is concerned, institutionalist analysis provides us with significant insights not only upon outcomes but also upon diversity. Earlier theoretical constructs acknowledge the influence of the post-socialist context, especially those emanating from outside economics (Gartner and Social Constructionism). Economic theories of the entrepreneur, with the notable exception of Schumpeter are weaker in the analysis of socio-cultural influences, which are of particular importance in the case of Russian entrepreneurs. However, the works of the Austrian tradition, and especially Mises, are particularly useful in the analysis of purposive action (i.e. starting from dissatisfaction with the present and aspiring to alter future states of affairs) in Russia.   Moreover, existing theoretical constructs rarely perceive context, as a complex and often multi-layered setting within which entrepreneurs act, in sharp contrast to empirical studies and the approach advanced here.   A uniform view of the context creates significant difficulties. We suggest that it is the notion of the position of the entrepreneurial agent, which emerges as of paramount importance in exploring the diverse impact of the context upon agency.

Notes

1 Early attempts at uncritical replication of Western theory in an Eastern setting (for an example see Green et al, 1996), have been criticised (Kalantaridis and Labrianidis, 2004) and subsequently replaced with the adoption of more cautious approaches.   Thus, some researchers in the field deploy an ethnocentric perspective (Kusnezova, 1999), whilst others engage in dialectic between theory (emanating predominantly from a Western context) and evidence from post-socialist regimes (Luthans et al, 2000; Smallbone and Welter, 2001).

2 Only sources of data published in English are reviewed here.   We are aware that there is a number of works – often of empirical nature – published in Russian that would be particularly useful in enhancing our understanding of the entrepreneur in post-socialist transformation.   Accessing these sources of data is difficult, whilst language erects additional boundaries. Given the importance of the issue under investigation an exhaustive research of the literature published in Russian is an essential task for the advancement of the field of entrepreneurial studies.

3 The Project funded by INTAS (99-0965) was entitled Rural Entrepreneurship and Employment in Transition.   The team members were: Labrianidis L., Kalantaridis C., Kalugina Z., Makhmutov A., and Pityulich M.   The project started on the 15/3/2000 and was completed on the 15/3/2002.

4 These areas by virtue of their diversity from other localities researched by scholars in the field provide a useful corrective to the literature.

5 The questionnaire included sections on the personal details of the respondent, educational and work experience, current employment status, and general perceptions of entrepreneurship. In addition to the harmonised part of the questionnaire a number of other 'case-specific' questions were included in the instrument.

6 This issue is more complex than may appear in the first instance.   In Russia there are many instances where entrepreneurial ventures may have registered but never started trading. Exploring the individuals behind such 'phantom' entities would be erroneous. However, we argue, there is merit in the study of real though marginal entrepreneurial pursuits.

7 The marginal emphasis placed upon regional comparisons is manifested in the neglect to identify the characteristics or even the types of location where research was carried out in some of the previous publications in the field (Shulus, 1996).

8 For a sympathetic view see Ageev et al (1995), whilst for a critical one Khotin (1996).

9 Leitzel illustrates this using a quote attributed to Leonid Brezhnev that 'no one lives on wages alone. I remember in my youth we earned money by unloading freight cars. So what did we do? Three bags or crates unloaded and one for ourselves' (Leitzel, 1998, p. 119).

10 This argument is somewhat different from the thesis advanced by new institutionalists such as North (1990) and Feige (1998) who suggest that change is primarily associated with formal institutions, whilst continuity is apparent in the case of informal ones.

11 In his work Mises (1922) suggested that without private property , there could be no real competitive markets and no prices to guide economic decision-making. Following on Mises' footsteps, Hayek (1944) argued that the rigidity of prices in planned economies diminish their usefulness in transferring localised information.

12 A practice reminiscent of Veblen's idea of sabotage by absentee-owners.

13 Khotin's paper draws upon from a number of empirical studies conducted in Russia between 1981-1990. During the mid 1980s he conducted a study with 208 emigres who were former Soviet managers. In 1990 he participated in a survey of 1,200 directors of Russian industrial enterprises. Thus his work concentrates heavily upon the very early stages of post-socialist transformation.

14 Kukolev's research was conducted during the 1992-1994 period and concentrated upon the business elite, which he defines as the top stratum of entrepreneurs. Thus, he pays little attention upon the ventures petty entrepreneurs. In his paper he provides previous few details regarding the research methods used or the geography of the study.

15 Four insightful illustrations of this process are presented by Clarke and Fairbrother, 1994.

16 Indeed, Ufa is located some 1,500 kilometres away from Moscow, making it one of the Eastern-most extremities of Europe (Kalantaridis and Labrianidis, 2004).

17 This process appears to be quite common in the countryside of Bashkortostan. In 2000, there were 3,286 large private agriculturists occupying some 15% of the total farming land.

18 Kryshtanovskaya and White deploy a different methodological approach from that deployed by most other studies. They concentrate upon the analysis a large number (3,610) of biographies from official directories, up to 1994.

19 The case is described in considerable detail by Coulloudon (2000).

20 For other examples of the process of enterprising science see Bruton and Rubanik, 1997; Coulloudon, 2000; Schweitzer, 2001.

21 Interestingly, he manifests several of the traits of the prototype entrepreneur, as conceptualised in large parts of the literature developed in capitalist economies, in a post-Socialist context.

22 Indeed, nearly two thirds are forty years old or more (Kalantaridis and Labrianidis, 2004).

23 See Chalidze, 1977; Handelman, 1994; Williams, 1997; Frisby, 1998; Volkov, 1998 and 2000.

24 He defines violent entrepreneurship as 'a set of organizational solutions and action strategies that convert organized force (or organized violence) into money or other valued assets' (Volkov, 2000, p. 710).

25 Evidence provided in Kalantaridis and Labrianidis (2004) suggests that it accounts for 38% of entrepreneurial ventures in the rural areas of the Novosibirsk region and 25% in the countryside of the Republic of Bashkortostan.

26 In fact, two thirds are below the age of 40, in comparison to 43% for the sample as a whole (Kalantaridis and Labrianidis, 2004).

27 Only 13% have a university education (Kalantaridis and Labrianidis, 2004).

28 Other suggestive cases of reluctant petty entrepreneurship are presened by Burawoy et al (2001).

29 Kalugina et al (2001) conceptualise this as a symbiotic relationship. This co-existence bears striking similarities with theses regarding the articulation of modes of production.

30 This thesis is different to that of new institutionalists, who fail to distinguish the differential impact of the changing institutional setting upon individuals (for an example see Feige, 1998).

31 Bashkortostan, being an autonomous republic of the Russian Federation, enjoyed a greater degree of control in economic policy than the regions. This enabled the 'conservative' political elite to slow down the pace of the reform, especially during the 1991-1996 period.

32 In fact, throughout the literature on Russian entrepreneurship there is only one paper (Radaev, 1997) explicitly addressing the impact of ethnic networks upon the process of starting and running a new business.

33 As a result of the total absence of any studies exploring the phenomenon outside the case study presented here we were concerned about how well this sub-Section fits within the Chapter. Although the problem is apparent to the reader, we believe that the advantages of including whatever little evidence there is regarding the diaspora entrepreneurs are greater than the disadvantage of the continuity in the manner the evidence is presented.

34 McCarthy et al (1997) discuss extensively her attributes in relation to that of her counterparts of either Russian or US origin. The influence of her US education and work experience appears to be stronger than that of her early socialisation in Russia.

35 Greenfield and Strickon were excluded from this exercise as they are considered among the antecedent s of an institutionalist approach in entrepreneurial studies.

36 A difference in objectives, between aspiring to make ends meet and pursuing profits, has significant implications upon the decision-making process of economic agents (for a suggestive discussion of this issue in the context of early revolutionary Russia see Chayanov, 1966).

Chapter 7

Conclusions

Understanding the Entrepreneur: An Institutionalist Approach

In an era marked by the emergence of new market economies, the diminishing influence of the State in the co-ordination of economic activity, and a shift away from the multinational towards 'flexible' and 'responsive' forms of business organisation, the importance attached to entrepreneurship by researchers and policy-makers has increased considerably. However, the revival[1] of interest in the 'life and works' of the entrepreneur is combined with the realisation of the limitations in the state of the art in the field. We know that the entrepreneur matters but the scholarly community can not reach agreement upon neither a definition of what he or she does nor on how best to investigate him or her. We believe that the growing imbalance between interest on the one side and the ability to provide answers on the other creates considerable tensions in the field. In fact, one could argue that the emergence of a multitude of pragmatic arguments in the last twenty years or so, could be perceived, at least in part, as a result of this tension. The proposed shift away from the entrepreneur towards the entrepreneurial process (discussed in Chapter 3), the pursuit of advanced mathematical models (Bygrave and Hoffer, 1991), and the increased pursuit of usefulness (Swedberg, 2000) undoubtedly fall within this context. The result has been a growing emphasis upon empirical research, which although necessary is not a sufficient condition for the advancement of the field of study[2].

Our purposeful review of the entrepreneurship literature has enabled us to identify theoretical constructs with precious little explanatory power. More specifically, the adoption of a mechanistic approach, such as that of mainstream economics that pursues universal laws has been proved unable to advance our understanding of the entrepreneur (see Chapter 2). As a consequence, well-respected scholars, such Baumol and Casson, are explicitly dealing with the dilemma of maintaining coherence and consistency whilst stretching the boundaries of the mainstream. Similarly mono-causal explanations, adopted in the exploration of either the sociology or the psychology of the entrepreneur, have proved unsuccessful. The emphasis upon either context or agency led to the creation of 'caricatures' of the entrepreneur: either performing socially prescribed roles or acting wilfully in abstraction.

In contrast, scholars who view the entrepreneur as a conscious but contextual economic agent who can exercise judgement have made significant inroads in understanding entrepreneurship. Within this context, there is a growing consensus regarding the usefulness of institutional analysis. Whilst most scholars derive their view of institutions from the New Institutional Economics, others tap into the works of the old institutionalists, such as Veblen.   In both instances however, institutions not only matter but institutional analysis enhances scholarly understanding of the entrepreneur.   Darwinian evolution has also become increasingly prominent in entrepreneurship research.   This is, in large part, a consequence of the realisation that typological views of entrepreneurship are unsatisfactory.   It is this acknowledgement that entrepreneurs are not the same, but, differ significantly from each other, that underpin the advancement of Darwin's idea of the uniqueness of everything in the organic world in the field of entrepreneurial studies.

The institutionalist approach advanced here perceives entrepreneurs as unified human beings, who are contextual but engage in purposive action.   Our entrepreneur is a rational economic agent but not in the manner of the neo-classical tradition.   The entrepreneur's rationality is influenced by his or her past as a member of a collective. Manifestations of time past are the cognitive framework of the individual, as well as his or her accumulated body of knowledge and experiences. However, the rational entrepreneur exists and operates in time present and in a specific social context. The characteristics of the institutional setting and the level of technological advancement outline the boundaries (which could also be viewed as a finite set of opportunities and constraints) of entrepreneurial decision-making. Whilst technological and institutional evolution are possible, in part on account of entrepreneurial actions, the entrepreneur sets out from the state of affairs that is present. Lastly, the rationality of the entrepreneur is deployed in order to influence future states of affairs. It is the pursuit of ends that drive entrepreneurial actions.   Interaction with other economic agents influences the outcomes of entrepreneurial actions creating new information and experiences that may instigate new entrepreneurial actions.

This rational entrepreneurial agent engages in purposive action. However, the purpose of his or her endeavour is not the outcome of fixed and unknowable 'pleasures and pains'.   Unlike neo-classical theoretical[3] constructs the approach advanced here enables us to explore the objectives (or ends) pursued by the entrepreneur. Whilst these objectives are defined by a set of universal instincts, their manifestation is context specific: whilst instincts are abstract drives of action, they are meaningless outside the reality of a socio-economic milieu. This interface between purpose and context is influenced in large part by the position of the individual. Moreover, institutionalist analysis enables us to view the purpose of human endeavour as both teleological and non-teleological. Thus, a specific entrepreneurial action is driven by given objectives (teleological). However, subsequent actions of the same entrepreneurial agent may be driven by different objectives developed in i) the light of new information or experiences (themselves the outcome of previous actions), ii) the partial or complete satisfaction of previous objectives, iii) a change in the interface between agency and context (non-teleological).

Our rational and purposive entrepreneurial agent is contextual but not context-driven. The approach adopted here enables us to decipher the entirety of manners that the context impacts upon agency. These include: i) the choice of objectives (and the scope offered to idle curiosity among them) that drive human endeavour, ii) the formation of cognitive frameworks that introduce meaning to information, iii) the flow of information, iv) and the boundaries of action in the process of economic interaction. More importantly, however, the impact of institutions and technology upon individuals is differential on account of their distinct positions. This notion constitutes a useful analytical instrument in exploring not only why some individuals engage in entrepreneurial pursuits whilst others are not but also the apparent disparity among economic agents falling within the entrepreneurs category.

The philosophical underpinning of Darwinian biology lies at he heart of the main attribute of the approach advanced here, i.e. its ability to deal with the impact of diverse environmental settings on the entrepreneur and his or her decision-making process. As already stressed in the introductory Chapter, we advocate a shift in emphasis away from all embracing theorisation, towards a more context-responsive approach. This concentrates upon the development of some general principles that drive the action of entrepreneurs, which can be combined with data regarding specific historical settings (for an example, see Chapter 6). Thus, our understanding of the entrepreneur depends upon the clarity of our key concepts and propositions and our sensitivity to the specificity of the context.

Directions of Future Research: An Institutionalist Agenda

In this book we have identified the intellectual core of an (old) institutionalist perspective in entrepreneurial studies. The approach developed here is, in our opinion, far from complete. In fact, the reader must have already identified a number of 'intellectual threads', potential lines of future scholarly enquiry, throughout the work. These constitute research issues that are essential for the exposition of our ideas but not sufficient so as to warrant detailed consideration here. Thus, in several instances the issue is raised and an outline argument is advanced but is not developed any further. In this Section we identify four such issues. Together, they make-up one of two directions for the advancement of institutionalist ideas in entrepreneurial studies.

The first concerns with the exploration of entrepreneurship in analytical units other than the individual economic agent. In the Introduction to this book, we suggested that alternative units of analysis should not be perceived as a collection of individuals. Research into other (than the individual) units of entrepreneurship may benefit from the treatise on institutions provided by Veblen and recently advanced by Hodgson (1998). Three assumptions, regarding alternative units of analysis in entrepreneurship research, provide the justification for the adoption of this approach. Firstly, these units, like institutions, have a number of characteristics and routines that are shared by those belonging to them. Secondly, they involve the interaction of individual economic agents, with crucial information feedback. Thirdly, these units of analysis though neither immutable nor immortal they are relatively durable, self-reinforcing structures.   The empirical observation that alternative entrepreneurial units often involve existing institutions, such as the family household, lend support to the approach advanced here. This approach opens a number of suggestive avenues of scholarly enquiry.   It enables the investigation of alternative entrepreneurial units, as collectives which are made up of individuals brought together by elements of commonality whilst also allowing us to explore friction that may lead to change. This, long overdue, area of research in the field of entrepreneurial studies forms an integral part of an institutionalist agenda.

The theme of entrepreneurial learning constitutes the second line of enquiry that warrants further investigation. In this book the importance of learning in the entrepreneurial decision-making has been illustrated.   Learning in the institutionalist context has two dimensions. The first dimension conceptualises learning as a social process (resulting in the formation of cognitive frameworks and the accumulation of knowledge), whereby the individual internalises information embodied in the institutional setting and the prevailing state of industrial arts.   The second dimension conceptualises learning as an individual process (producing experiences). At the heart of the second dimension is a process of 'learning by doing' whereby individuals take actions and learn from the outcomes (intended or unintended) of actions. Both dimensions of entrepreneurial learning require further development.   What are the specific processes at work in each of the two dimensions?   Indeed, the issue of how do human beings learn is becoming increasingly important in the social sciences. What is the interface between learning as a social and as an individual process?   The distinction between social and individual learning processes has been proved a useful one for the purposes of our approach.   However, further investigation is required to examine both the distinctiveness and similarity between the two dimensions. Lastly, how learning influences the position of the individual within his or her context?

Another (third) potentially fruitful area of future research concerns with the choice and nature of relationships among entrepreneurs as well as between entrepreneurs and other economic agents.   The New Institutional Economics have made a significant positive contribution in the advancement of our knowledge in this direction through the use of the concept the cost of transacting. However, New Institutional Economics is - like all mainstream approaches - an efficiency argument.   Moreover, whilst New Institutional Economics enhance our understanding of relationships of power it has been less successful in exploring relationships based upon trust. The old institutionalist approach advanced here, by virtue of its core conceptual assumptions, offers a wider scope for the investigation of the choice and nature of relationships in the process of entrepreneurial decision-making.   It conceptualises the economic agent in a more complex manner than the New Institutional Economics: advancing the notion of a unified being with only partial information regarding the current state of affairs and little information about the future actions of other economic agents. In our context, the economic agent has a cognitive framework in order to interpret information and only limited computational capabilities (bounded rationality). More importantly, however, self-interest is not the only motivational factor that drives the economic agent: other-regarding instincts offer a contrary pull, whose strength is influenced in part by the context within which the agent operates. Moreover, the approach advanced here explores the choice, as well as the nature of relationships developed by entrepreneurial economic agents. In doing so, it utilises the notion of reducing the level of fundamental uncertainty experienced by the economic agent. This raises the questions of how do entrepreneurs choose other economic agents for relationship building? Given the limited (in the sense it is not boundless and thus selectivity is essential) relationship building capabilities of economic agents this issue requires careful consideration. What is the nature of the relationship between the entrepreneur and other economic agents, and how does this influence the flow of information? This question places the emphasis upon the exploration of the multitude of hybrid (between power and trust) forms of governing relationships.

The final line of future enquiry concerns with influence of entrepreneurial actions upon the prevailing context. Indeed, there is a large and ever expanding awareness in the field of entrepreneurial studies that whilst there is a growing body of knowledge on the influence of institutions upon the entrepreneur, there is very little on how entrepreneurs may shape their institutional setting. At the same time, empirical observation especially from post-socialist economies suggests that entrepreneurs can themselves influence the environment within which they operate. In a number of instances entrepreneurs in these settings influence directly the rules of the competitive game. In this book, we have presented, drawing upon Veblen's pioneering work, one possible manner by which entrepreneurs may influence the institutional setting. This constitutes of a two-move process, whereby the prevailing technology constitutes the lever through which entrepreneurs influence institutions. More specifically, the entrepreneur through his or her actions instigates change in the state of industrial arts, which in turn necessitates a change in the institutional setting. Although the evolution of institutions in response to the change of technological development is not automatic it is ultimately inevitable. However, this manner of entrepreneur-instigated evolution of the institutional setting, evident in a number of instances in advanced industrialised countries remains agnostic regarding the process commonly reported in, though not exclusive to, post-socialist regimes. Therefore, further research is needed, probably drawing from insights gained by the political sciences, as to how the entrepreneur both individually and collectively influences directly the institutional setting.

An altogether different direction for the advancement of institutionalist ideas in entrepreneurial studies involves the conduct of empirical research. Indeed, both the old institutionalist tradition and the area of entrepreneurship research demonstrate a strong propensity towards the pursuit and interpretation of empirical evidence. Thus, it must come as something of a surprise to the informed reader the absence of a body of empirical evidence, generated explicitly to underpin the approach advanced here. Chapter 6 provided a glimpse of the explanatory power of the institutionalist ideas advanced, based on data acquired in a generic, rather than purposive, manner. Although useful as the first step in this direction, this is by no means sufficient. Instead, a dedicated programme of empirical study is essential in order to generate the body of robust empirical data. Each study focusing upon a specific historical, geographic and industrial context offers us an opportunity to explore the ability of institutionalism to enhance our understanding of the entrepreneur and the entrepreneurial decision-making process. However, it is the ability of to provide insights into a multitude of contexts which constitutes the ultimate criterion for the evaluation of the usefulness of institutionalism in entrepreneurial studies.

Implications for Policy-making

Research in the field of entrepreneurial studies is driven, in large part, by a desire to create theoretical constructs that possess predictive power. Given that entrepreneurs are instrumental in engineering change and generating growth in a market economy, increasing the incidence of entrepreneurship is assumed to be beneficial for economic advancement. Indeed an influential OECD study identifies a number of reasons why governments are interested in promoting entrepreneurship. The argument goes that

> [w]hile seen as a means of combating unemployment and poverty, the adoption of entrepreneurship is perceived to yield additional benefits such as raising the degree of competition in a given market, fuelling the drive for new economic opportunities, and helping to meet the challenges of rapid change in a globalising economy. A reliance on private initiative as a source of employment creation is also very clearly attractive in a context both of restricted public expenditures and a preference among policymakers for supply-side solutions to unemployment. Promoting entrepreneurship is thus viewed as part of a formula that will reconcile economic success with social cohesion (OECD, 1997, p. 34).

It is this view that underpins the pursuit of 'useful' theories that enable the development of policies, which in turn may enhance entrepreneurial activity in specific socio-economic contexts.

The approach adopted here does not fit well within this policy-oriented environment, as it is not useful in the sense of being problem-solving and prescriptive. Instead, it raises concerns and advances an alternative mode of viewing entrepreneurship policy but does not put forward prescriptive solutions. Three such policy issues merit careful consideration. The first issue concerns with the identification of the parameters that define entrepreneurship policy: involving both its objectives and its realm. As far as the issue of objectives of entrepreneurship policy is concerned, the OECD quotation above encapsulates the nature of the problem. Entrepreneurship is undoubtedly a means of exploiting opportunities, raising the degree of competition, and increasing economic prosperity. However, entrepreneurship may have little - and in some cases none - influence upon unemployment or poverty alleviation. Entrepreneurs may adopt labour-saving technologies that may lead to labour-shedding rather than new recruitment. The skills needed by entrepreneurial ventures may prevent employment of individuals from the lowest social strata, thus, preventing any positive outcomes in combating poverty. Entrepreneurship may also be a means rupturing social cohesion. Thus, it is of paramount importance that there is clarity and appropriateness of objectives of entrepreneurship policy. The issue of the realm of entrepreneurship policy impacts directly upon its effectiveness. Indeed, there is widespread agreement among scholars in the field that entrepreneurship policy focuses upon only a fraction of the factors that influence the incidence of enterprising individuals. Hart (2001) argues that

> [n]ot all public policy that shapes the context for entrepreneurship and the supply of potential entrepreneurs is entrepreneurship policy ... Education policy, for instance, may influence the legitimacy of entrepreneurial ventures and the knowledge, skills, and networks possessed by individuals .... Macroeconomic policy ... affects short-term capital availability and the conditions of international trade (Hart, 2001, p. 12).

As a consequence, a host of issues that influence heavily the incidence and direction entrepreneurship remain outside the confines of entrepreneurship policy. It is the adoption of an approach that places entrepreneurship as a key consideration in the formulation of all policy, which is going to have significant long-term effects upon entrepreneurial agents. This requires a shift in the time-scope of entrepreneurship policy away from the medium-term, which allows policy-makers to evaluate (and perhaps take credit for) the consequences of their actions, towards the long-term.

The second issue, deriving in large part from the concerns regarding the generalisability of policy, involves the level and nature of action undertaken. Within the broader contemporary tendency towards growing regional economic and political integration, there is a pursuit of entrepreneurship policy at the highest level. Thus, the European Unions has recently become the latest in a long list of organisations which influence directly or indirectly policy across national frontiers to develop an entrepreneurship policy. In contrast, the approach advanced here lends support to the thesis that direct attempts to encourage entrepreneurial behaviour can be the remit of regional and local institutions. In fact, governance (in the sense of collective action of businesses, communities etc) may be preferable to public policy.

The third issue revolves around the appropriateness of over-arching and all-embracing policy initiatives. Not all entrepreneurs, even those working within the same socio-economic milieu, go through the same processes and inevitably reach the point of conforming to the typological characteristics of pre-conceived categories. This is nowhere more apparent than in some of the instances of Russian entrepreneurship (discussed in Chapter 6), where individuals operating within the same local context report profoundly different experiences. Thus, in our view, the individuality of the agent, as well as his or her position in relation to the context are not to be assumed. The actions of entrepreneurs may vary on account of differences both in the degree of internalisation of socio-cultural norms, and in the ability to tap into sources of capital, labour and information. Moreover, change in the entrepreneurial process, though inherent, is not necessarily taken to be directional nor is it assumed to be convergent. As a consequence, policy based upon the characteristics of an ideal representation of entrepreneurship may be inappropriate on account of the mere variation of actual entrepreneurs from this ideal representation. Recent research in the field of entrepreneurial studies indicate a realisation of the difficulty of overarching policy initiatives. Specifically, Bridge, O'Neil and Cromie (1998) conclude that existing policy frameworks make no attempt to relate intervention measures to the stages of growth of a business or to the pre-start-up stage. Stevenson and Lundstrom (2002) take this point further by developing a taxonomy of entrepreneurship policy. Similarly, scholars in the past emphasised the importance of diverse industrial or spatial contexts upon policy[4] (Smallbone et al, 1998).

Notes

1 A term not strictly accurate as earlier growth periods did not involve comparable levels (at least in terms of numbers of scholars involved and quantity of outputs) to those attained in the late twentieth century.

2 We would like to stress here that the pursuit of empirical evidence is strongly endorsed here. However, we believe that the insights produced by empirical data can be maximised in most instances only if placed within a body of theoretical knowledge.

3 We must stress here however, that the ability to decipher the objectives that drive human agency matters more in the theory (any suggestive theory) of the entrepreneur than in neo-classical economics. This is because, the former focuses upon actions (in pursuit of ends) that distinguish individual economic agents from one another, whilst the latter centres upon (re-)actions that are common to entirety of men.

4 In response, Atherton and Lyon (2001) emphasise the importance of segmentation in policy support, providing a comprehensive list of segmentation strategies. However, they go on to conclude that 'segmentation using more than four different criteria was considered in many cases to be overly complex and, as a result, overly complex to implement' (Atherton and Lyon, 2001, p. 6).

Bibliography

Ackerman, F. (1999) 'Still Dead After All These Years' Global Development and Environment Institute Working Paper, Tufts University, No. 99-01.

Ad, E. (1997) 'SGI Acquires Russian ParaGraph' *Primeur Monthly*, May, p. 22.

Ageev A. I., Gratchev, M. V. and Hisrich, R. D. (1995) 'Entrepreneurship in the Soviet Union and Post-Socialist Russia', *Small Business Economics*, 7 (5), pp. 365-376.

Aldrich, H. (1999) *Organizations Evolving*, London: Sage.

Aldrich, H. and Martinez, M. A. (2001) 'Many are Called but Few are Chosen: An Evolutionary Perspective for the Study of Entrepreneurship' *Entrepreneurship Theory and Practice*, 25 (4), pp. 41-56.

Anderski, S. (1972) *Social Sciences as Sorcery*, New York: St Martin's Press.

Ashworth, W. (1975) *A Short History of the International Economy Since 1850*, London: Longman.

Atherton, A. and Lyon, F. (2001) 'Segmenting Support for Small and Medium Enterprises' Durham: The Foundation for Small and Medium Enterprise Development.

Audretsch, D. B. (2002) 'Entrepreneurship: A Survey of the Literature' Prepared for the European Commission, Enterprise Direcotrate General.

Audretsch, D. B. and Thurik, R. (2002) 'Linking Entrepreneurship to Growth' OECD STI Working Paper, 2081/2.

Babe, R. E. (1993) 'Information Theory in Economics' in Hodgson, G. M., Samuels, W. J. and Tool, M. C. (eds) *The Elgar Companion to Institutional and Evolutionary Economics*, Aldershot: Edward Elgar, pp. 360-366.

Babe, R. E. (1998) 'Economics and Information: Toward a New (and More Sustainable) Worldview' *Canadian Journal of Communication*, 21 (2), pp. 120-133.

Backhouse, R. (1985) *A History of Modern Economic Analysis*, Oxford: Blackwell.

Barreto, H. (1989) *The Entrepreneur in Microeconomic Theory*, London: Routledge.

Batstone, S. and Pheby, J. (1996) 'Entrepreneurship and decision-making: the contribution of G.L.S. Shackle' *International Journal of Entrepreneurial Behaviour and Research*, 2(2), pp. 34-51.

Baumol, W. J. (1968) 'Entrepreneurship in Economic Theory' *American Economic Review*, 58, pp. 64-71.

Baumol, W. J. (1990) 'Entrepreneurship: Productive, Unproductive and Destructive' *Journal of Political Economy*, 98 (5), pp. 893-921.

Baumol, W. J. (1995) 'Formal Entrepreneurship Theory in Economics: Existence and Bounds' in Bull I., Thomas, H. & Willard, G. (eds) (1995) *Entrepreneurship Perspectives on Theory Building*, New York: Pergamon, pp. 17-33.

Begley, T. M. and Boyed, D. B. (1987) 'Psychological characteristics associated with performance in entrepreneurial firms and small businesses' *Journal of Business Venturing*, 2 (1), pp. 79-93.

Berliner, J. S. (1957) *Factory and Manager in the USSR*, Cambridge, Mass: Harvard University Press.

Berliner, J. S. (1976) *The Innovation Decision in the Soviet Industry*, Cambridge, Mass: MIT Press.

Binks, M. and Vale, P. (1991) *Entrepreneurship and Economic Change*, London: McGraw-Hill.

Birch, D. (1981) 'Who Creates Jobs?' *The Public Interest*, 65, Fall, pp. 3-14.

Blackwell, W. (1970) *The Industrialization of Russia: An Historical Perspective*, Arlington Heights: Harlan Davidson Press.

Blaug, M. (1986) 'Entrepreneurship before and after Schumpeter' in Blaug, M. (ed) *Economic History and the History of Economics*, New York: New York University Press.

Boettke, P. J. (1993) *Why Perestroika Failed: The Politics and Economics of Socialist Transformation*, London: Routledge.

Boettke P. J., Lavoie, D. and Storr, H. V. (2001) 'The Subjectivist Methodology of Austrian Economics and Dewey's Theory of Inquiry' First Annual Symposium on the Foundation of Behavioral Sciences, Great Barrington, MA.

Boettke, P. J. and Butkevich, B. I. (2001) 'Entry and Entrepreneurship: The Case of Post-Communist Russia' *Journal des Economistes et des Etudes Humaines*, 11(1), pp. 91-114.

Boland, L. A. (1979) 'Knowledge and the Role of Institutions in Economic Theory' *Journal of Economic Issues*, 13 (4), pp. 957-972.

Bolton, J. E. (1971) *Report of the Committee of Inquiry on Small Firms*, CMND, 4811, London: HMSO.

Bouchikhi, H. (1993) 'A constructivist framework for understanding entrepreneurship performance' *Organizational Studies*, 14 (4), pp. 551-569.

Boulding, K. E. (1961) *The image: knowledge and life in society*, Ann Arbor, MI: University of Michigan Press.

Bound, J., Cummins, C., Grilliche,s Z., Hall, B. H. and Jaffe, A. (1984) 'Who does R & D and who patents?' in Grilliches, Z. (ed) *R & D, Patents and Productivity*, Chicago: University of Chicago Press, pp. 21-54.

Brazeal, D. V. and Herbert, T. T. (1999) 'The Genesis of Entrepreneurship' *Entrepreneurship Theory and Practice*, 23 (3), pp. 29-45.

Bridge S., O'Neil, K. and Cromie, S. (1998), *Understanding Enterprise, Entrepreneurship and Small Business*, London: Macmillan.

Bruton, G. D. and Rubanik, Y. (1997) 'High Technology Entrepreneurship in Transitional Economies: The Russian Experience' *Journal of High Technology Management Research*, 8 (2), pp. 213-224.

Bull, I. and Willard, G. (1995) 'Towards a Theory of Entrepreneurship' in Bull I., Thomas H. and Willard G. (eds) *Entrepreneurship Perspectives on Theory Building*, New York: Pergamon, pp. 1-15.

Burawoy M., Krotov, P. and Lytkina, T. (2001) 'Involution and Destitution: Russia's Gendered Transition to Capitalism', *Ethnography*, 1 (1), pp. 43-65.

Buss, T. F., and Yasner, L. C. (1999) 'Microenterprise in Russia During its Economic Transition, 1991-1993' *International Journal of Economic Development*, 1 (2), pp. 221-237.

Bygrave, W. (1995) 'Theory Building in the Entrepreneurship Paradigm' in Bull I., Thomas H. and Willard G. (eds) *Entrepreneurship Perspectives on Theory Building*, New York: Pergamon.

Bygrave, W. D. and Hoffer, C. W. (1991) 'Theorizing about entrepreneurship' *Entrepreneurship Theory and Practice*, 16 (2), pp. 13-22.

Camerer, C. and Weber, M. (1992) 'Recent developments in modelling preferences: uncertainty and ambiguity' *Journal of Risk and Uncertainty*, 5 (4), pp. 325-370.

Cantillon, R. (original 1755, 1932) *Essai sur la nature de commerce en general*, London: Macmillan.

Casson, M. (1982) *The Entrepreneur an Economic Theory*, London: Gregg Revivals.

Casson, M. (1993) 'Entrepreneurship and Business Culture' in Brown, J. and Rose, M. (eds) *Entrepreneurship, networks and modern business*, Manchester: Manchster University Press.

Casson, M. (1995) *Entrepreneurship and Business Culture*, Aldershot: Edward Elgar.

Casson, M. (1998) 'An Entrepreneurial Theory of the Firm', DRUID Summer Research Conference, Bornholm, Denmark.

Chalidze, V. (1977) *Criminal Russia: Essays on Crime in the Soviet Union*, New York: Random House.

Chayanov, A. V. (1966) *The Theory of the Peasant Economy*, Madison, Wisc: University of Wisconsin Press.

Chell, E. (1985) 'The Entrepreneurial Personality: A Few Ghosts Laid to Rest' *International Small Business Journal*, 3 (3), pp. 43-54.

Chell, E. (2000) 'Towards researching the "opportunistic entrepreneur": a social constructionist Approach and research agenda' *European Journal of Work and Organizational Psychology*, 9 (1), pp. 63-80.

Choi, Y. B. (1993) *Paradigms and Conventions Uncertainty, Decision Making and Entrepreneurship*, Ann Arbor: The University of Michigan Press.

Clarke, S. and Fairbrother, P. (1994) 'The Privatisation of Industrial Enterprises in Russia: Four Case-Studies' *Europe-Asia Studies*, 46 (2), pp. 179-215.

Coase, R. H. (1937) 'The Nature of the Firm' *Economica*, 4, pp. 386-405.

Coase, R. H. (1992) 'The Institutional Structure of Production' *American Economic Review*, 82 (4), pp. 713-719.

Cochran, T. C. (1949) 'Role and Sanction in American Entrepreneurial History' *Change and the Entrepreneur*, edited by the Harvard University Research Center in Entrepreneurial History, pp. 153-175.

Cochran, T. C. (1955) 'The Entrepreneur in American Capital formation' *Capital Formation and Economic Growth*, A Conference of the Universities-National Bureau Committee for Economic Research.

Cochran, T. C. (1966) 'The Entrepreneur in Economic Change' *Explorations in Entrepreneurial History*, Vol. III (Second series).

Cole, A. H. (1949) 'Entrepreneurship and Entrepreneurial History' *Change and the Entrepreneur*, edited by the Harvard University Research Center in Entrepreneurial History, pp. 85-107.

Commons, J. R. (1959) *Institutional Economics*, Madison: The University of Wisconsin Press.

Conyngham, W. J. (1982) *The Modernization of Soviet Industrial Management*, Cambridge: Cambridge University Press.

Cosgel, M. M. (1996) 'Metaphors, Stories and the Entrepreneur in Economics' *History of Political Economy*, 28 (1), pp. 57-76.

Coulloudon, V. (2000) 'The Divided Russian Elite: How Russia's Transition Produced a Counter-Elite' in Sperling, V. (ed) *Building the Russian State: Institutional Crisis and the Quest for Democratic Governance*, Boulder, Co: Westview Press, pp. 67-87.

Cox, S. M. (2000) 'The Politics of Russia's Financial-Industrial Groups' *Dogus University Journal*, 1, pp. 27-32.

Demsetz, H. (1983) 'The Neglect of the Entrepreneur' in Ronen, J. (ed) *Entrepreneurship*, Lexington, Mass: Lexington Books, pp. 275-288.

Demsetz, H. (1996) 'Rationality Evolution and Acquistiveness' *Economic Inquiry*, 34 (3), pp. 484-495.

Dequech, D. (2001) 'Bounded Rationality, institutions and uncertainty' Discussion Paper No. 100, IE/UNICAMP, pp. 1-23.

Dibben, M. R. (2000) *Exploring Interpersonal Trust in the Entrepreneurial Venture*, London: Macmillan.

Dorn, J. A. (1991) 'From Plan to Market: The Soviet Challenge', *Cato Journal*, 11 (2), pp. 175-193.

Drucker, P. F. (1986) *Innovation and Entrepreneurship*, New York: Harper & Row.

Duchesnau, D. A. and Gartner, W. B. (1990) 'A profile of new venture success and failure in emerging industry, *Journal of Business Venturing*, 5 (2), pp. 297-312.

Earl, P. E. (1994) 'Simon, Herber, Alexander' in Hodgson, G. M, Samuels, W. J, and Tool, M. R. (eds) *The Elgar Companion to Institutional and Evolutionary Economics*, Aldershot: Edward Elgar, pp. 284-286

EC (1998) *Fostering Entrepreneurship in Europe: Priorities for the Future.* Communication from the Commission to the Council. Brussels: COM(98) 222.

Egashira, S. and Hashimoto, T. (2001) 'The Formation of Common Norms on the Assumption of Fundamentally Imperfect Information' in Conte, R. and Dellarocas, C. (eds) *Social Order in Multiagent Systems*, Doldrecht: Luwer Academic, pp. 160-192.

Ekelund, R. B. and Herbert, R. F. (1997) *A History of Economic Theory and Method*, New York: McGraw-Hill.

Eliasson, G. and Henrekson, M. (2004) 'William J. Baumol: An entrepreneurial economist on the economics of entrepreneurship' *Small Business Economics* (forthcoming).

Falk, R. W. (1996) 'An Inquiry into the Political Economy of World Order' *New Political Economy*, 1 (1), pp. 13-26.

Feige, E. L. (1998) 'Underground Activity and Institutional Change: Productive, Protective and Predatory Behavior in Transition Economies' in Nelson, J. M., Tilly, C. and Walker, L. (eds) *Transforming Post-Communist Political Economies*, Washington DC: National Academy Press, pp. 19-34.

Foss, N. (1994) *The Austrian School and Modern Economics: Essays in Reassessment*, Copenhagen: Handelshojskolens Forlag.

Franz, R. (2002) 'Frank Knight on the Importance and Difficulty of Doing Behavioral Economics' History of Economics Society Conference, Davis California, USA.

Frisby, T. (1998) 'The Rise of Organised Crime in Russia: its roots and social significance' *Europe-Asia Studies*, 50 (1), pp. 27-49.

Fuller, T. (2002) 'Social constructionism and reflexivity? Researchers and owner-managers are not immune: but it is science?' RENT XVI Conference, Barcelona, Spain.

Galbraith, J. K. (1956) *The Affluent Society*, Boston, Mass: Houghton Mifflin.

Gardner, W. B. (2001) 'Is There an Elephant in Entrepreneurship? Blind Assumptions in Theory Development' *Entrepreneurship Theory and Practice*, 25 (4), pp. 27-39.

Gartner, W. B., (1985) 'A Conceptual Framework for Describing the Phenomenon of New Venture Creation' *Academy of Management Review*, 10 (4), pp. 696-706.

Geiger, H. (1968) *The Family in Soviet Russia*, Cambridge, Mass: Cambridge University Press.

Gerschenkron, A. (1954) 'Social Attitudes, Entrepreneurship and Economic Development', *Explorations in Entrepreneurial History*, VI, pp. 1-19.

Gilad, B. S. (1982) 'On encouraging entrepreneurship: an interdisciplinary approach' *Journal of Behavioural Economics*, 11 (1), pp. 132-163.

Gimpelson, V. and Schultz, A. (1994) 'New Russian Entrepreneurship' *Russian Social Science Review*, 35 (3), pp. 19-36.

Glade, W. P. (1967) 'Approaches to a theory of entrepreneurial formation' *Explorations in Entrepreneurial History*, 2nd Series, 4 (3), pp. 245-259.

Glancey, K. S. and McQuaid, R. W. (2001) *Entrepreneurial Economics*, London: Macmillan.

Gloria-Palermo, S. (1998) *The Evolution of Austrian Economics From Menger to Lachmann*, London: Routledge.

Granick, D. (1960) *The Red Executive*, NewYork: Doubleday & Company.

Granick, D. (1972) *Managerial Comparisons of Four Developed Countries: France, Britain, United States and Russia*, Cambridge: Cambridge University Press.

Granovetter, M. (1985) Economic action and social structure: the problem of embeddedness' *American Journal of Sociology*, 91, pp. 481-510 .

Green, R. David, J. and Dent, M. (1996) 'The Russian entrepreneur: a study of psychological characteristics', *International Journal of Entrepreneurial Behaviour & Research*, 2 (1), pp. 49-58.

Greenfield, S. M. and Strickon, A. (1981) 'A new paradigm for the study of entrepreneurship and social change' *Economic Development and Cultural Change*, 29 (3), pp. 467-499.

Gregori, de T. R. and Shepherd, D. A. (1993) 'Technology, Theory of' in Hodgson G. M., Samuels, W. J. and Tool M. R. (eds) *The Elgar Companion to Institutional and Evolutionary Economics*, Aldershot: Edward Elgar.

Gregory, P. R. and Stuart, R. C. (1981) *Soviet Economic Structure and Performance*, New York: Harper and Row.

Grimes, S. (2000) 'Rural areas in the information society: diminishing distance or increasing learning capacity' *Journal of Rural Studies* 16(1), pp. 13-21

Grossman, G. (1976) 'Notes on the Illegal Private Economy and Corruption' in Joint Economic Committee (ed) *Soviet Economy in a Time of Change*, Washington: Government Printing Office, pp. 834-855.

Gunning, P. J. (1997) 'The Theory of Entrepreneruship in Austrian Economics' in Keizer, W. Tieben, B. and van Zijp, R. (eds) *Austrian Economics in Debate*, London: Routledge, pp. 172-191.

Gurroff, G., and Carstensen, F. (eds) (1983) *Entrepreneurship in Imperial Russia and the Soviet Union*, Princeton: Princeton University Press.

Habakkuk, H. J. (1953) 'Economic Functions of English Landowners in the Seventeenth and Eighteenth Centuries' *Explorations in Entrepreneurial History*, VI, pp. 92-102.

Habakkuk, H. J. (1962) *American and British Technology in the 19th century*, Cambridge: Cambridge University Press.

Hagen, E. E. (1962) *On the Theory of Social Change: How Economic Growth Begins*, Homewood, IL: Dorsey Press.

Hampson, S. E. (1982) *The construction of personality*, London: Routledge.

Handelman, S. (1994) *Comrade Criminal. The Theft of the Second Russian Revolution*, London: Michael Joseph.

Hands, D. W. (1987) 'A Review of Charles Taylor's Philosophical Papers I and II' *Economics and Philosophy*, 3, pp. 172-175.

Hannan, M. T., and Freeman, J. H. (1977) 'The population ecology of organizations' *American Journal of Sociology*, 82 (5), pp. 929-964.

Harper, D. H. (1996) *Entrepreneurship and the Market Process*, London: Routledge.

Hart, D. M. (2001) 'Entrepreneurship Policy: What it is and Where it Came from' in Hart, D. M. (ed) *The Emergence of Entrepreneurship Policy Governance, Start-ups and*

Growth in the US Knowledge Economy, Cambridge: Cambridge University Press, pp. 3-19.

Hawley, F. B. (1907) *Enterprise and the Productive Process*, New York: Putnam

Hayek, von F. A. (1937) 'Economics and Knowledge' *Economica*, 4, pp. 33-54.

Hayek, von F. A. (1944) *The Road to Serfdom*, Chicago: University of Chicago Press.

Hayek ,von F. A. (1949) *Individualism and Economic Order*, London: Routledge.

Hebert, R. F. and Link, A. N. (1988) *The Entrepreneur: Mainstream Views and Radical Critiques*, Westport, Conn: Praeger.

Hey, J. D. (1979) *Uncertainty in Microeconomics*, New York: New York University Press.

Heilbroner, R. L. (1956) *The Wordly Philosophers. The lives times and ideas of the great economic thinkers*, New York: Penguin Books.

Heiner, R. A. (1983) 'The Origin of Predictable Behavior' *American Economic Review*, 73 (4), pp. 560-595.

Herron L., Sapienza, H. J. and Smith-Cook, D. (1991) 'Entrepreneurship Theory from an Interdisciplinary Perspective: Volume I' *Entrepreneurship Theory and Practice*, 16, (2), pp. 7-12.

Hodgson, G. M. (1992) 'Thorstein Veblen and Post-Darwinian Economics' *Cambridge Journal of Economics*, 16, pp. 285-301.

Hodgson, G. M. (1993) 'Institutional Economics: Surveying the 'Old' and the 'New'' *Metroeconomica*, 1, pp. 1-28.

Hodgson, G. M. (1998) 'The Approach of Institutional Economics' *Journal of Economic Literature*, 36, pp. 166-192.

Hodgson, G. M. (2003) 'Veblen and Darwisnism' paper presented to the International Review of Sociology Conference on Veblen as a Systematic Social Thinker.

Hoselitz, B. F. (1963) 'Entrepreneurship and Traditional Elites' *Explorations in Entrepreneurial History*, 2 (1).

Hough, J. F. (1986) 'Economic Reform and Soviet Foreign Policy' in Hohma, H. H., Nove, A. and Vogel, H. (eds) *Economics and Politics in the USSR. Problems of Interdependence*, Boulder, Co: Westview Press.

Hughes, J. (1997) 'Sub-national Elites and Post-Communist Transformation in Russia: A Reply to Kryshtanovskaya & White' *Europe-Asia Studies*, 49 (6), pp. 1017-1036.

Ingrao, B. and Israel, G. (1990) *The Invisible Hand*, Cambridge, Mass: MIT Press.

Ito, T. M. (1997) 'From Russia, with very advanced degrees' *News and World Report*, 122 (21), p. 53.

Izyumov, A. Razumnova, I. (2000) 'Women entrepreneurs in Russia: learning to survive the market' *Journal of Developmental Entrepreneurship*, 5 (1), pp. 1-19.

Jenks, L. (1949) 'Role Structure of Entrepreneurial Personality' *Change and the Entrepreneur*, edited by the Harvard University Research Center in Entrepreneurial History, pp. 108-152.

Jensen, H. E. (1987) 'The Theory of Human Nature' *Journal of Economic Issues*, 21 (3), pp. 1039-1073.

Johannisson, B. (1995) 'Paradigms and entrepreneurial networks – some methodological challenges' *Entrepreneurship and Regional Development*, 7 (3), pp. 215-231.

Johannisson, B. (1990) 'Community entrepreneurship – cases and conceptualisation' *Entrepreneurship and Regional Development*, 2 (1), pp. 71-88.

Johnson S., McMillan, J. and Woodruff, C. (2000) 'Entrepreneurs and the ordering of institutional reform Poland, Slovakia, Romania, Russia, and Ukraine compared', *Economics of Transition*, 8 (1), pp. 1-36.

Julien, P. A. (1998) *The State of the Art in Small Business and Entrepreneurship*, Aldershot: Ashgate.

Kalantaridis, C. (1997) 'Between the Community and the World Markets: Entrepreneurs in a Garment Producing District of Greece', *Entrepreneurship and Regional Development*, 9 (1), pp. 25-44.

Kalantaridis, C. and Bika, Z. (2003) 'The Case of Cumbria' in Labrianidis, L. (ed) *The Future of Europe's Rural Periphery, Part II*, Thessaloniki: University of Macedonia, pp. 312-346.

Kalantaridis, C. and Labrianidis, L. (2004) 'Rural Entrepreneurship in Post-Socialist Regimes: A Comparative Study from Russia and the Ukraine' *Journal of Economic Issues* (forthcoming).

Kalugina, Z. I., Arsentieva, N. M,. Koshleva, O. P., Oleh, A. L. and Fadeeva, O. P. (2001) Rural Entrepreneurship and Employment in Transition Economies The Case of the Novosibirsk Region, INTAS Project 99-00965.

Katzenelinboigen, A. (1977) 'Coloured Markets in the Soviet Union' *Soviet Studies*, 29 (1), pp. 62-85.

Kent, C. A. (1989) 'The Treatment of Entrepreneurship in Principles of Economics textbook' *Journal of EconomicEducation*, 20 (2), pp. 153-164.

Kent, C. A. and Rushing F. W. (1999) 'Coverage of Entrepreneruship in Economics Textbooks: an Update' *Journal of Economic Education*, 30 (30), pp. 184-188.

Kets de Vries, M. (1977) 'The Entrepreneurial Personality: A Person at the Crossroads' *Journal of Management Studies*, 14 (1), pp. 34-57.

Keynes, J. M. (1937) 'The General Theory of Employment', *Quarterly Journal of Economics*, 51 (3), pp. 209-223.

Khalil, E. (1994) 'Trust' in Hodgson G. M., Samuels, W. J. and Tool, M. C. (eds) *The Elgar Companion to Institutional and Evolutionary Economics*, Aldershot: Edward Elgar.

Khanin, G. I. (2000) 'The Splendor and Poverty of the Russian Bourgeoisie' *Russian Social Science Review*, 41 (5), pp. 67-84.

Khotin, L. (1996) 'Old and New Entrepreneurs in Today's Russia' *Problems of Post Communism*, 43 (1), pp. 49-57

Kihlstrom, R. E. and Laffont, J. J. (1979) 'A General Equilibrium Entrepreenurial Theory of Firm Formation Based on Risk Aversion' *Journal of Political Economy*, 87 (4), pp. 719-748.

Kilby, P. (1971) 'Hunting the Heffalump' in Kilby, P. (ed) *Entrepreneurship and Economic Development*, New York: Free Press, pp. 1-40.

Kirkby, D. (2002) *Entrepreneurship*, London: McGraw-Hill.

Kirzner, I. M. (1973) *Competition and Entreprneurship*, Chicago: University of Chicago Press.

Kirzner, I. M. (1979) *Perception, Opportunity and Profit*, Chicago: University of Chicago Press.

Kirzner, I. M. (1997) 'Entrepreneurial discovery and the competitive market process: an Austrian Approach, *Journal of Economic Literature*, 35, pp. 60-85.

Kitching, G. (1989) *Development and Underdevelopment in Historical Perspective. Populism, Nationalism and Industrialisation*, London: Routledge.

Knight, F. (1921) *Risk, Uncertainty and Profit*, NY: Houghton Mifflin.

Knight, F. (1935) *The Ethics of Competition and Other Essays*, London: Allen and Unwin.

Koolman, G. (1971) 'Say's Conception of the role of the entrepreneur' *Economica*, New Series 38, pp. 282-286.

Kotz, D. and Weir, F. (1997) *Revolution from Above: The Demise of the Soviet System*, London: Routledge.

Kryshtanovskaya, O. (1995) 'The New Russian Elite' *Sociological Research*, 34, pp. 6-26.

Kryshtanovskaya, O. and White, S. (1996) 'From Soviet Nomenklatura to Russian Elite' *Europe-Asia Studies*, 48 (5), pp. 711-734.

Kuhn, T. (1970) *The Structure of Scientific Revolutions*, Chicago: University of Chicago Press.

Kukolev, I. V. (1997) 'The Formation of the Business Elite' *Russian Social Science Review*, 38 (4), pp. 62-83.

Kuratko, D. F. and Hodgetts, R. M. (1994) *Entrepreneurship A Contemporary Approach*, Fort Worth: Dryden Press.

Kusnezova, N. (1999) 'Roots and philosophy of Russian entrepreneurship', *Journal for East European Management Studies*, 4 (1), pp. 45-72.

Kyrro, P. (1998) 'The Identity and Role of Entrepreneurship in Post-Modern Society' 43rd ICSB World Conference, Singapore.

Lachmann, L. M. (1991) 'Austrian Economics as a Hermeneutic Approach' in Lavoie, D. (ed) *Economics and Hermeneutics*, London: Routledge.

Landes, D. S. (1951) 'French Business and the Businessman: A Social and Cultural Analysis' in Earle, E. M. (ed) *Modern France*, Princeton: Princeton University Press.

Lavoie, D. (1991) 'The Discovery and Interpretation of Profit Opportunities: Cutlure and the Kirznerian Entrepreneur' in Berger, B. (ed) *The Culture of Entrepreneurship*, San Fansisco: ICS Press.

Ledeneva, A. (1998) *Russia's Economy of Favours*, Cambridge: Cambridge University Press.

Leff, N. H. (1979) 'Entrepreneurship and Economic Development: The Problem Revisited' *Journal of Economic Literature*, 17 (1-2), pp. 46-64.

Leibenstain, H. (1968) 'Entrepreneurship and Economic Development, *American Economic Review*, 58 (2), pp. 72-83.

Leibenstain, H. (1987) *Inside the Firm: The Inefficiencies of Hierarchy*, Cambridge, MA: Harvard University Press.

Leitzel, J. (1998) 'Rule Evasion in Transitional Russia' in Nelson, J. M., Tilly, C. and Walker, L. (eds) *Transforming Post-Communist Political Economies*, Washington DC: National Academy Press, pp. 118-130.

Lounsbury, M. (1998) 'Collective Entrepreneurship: The Mobilisation of College and University Recycling Coordinators' *Journal of Organisational Change Management*, 11 (1), pp. 23-36.

Low, B. and McMillan, I. C. (1988) 'Enrepreneurship: past research and future challenges' *Journal of Management*, 14, pp. 139-161.

Lukas, R. E. (1978) 'On the size distribution of business firms' *Bell Journal of Economics*, 9, pp. 508-523.

Lundstrom, A. and Stevenson, L. (2001) 'Entrepreneurship Policy for the Future' Stockholm: Swedish Foundation for Small Business Research.

Luthans F., Staikovic, A. D. and Ibrayeva, E. (2000) Environmental and psychological challenges facing entrepreneurial development in transitional economies, *Journal of World Business*, 35 (1), pp. 95-110.

Makhmutov, A. (2002) Final Report of the National Team of the Republic of Bashkortostan, INTAS Project 99-00965.

Margolis, H. (1987) *Patterns, Thinking and Cognition: A Theory of Judgement*, Chicago: University of Chicago Press.

Martin, R. (1977) *The Sociology of Power*, London: Routledge & Kegan Paul.

Martinelli, A. (1994) 'Entrepreneurship and Management' in Smelser, N. J. and Swedberg, R. (eds) *The Handbook of Economic Sociology*, Princeton: Princeton University Press, pp. 476-503.

Mayberry, T. C. (1969) 'Thorstein Veblen on Human Nature' *American Journal of Economics and Sociology*, 28 (3), pp. 315-323.

Mayhew, A. (1989) 'Contrasting origins of the two institutionalisms: the social science context' *Review of Political Economy*, 1 (3), pp. 319-335.

Mayr, E. (1976) *Evolution and the Diversity of Life*, Cambridge, Mass: Harvard University Press.

McCarty D. J., Puffer, S. M. and Naumov, A. I. (1997) 'Orga Kirova: A Russian Entrepreneur's Quality Leadership' *The International Journal of Organisational Analysis*, 5 (3), pp. 267-290.

McClelland, D. (1961) *The Achieving Society*, Princeton: D. Van Nostrad Co.

McMylor, P., Mellor, R. and Barkhatova, N. (2000) 'Familialism, Friendship and the Small Firm in the New Russia' *International Review of Sociology*, 10 (1), pp. 125-146.

Meier, P. (2002) 'The Brothers Pachikov' E-Europe A Time Special Report.

Mirowski, P. (1989) *More Heat than Light*, New York: Cambridge University Press.

Mises, von L. (1922 reprinted 1981) *Socialism: An Economic and Sociological Analysis*, Indianapolis: Liberty Classics.

Mises, von L. (1949) *Human Action: A Treatise on Economics*, New Haven: Yale University Press.

Mises, von L. (1958) 'Liberty and Capitalism' Lecture for the 9th Meeting of the Mont Pelerin Society, Princeton University.

Mises, von L. (1990) *Money Method and the Market Process: Essays by L. Mises*, (edited by Ebeling, R. M.) Auburn, AL: Praxeology Press.

Mitchell, W. C. (1937) *The Backward Art of Spending Money and Other Essays*, New York: McGraw-Hill.

Mugler, J. (2000) 'The Climate for Entrepreneurship in European Countries in Transition' in Sexton, D. L. and Landstom, H. (eds) *The Blackwell Handbook of Entrepreneurship*, Oxford: Blackwell, pp. 150-175.

Myrdall, G. (1957) *Economic Theory and Underdeveloped Regions*, London: Duckworth.

Neale, W. C. (1994) 'Institutions' in Hodgson G. M., Samuels W. J., and Tool, M. C. (eds) *The Elgar Companion to Institutional and Evolutionary Economics*, Aldershot: Edward Elgar, pp. 402-406.

Newcomer, M. (1952) 'The Chief Executive of Large Business Corporations' *Explorations in Entrepreneurial History* Vol. IV, pp.1-33.

Newman, G. (1976) 'An Institutional Perspective on Information' *International Social Science Journal*, 28 (3), pp. 466-492.

North, D. C. (1990) *Institution, Institutional Change and Economic Performance*, Cambridge: Cambridge University Press.

O'Hara, P. A. (1999) 'Thorstein Veblen's Theory of Collective Social Wealth, Instincts and Property Relations' *History of Economic Ideas*, 7 (3), pp. 153-179.

O'Donnell, L. A. (1993) 'Rationalism, Capitalism and the Entrepreneur: the Views of Veblen and Schumpeter', in Hodgson, G. M. (ed) *The Economics of Institutions*, Aldershot: Edward Elgar.

Oakley, A. (1996) *The Foundations of Austrian Economics from Menger to Mises A Critic-Historical Perspective of Subjectivism*, Cheltenham: Edward Elgar.

OECD, (1997) *Fostering Entrepreneurship*, Paris: OECD Publications.

OECD, (1998) *Entrepreneurship and Small Business in the Russian Federation*, Paris: OECD Publications.

Owen, T. (1981) *Capitalism and Politics in Russia: A Social History of Moscow Merchants, 1855-1905*, New York: Cambridge University Press.

Pavitt K., Robson, M. and Townsend, J. (1987) 'The size of innovating firms in the UK: 1945-1983' *Journal of Industrial Economics*, 55, pp. 297-316.

Peirce, C. S. (1958*) Collected Papers Volumes VII & VIII*, Harvard: Arthur W. Burks.

Pepper, S. C. (1942) *World Hypotheses*, Berkeley: University of California Press.

Phares, E. J. (1976) *Locus of Control in Personality*, Morristown, NJ: General Learning Press.

Piore, M. and Sabel, C. (1984) *The Second Industrial Divide: Possibilities for Prosperity*, New York: Basic Books.

Polanyii, K. (1944) *The Great Transformation*, New York: Rinehart.

Portes, A. and Min Zhu (1992) 'Gaining the upper Hand: Economic Mobility Among Immigrant and Domestic Minorities' *Ethnic and Racial Studies*, 15, pp. 491-522.

Pressman, S. (1997) 'Paradigms, Conventions and the Entrepreneur' *American Journal of Economics and Sociology*, 56 (1), pp. 51-58.

Radaev, V. (1997) Practicing and potential entrepreneurs in Russia, *International Journal of Sociology*, 27 (3), pp. 15-21.

Radaev, V. (2001) The Development of Small Entrepreneurship in Russia, WIDER Discussion Paper 135.

Rauch, A. and Frese, M. (2000) 'Psychological approaches to entrepreneurial success: a general model and an overview of findings' in Cooper, C. L. and Robertson, I. T. (eds) *International Review of Industrial and Organizational Psychology*, Chichester: Wiley, pp. 101-142.

Reynolds, P. D. (1991) 'Sociology and entrepreneurship: concepts and contributions' *Entrepreneurship Theory and Practice*, 16 (2), pp. 47-70.

Reynolds P. D., Camp M., Bygrave D., Autio, E. and Hay, M. (2002) *Global Entrepreneuship Monitor*, Kansas City: Kaufman Centre.

Ricketts, M. (1987) *The Economics of Business Enterprise*, Brighton: Wheatsheaf.

Roll, E. (1992) *A History of Economic Thought*, New Jersey: Prentice-Hall.

Rona-Tas, A. and Lengyel, L. (1998) 'Guest Editors' Introduction: Entrepreneurs & entrepreneurial inclinations in post-communist East-Central Europe*, International Journal of Sociology*, 27 (3), pp. 3-14.

Rothschild, K. W. (ed) (1971) *Power in Economics*, Harmondsworth: Penguin.

Rothwell, R. and Zeveld, W. (1982) *Innovation and Small and Medium Sized Enterprises*, London: Pinter.

Rotter, J. B. (1954) *Social Learning and Clinical Psychology*, New York: Prentice Hall.

Rotter, J. B. (1966) 'Generalized expectations for internal versus external control of reinforcement' *Psychology Monographs*, 80 (1), pp. 1-28.

Runde, J. (1998) 'Clarifying Frank Knight's discussion of the meaning of risk and uncertainty' *Cambridge Journal of Economics*, 22, pp. 539-546.

Sarachek, B. (1978) 'American Entrepreneurs and the Horatio Alger Myth' *Journal of Economic History*, 38, pp. 439-456.

Say, J. B. (1830 original 1803) *A Treatise on Political Economy*, New York: Augustus M. Kelley.

Scase, R. (1997) 'The role of small businesses in the economic transformation of Eastern Europe: real but relatively unimportant', *International Small Business Journal*, 16 (1), pp. 13-21.

Schackle, G. (1970) *Expectation, Enterprise and Profit*, London: Allen and Unwin.

Schmid, A. A. (1987) *Property, Power and Public Choice: An Inquiry into Law and Economics*, New York: Praeger.

Schumpeter, J. A. (1928) 'The Instability of Capitalism' *Economic Journal*, 38, pp. 361-386.

Schumpeter, J. A. (1947) 'The Creative Response in Economic History' *Journal of Economic History*, 7 (2), pp. 149-159.

Schumpeter, J. A. (1949) 'Economic Theory and Entrepreneurial History' *Change and the Entrepreneur*, edited by the Harvard University Research Center in Entrepreneurial History, pp. 63-84.

Schumpter, J. A. (1994 original 1954) *History of Economic Analysis*, London: Allen and Unwin.

Schweitzer, G. E. (2000) *Swords into Market Shares Technology, Economics, and Security in the New Russia*, Washington DC: Joseph Henry Press.

Seckler, D. (1975) *Thorstein Veblen and the Institutionalists A Study in the Social Philosophy of Economics*, London: Macmillan.

Shulus, A. (1996) 'Entrepreneurship in the former Soviet Union and Russia (1985-1994)', in Klandt, H., Rosa, P. and Scott, M. (eds) *Educating Entrepreneurs in Modernising Economies*, Aldershot: Avebury, pp. 105-112.

Simon, H. (1959) *Administrative Behavior: A Study of Decision-Making Processes in Administrative Organization*, New York: Macmillan.

Simon, H. (1982) *Models of Bounded Rationality*, 2 vols, Cambridge, MA: MIT Press.

Smallbone D., North, D. and Kalantaridis, C. (1997) 'Survival and Growth of Manufacturing SMEs' Salisbury: Rural Development Commission.

Smallbone, D. and Welter, F. (2001) 'The distinctiveness of entrepreneurship in transition economies', *Small Business Economics*, 16, pp. 249-262.

Smith, A. (1998) 'Breaking the Old and Constructing the New? Geographies of Uneven Development in Central and Eastern Europe' in Lee, R. and Wills, J. (eds) *Geographies of Economies*, London: Arnold.

Sombart, W. (1916-1927) *Der Moderne Kapitalismus*, 6 volumes, Munich: Deutscher Taschenbuch Verlag.

Sorensen, O. J., and Popova, J. F. (2002) 'Networks in the Management of Russian Enterprises' Centre for International Studies, Aalborg University, Reprint Series, No. 31.

Stam, E. (2002) 'An outline of a contextual approach on entrepreneurship' 98th Annual Meeting of the Association of American Geographers, Los Angeles CA.

Stevenson, L. and Lundstrom, A. (2002) 'Entrepreneurship Policy-Making: Frameworks, Approaches and Performance Measures' International Council for Small Business, 47th World Conference.

Stigler, G. J. (1961) 'The Economics of Information, *Journal of Political Economy*, 69, pp. 213-225.

Stiglitz, J. E. (1994) *Wither socialism?* Cambridge, MA: MIT Press.

Stolper, W. (1968) *International Encyclopaedia of the Social Sciences*, New York.

Storey, D. (2003) 'Entrepreneurship, Small and Medium Sized Enterprises and Public Policy' in Acs, Z. J. and Audretsch, D. B. (eds) *International Handbook of Entrepreneurship Research*, Dordrecht: Kluwer Academic (forthcoming).

Strayer, R. (2001) 'Decolonization, Democratizaion and Communist Reform: The Soviet Collapse in Comparative Perspective' *Journal of World History*, 12 (2), pp. 375-406.

Swain, A. and Hardy, J. (1998) 'Globalisation, institutions, Foreign Investment and the Reintegration of East and Central Europe and the Former Soviet Union with the World Economy' *Regional Studies*, 32 (7), pp. 587-590.

Swedberg, R. (ed) *Entreprneurship The Social Science View*, Oxford: Oxford University Press.

Tansey, M. (2002) 'Information Limits on Entrepreneurs: An Economic Perspective' Rockhurs University Working Papers.

Thurik, R. (1994) 'Small Firms, entrepreneruship and Economic Growth' F. De Vries Lecture, Erasmus University, Rotterdam.

Thomas, H. and Willard, G. (1995) 'Conclusions and Reflections' in Bull I., Thomas, H. and Willard, G. (eds) *Entrepreneurship Perspectives on Theory Building*, New York: Pergamon, pp. 167-173.

Thornton, P. H. (1999) 'The Sociology of Entrepreneurship' *Annual Review of Sociology*, 25, pp. 19-46.

Veblen, T. B. (1898) 'Why is Economics Not An Evolutionary Science?' *Quarterly Journal in Economics*, 12 (3), pp. 373-397.

Veblen, T. B. (1899) *The theory of the leisure class: an economic analysis in the evolution of institutions*, New York: Macmillan.

Veblen, T. B. (1908) *The Place of Science in Modern Civilization and other Essays*, New York: Viking Press.

Veblen, T. B. (1914) *The Instinct of Workmanship, and the State of the Industrial Arts*, New York: Augustus Kelley.

Volkov, V. (2000) 'The Political Economy of Protection Rackets in the Past and the Present' *Social Research*, 67 (3), pp. 709-744.

Volkov, V. (1998) 'Who is Strong When the State is Weak: Violent Entrepreneurs in Post-Communist Russia' paper presented at the Conference 'Russia at the End of the Twentieth Century' Stanford University.

Waldinger R., Aldrich, H. and Ward, R. (1990) *Ethnic entrepreneurs: immigrant business in industrial societies*, London: Sage.

Waller, W. T. (1982) 'The Evolution of the Veblenian Dichotomy' *Journal of Economic Issues*, 16 (3), pp. 757-771.

Waller, W. T. (1988) 'The Concept of Habit in Economic Analysis' *Journal of Economic Issues*, 22 (2), pp. 113-126.

Ward, R. and Jenkins, R. (eds) (1984) *Ethnic Communities in Business: Strategies for Economic Survival*, Cambridge: Cambridge University Press.

Weber, M. (original 1922, 1978) *Economy and Society: An Outline of Interpretive Sociology*, Berkely: University of California.

Wickham, P. A. (2000) *Strategic Entrepreneurship A Decision-Making Approach to New Venture Creation and Management*, Harlow: Prentice Hall.

Williams, P. (ed) (1997) *Russian Organized Crime: The New Threat*? Portland: Frank Cass.

Williamson, O. E. (1968) 'Economies as an Antitrust Defence: The Welfare Tradeoffs' *American Economic Review*, 58 (1), pp. 18-36.

Williamson, O. E. (1985) *The Economic Institutions of Capitalism*, New York: The Free Press.

Williamson, O. E. (1993) 'The economic analysis of institutions and organizations – in general and with respect to country studies' OECD working paper No. 133.

Wortman, M. Jr, (1987) 'Entrepreneurship: an integrating typology and evaluation of the empirical research in the field' *Journal of Management*, 13.

Wortman, M. Jr, (1992) 'The state of the art in entrepreneurship' paper presented at the Annual Meeting of the Academy of Management, Las Vegas, August.

Young, F. V. (1971) 'A Macro-Sociological Interpretation of Entrepreneurship' Kilby P (ed) *Entreprenreurship and Economic Development*, New York: Free Press, pp. 139-149.

Index